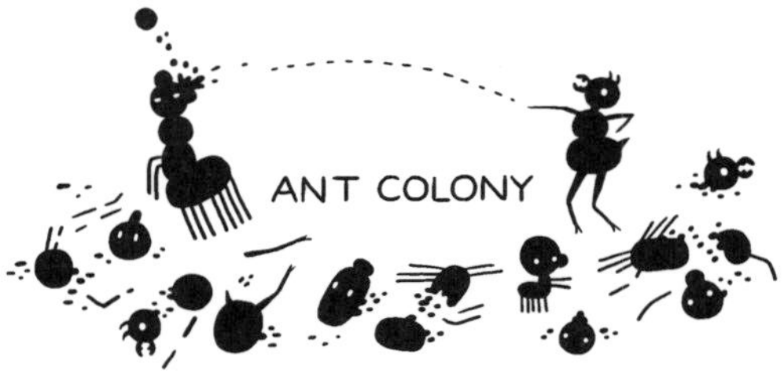
ANT COLONY

WWW. DRAWNANDQUARTERLY.COM

FIRST HARDCOVER EDITION: JANUARY 2014
PRINTED IN CHINA
10 9 8 7 6 5 4 3 2 1

DRAWN & QUARTERLY ACKNOWLEDGES THE FINANCIAL CONTRIBUTION OF THE GOVERNMENT OF CANADA THROUGH THE CANADA BOOK FUND
AND THE CANADA COUNCIL FOR THE ARTS FOR OUR PUBLISHING ACTIVITIES AND FOR SUPPORT OF THIS EDITION.

LIBRARY AND ARCHIVES CANADA CATALOGUING IN PUBLICATION
DEFORGE, MICHAEL, 1987-, AUTHOR, ARTIST
    ANT COLONY / MICHAEL DEFORGE
ISBN 978-1-77046-137-6 (BOUND)
    I. GRAPHIC NOVELS I. TITLE
PN6733.D435A57 2013   741.5'971   C2013-902768-8

PUBLISHED IN THE USA BY DRAWN & QUARTERLY
A CLIENT PUBLISHER OF
FARRAR, STRAUS AND GIROUX
ORDERS: 888.330.8477

PUBLISHED IN CANADA BY DRAWN & QUARTERLY
A CLIENT PUBLISHER OF
RAINCOAST BOOKS
ORDERS: 800.663.5714

PUBLISHED IN THE UNITED KINGDOM BY DRAWN & QUARTERLY
A CLIENT PUBLISHER OF
PUBLISHERS GROUP UK
ORDERS: INFO@PGUK.CO.UK

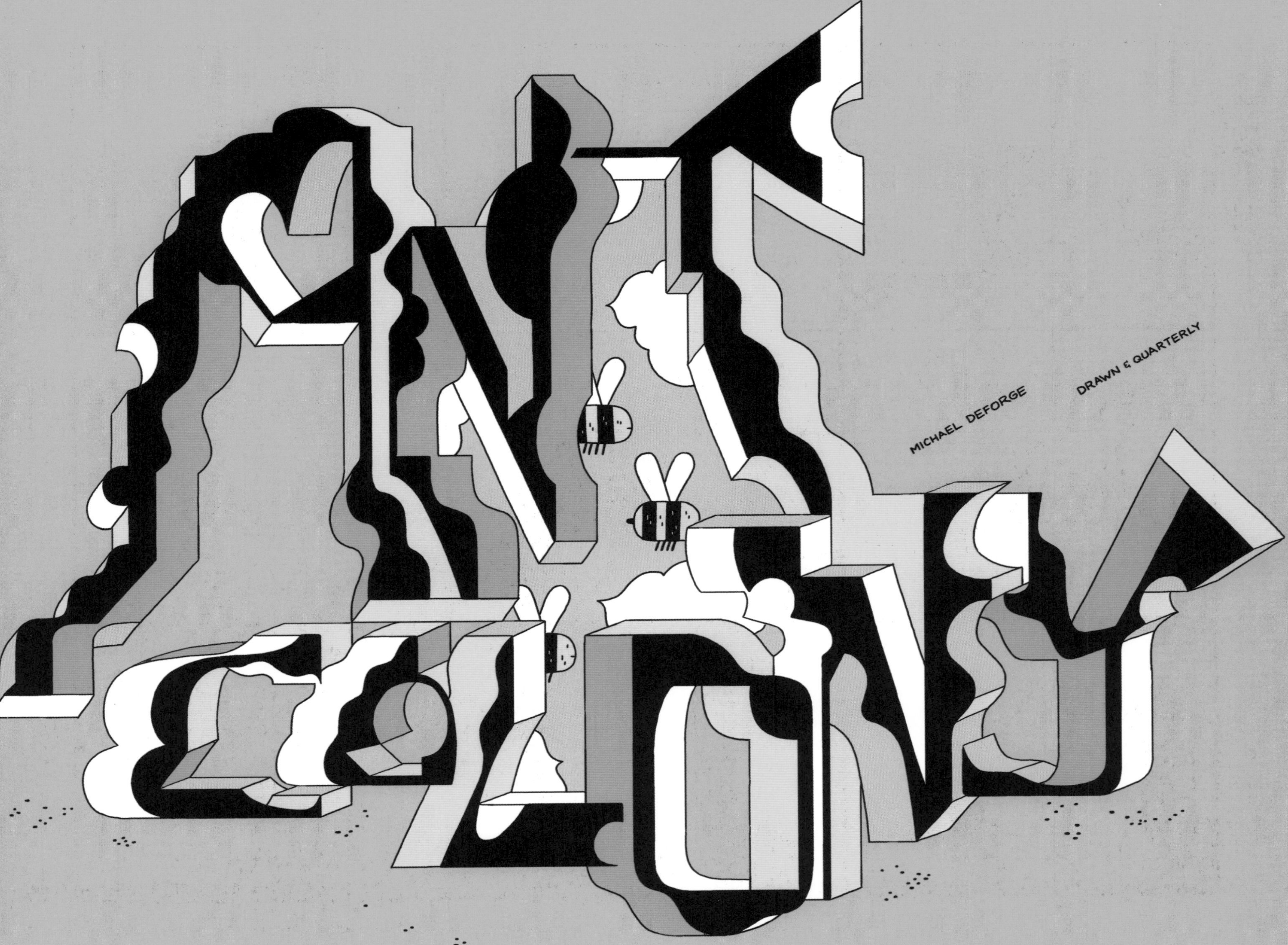
ANT COLONY
MICHAEL DEFORGE
DRAWN & QUARTERLY

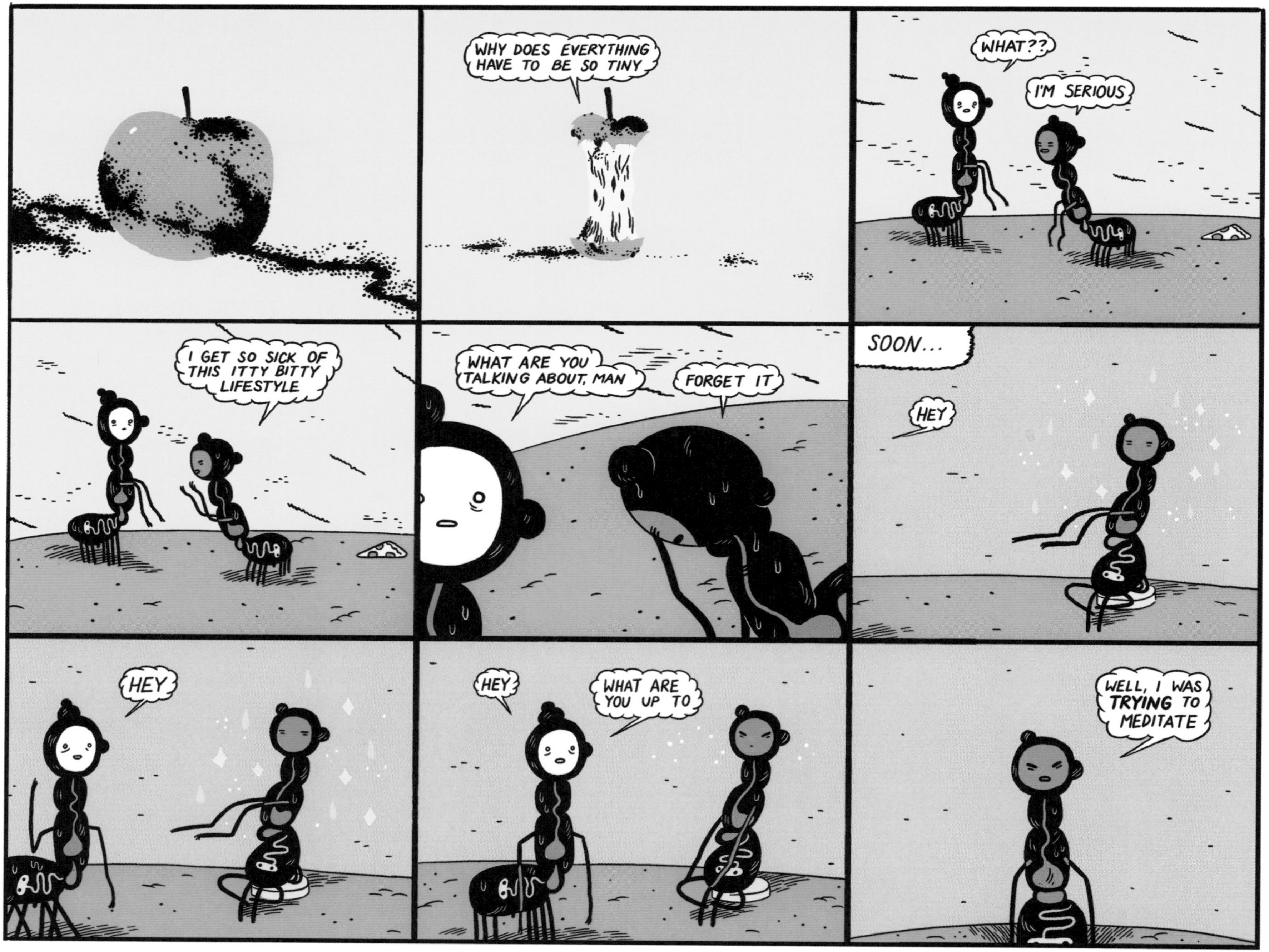
WHY DOES EVERYTHING HAVE TO BE SO TINY
WHAT??
I'M SERIOUS
I GET SO SICK OF THIS ITTY BITTY LIFESTYLE
WHAT ARE YOU TALKING ABOUT, MAN
FORGET IT
SOON...
HEY
HEY
HEY
WHAT ARE YOU UP TO
WELL, I WAS **TRYING** TO MEDITATE

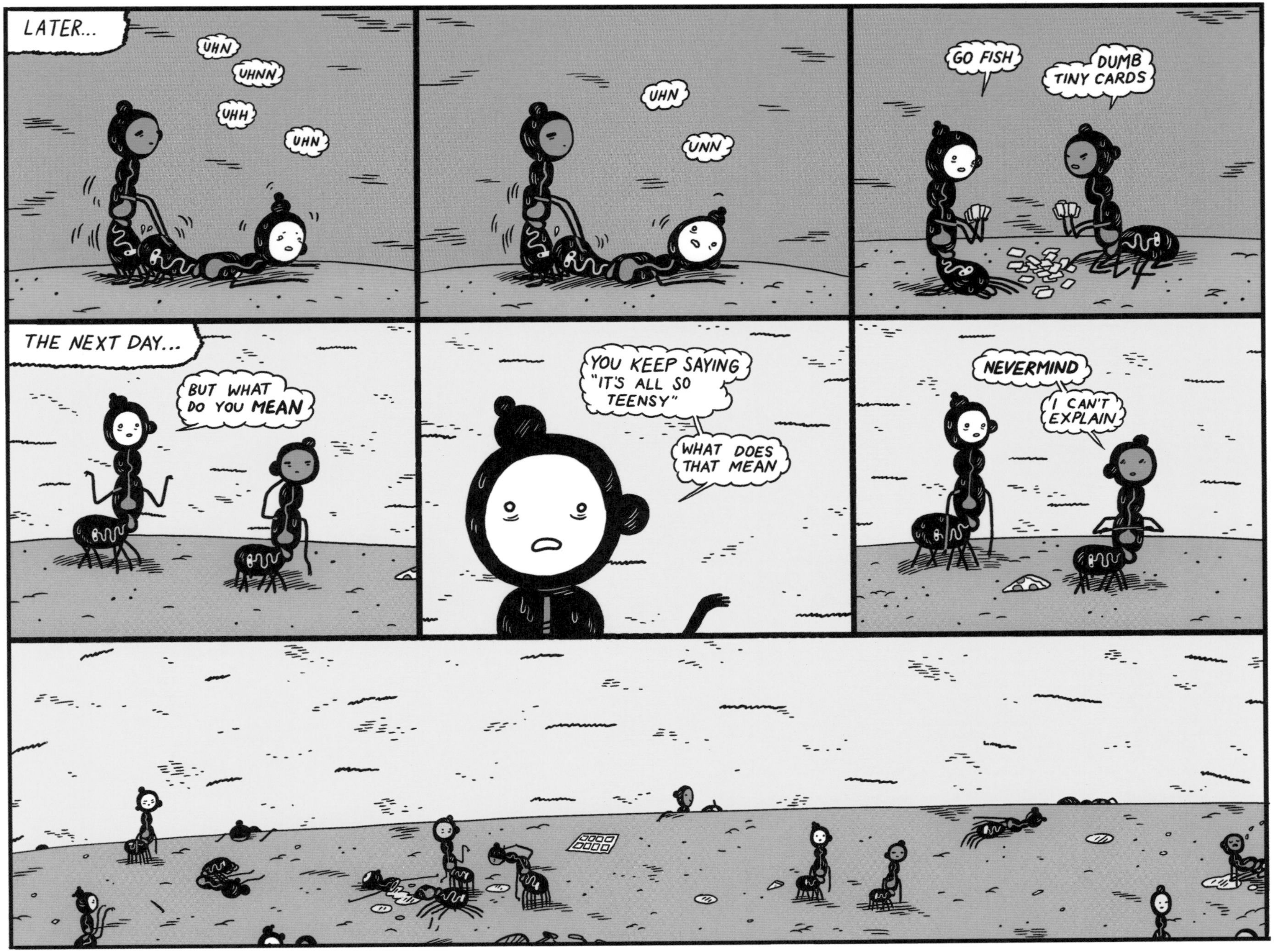
LATER...
UHN
UHNN
UHH
UHN
UHN
UNN
GO FISH
DUMB TINY CARDS
THE NEXT DAY...
BUT WHAT DO YOU MEAN
YOU KEEP SAYING "IT'S ALL SO TEENSY"
WHAT DOES THAT MEAN
NEVERMIND
I CAN'T EXPLAIN

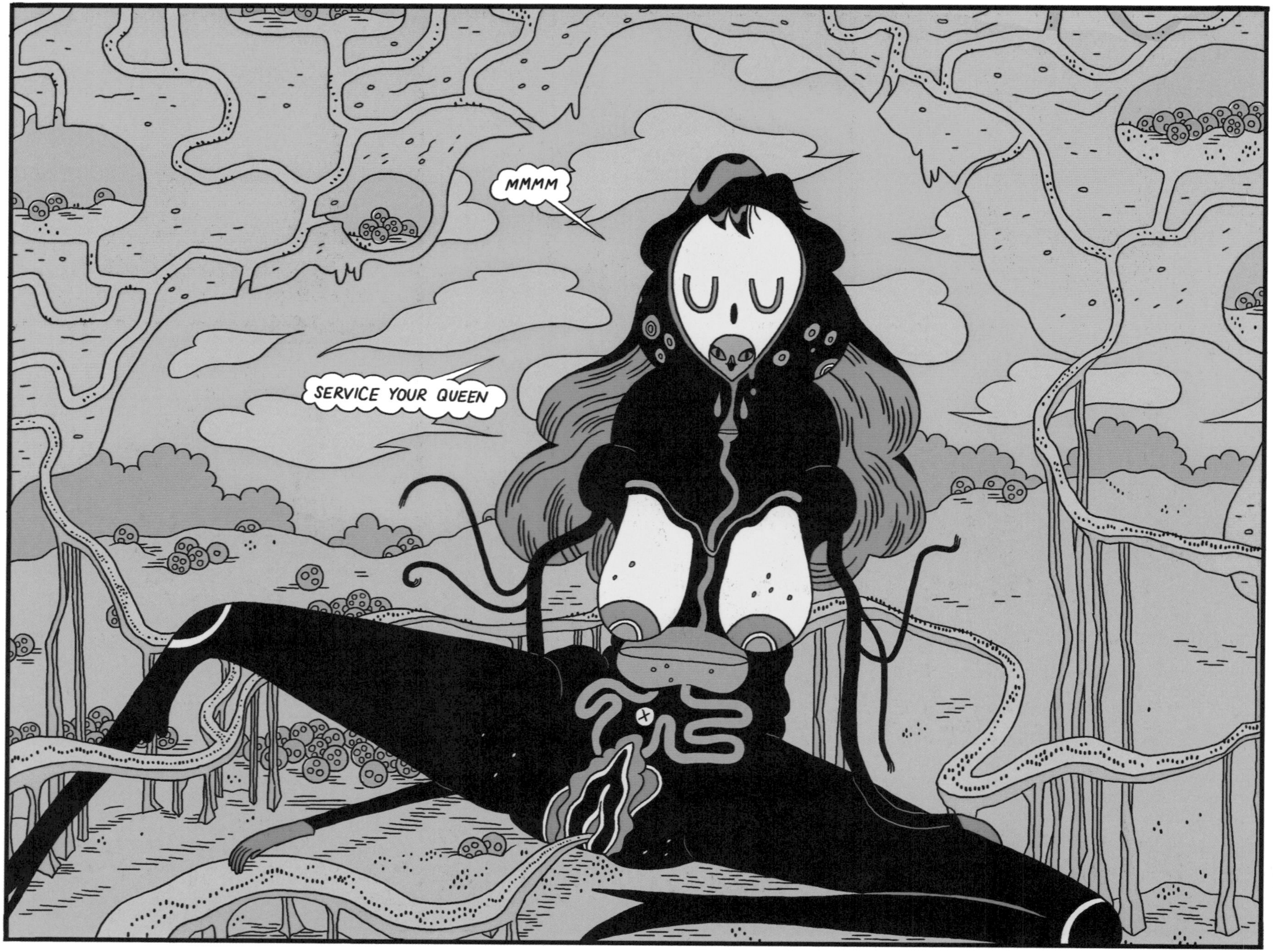
MMMM
SERVICE YOUR QUEEN

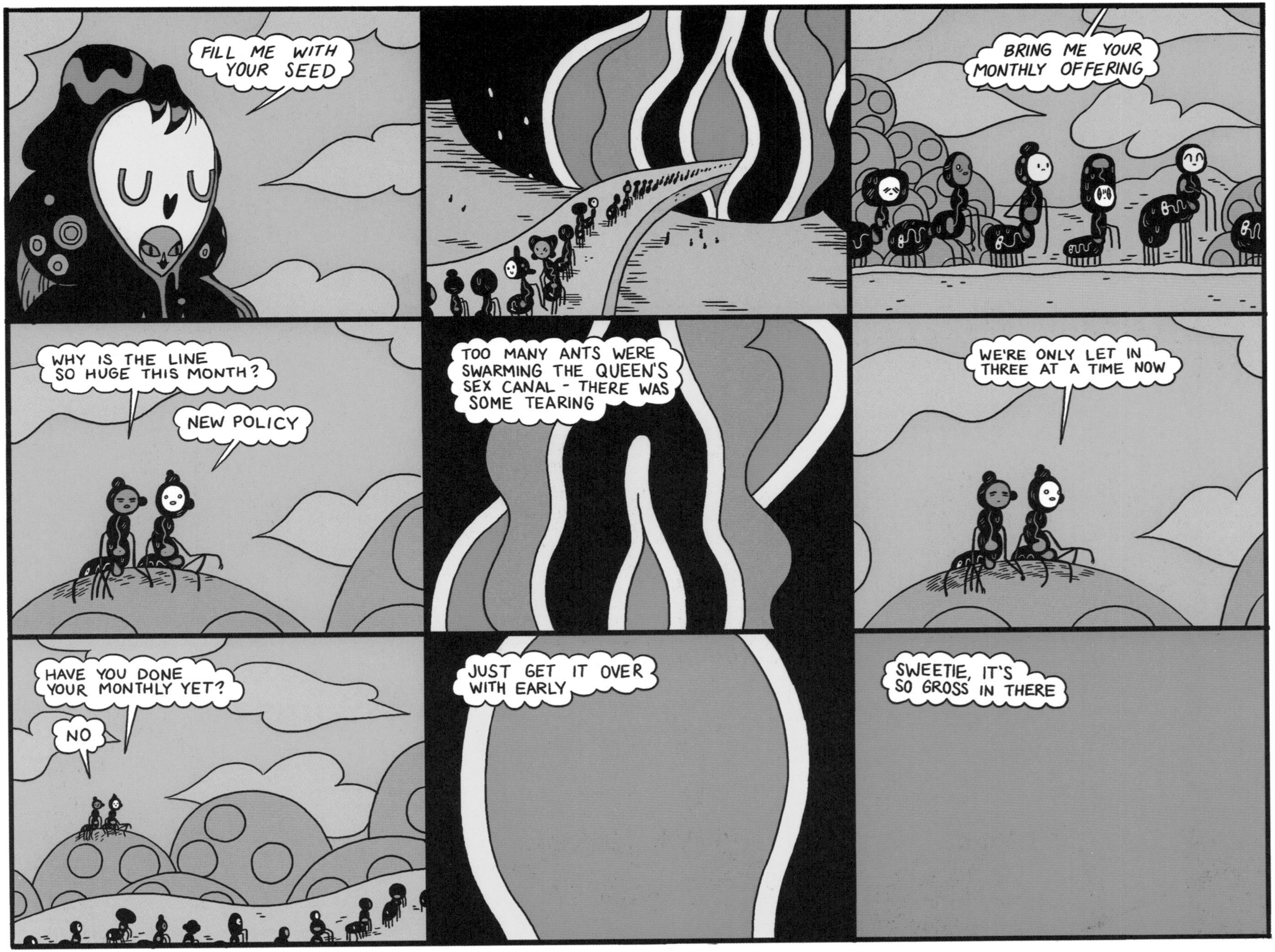
FILL ME WITH YOUR SEED
BRING ME YOUR MONTHLY OFFERING
WHY IS THE LINE SO HUGE THIS MONTH?
NEW POLICY
TOO MANY ANTS WERE SWARMING THE QUEEN'S SEX CANAL - THERE WAS SOME TEARING
WE'RE ONLY LET IN THREE AT A TIME NOW
HAVE YOU DONE YOUR MONTHLY YET?
NO
JUST GET IT OVER WITH EARLY
SWEETIE, IT'S SO GROSS IN THERE

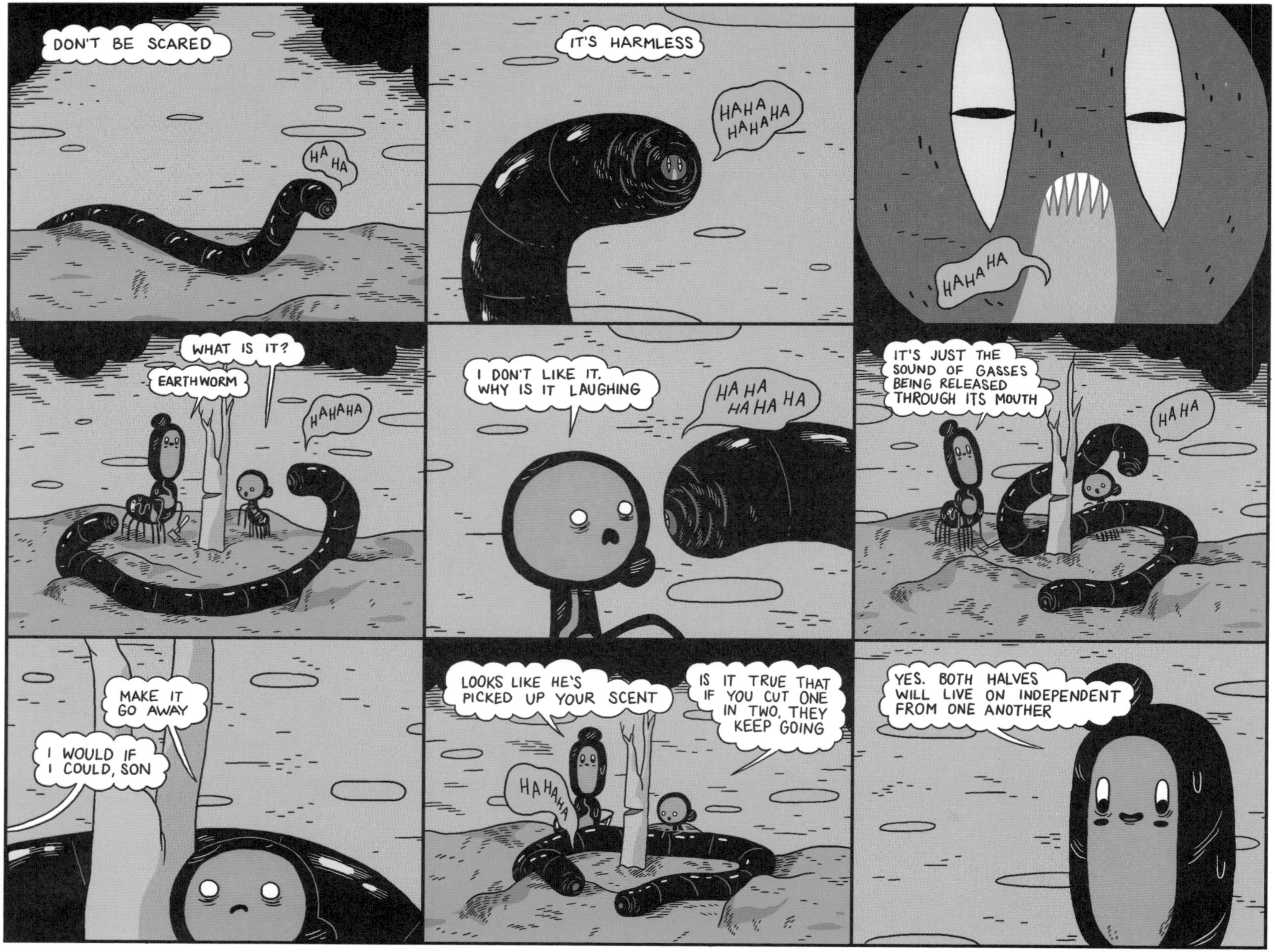
DON'T BE SCARED
HA HA
IT'S HARMLESS
HAHA HAHAHA
HAHAHA
WHAT IS IT?
EARTHWORM
HAHAHA
I DON'T LIKE IT. WHY IS IT LAUGHING
HA HA HA HA HA
IT'S JUST THE SOUND OF GASSES BEING RELEASED THROUGH ITS MOUTH
HA HA
MAKE IT GO AWAY
I WOULD IF I COULD, SON
LOOKS LIKE HE'S PICKED UP YOUR SCENT
IS IT TRUE THAT IF YOU CUT ONE IN TWO, THEY KEEP GOING
HAHAHA
YES. BOTH HALVES WILL LIVE ON INDEPENDENT FROM ONE ANOTHER

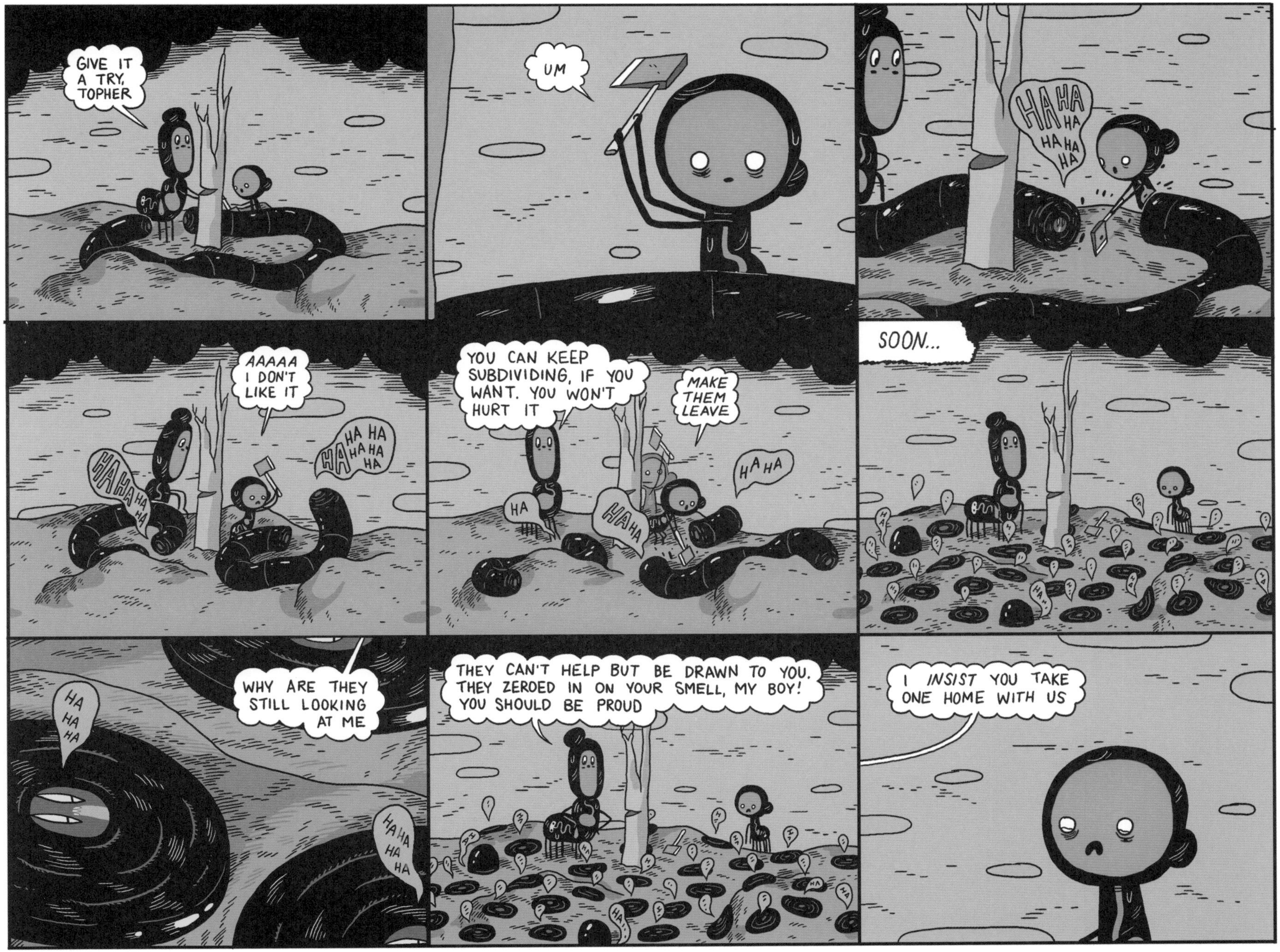
GIVE IT A TRY, TOPHER
UM
HA HA HA HA HA HA HA
AAAAA I DON'T LIKE IT
HA HA HA HA HA HA HA
HA HA HA HA
YOU CAN KEEP SUBDIVIDING, IF YOU WANT. YOU WON'T HURT IT
MAKE THEM LEAVE
HA
HA HA
HA HA HA
SOON...
HA HA HA
WHY ARE THEY STILL LOOKING AT ME
HA HA HA HA
THEY CAN'T HELP BUT BE DRAWN TO YOU. THEY ZEROED IN ON YOUR SMELL, MY BOY! YOU SHOULD BE PROUD
I *INSIST* YOU TAKE ONE HOME WITH US

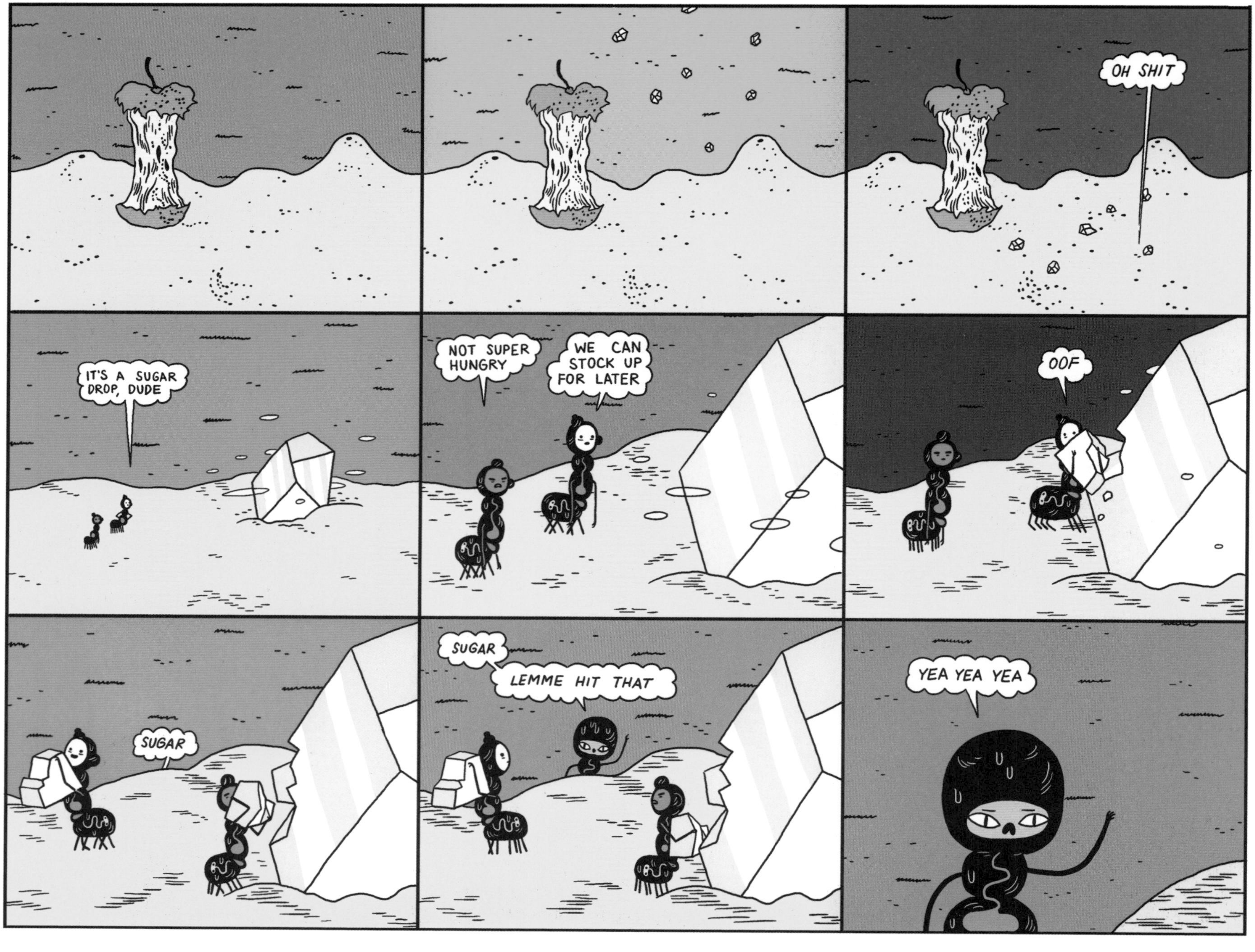
OH SHIT
IT'S A SUGAR DROP, DUDE
NOT SUPER HUNGRY
WE CAN STOCK UP FOR LATER
OOF
SUGAR
SUGAR
LEMME HIT THAT
YEA YEA YEA

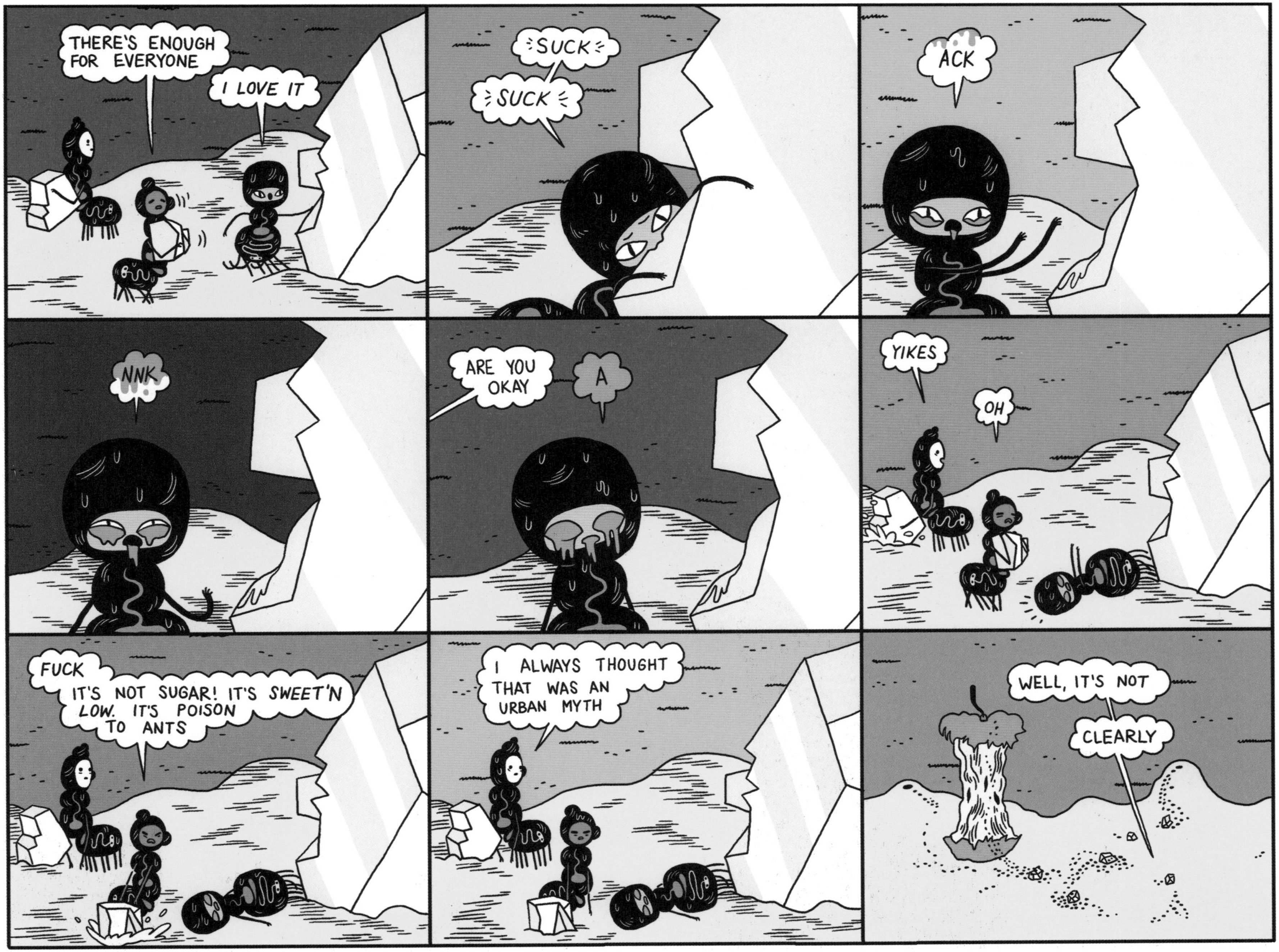
THERE'S ENOUGH FOR EVERYONE
I LOVE IT
SUCK
SUCK
ACK
NNK
ARE YOU OKAY
A
YIKES
OH
FUCK
IT'S NOT SUGAR! IT'S SWEET'N LOW. IT'S POISON TO ANTS
I ALWAYS THOUGHT THAT WAS AN URBAN MYTH
WELL, IT'S NOT
CLEARLY

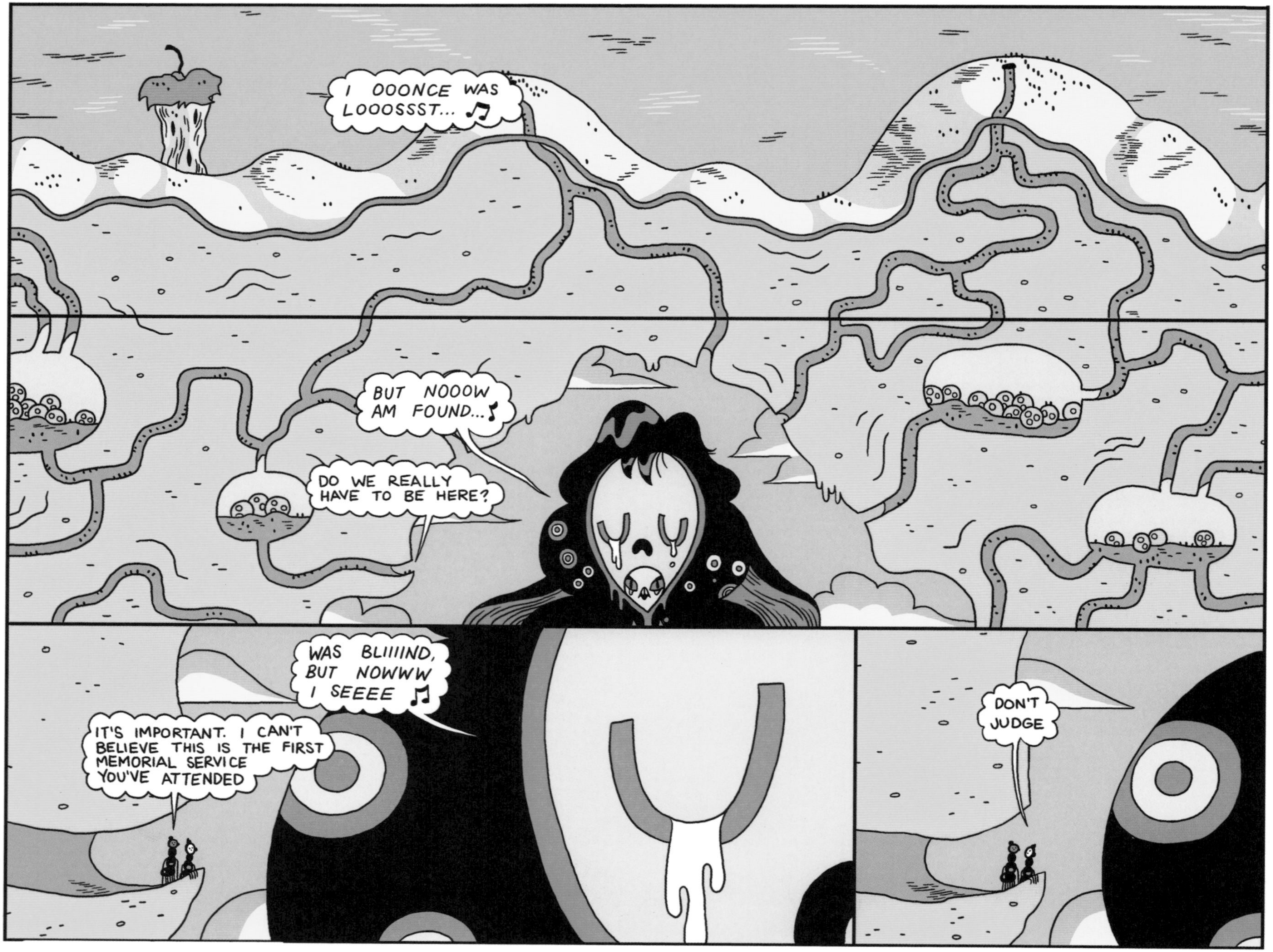

I OOONCE WAS LOOOSSST... ♫
BUT NOOOW AM FOUND... ♪
DO WE REALLY HAVE TO BE HERE?
WAS BLIIIIND, BUT NOWWW I SEEEE ♫
IT'S IMPORTANT. I CAN'T BELIEVE THIS IS THE FIRST MEMORIAL SERVICE YOU'VE ATTENDED
DON'T JUDGE

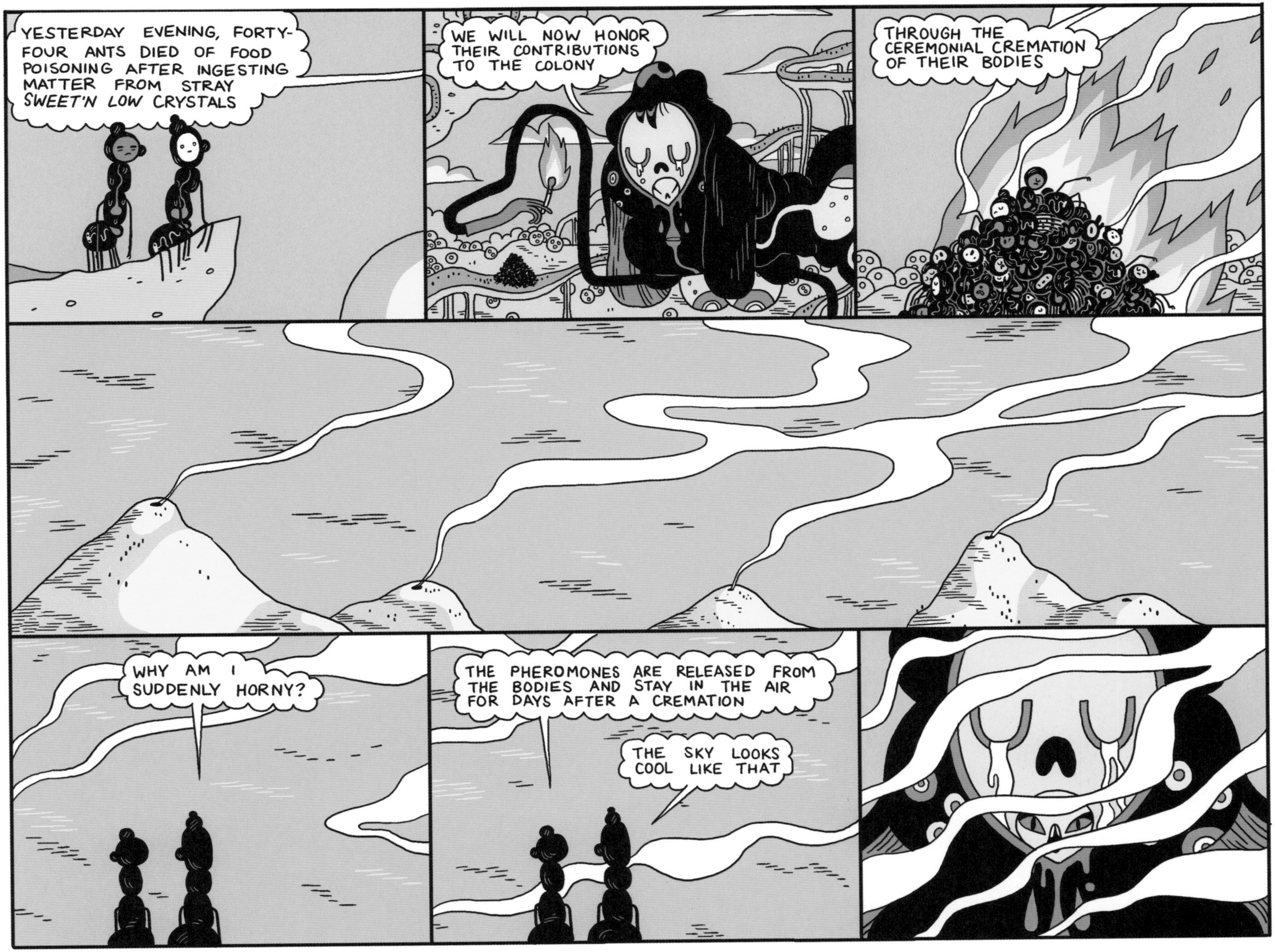
YESTERDAY EVENING, FORTY-FOUR ANTS DIED OF FOOD POISONING AFTER INGESTING MATTER FROM STRAY *SWEET'N LOW* CRYSTALS
WE WILL NOW HONOR THEIR CONTRIBUTIONS TO THE COLONY
THROUGH THE CEREMONIAL CREMATION OF THEIR BODIES
WHY AM I SUDDENLY HORNY?
THE PHEROMONES ARE RELEASED FROM THE BODIES AND STAY IN THE AIR FOR DAYS AFTER A CREMATION
THE SKY LOOKS COOL LIKE THAT

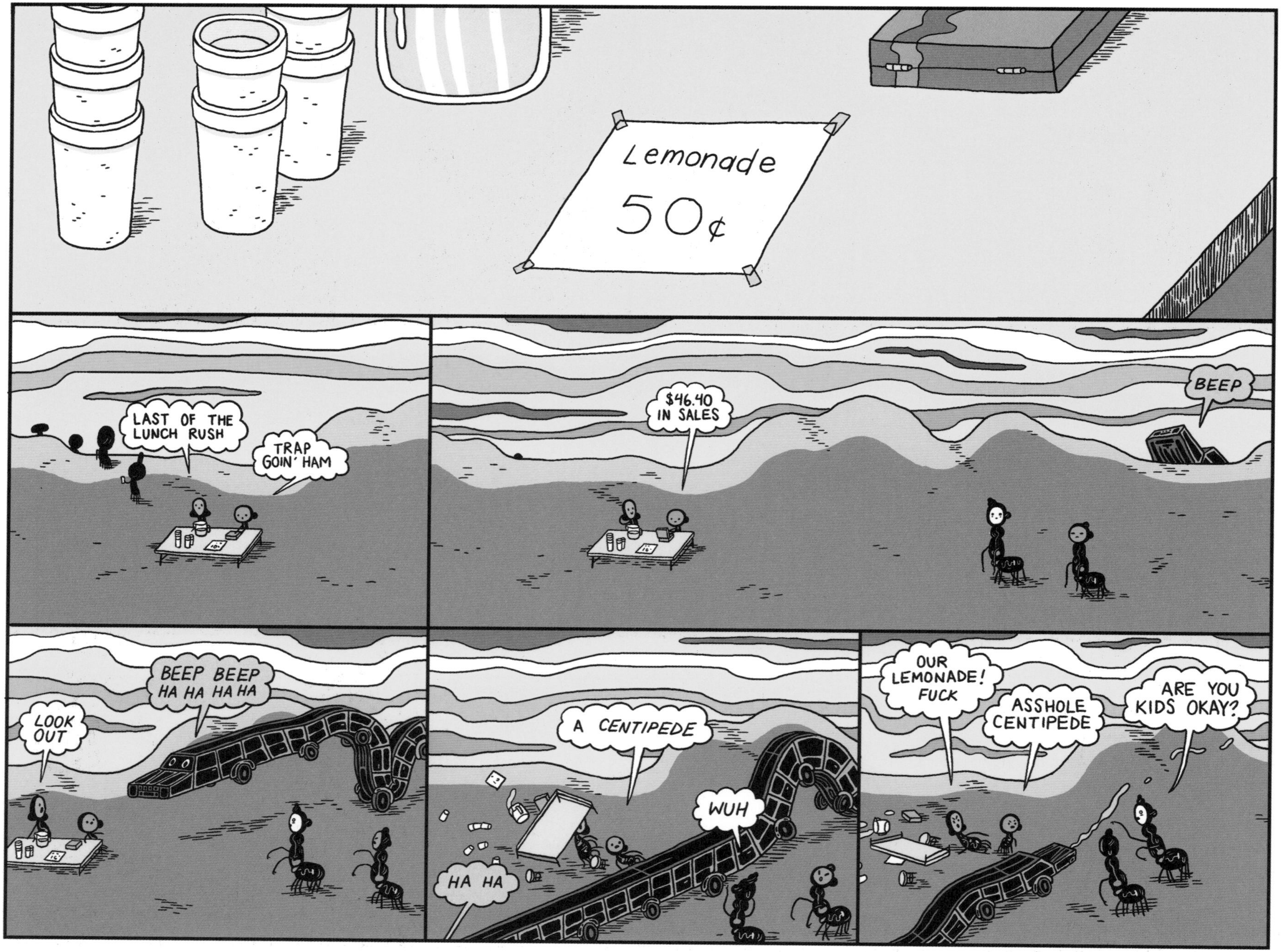
Lemonade
50¢
LAST OF THE LUNCH RUSH
TRAP GOIN' HAM
$46.40 IN SALES
BEEP
LOOK OUT
BEEP BEEP HA HA HA HA
A CENTIPEDE
HA HA
WUH
OUR LEMONADE! FUCK
ASSHOLE CENTIPEDE
ARE YOU KIDS OKAY?

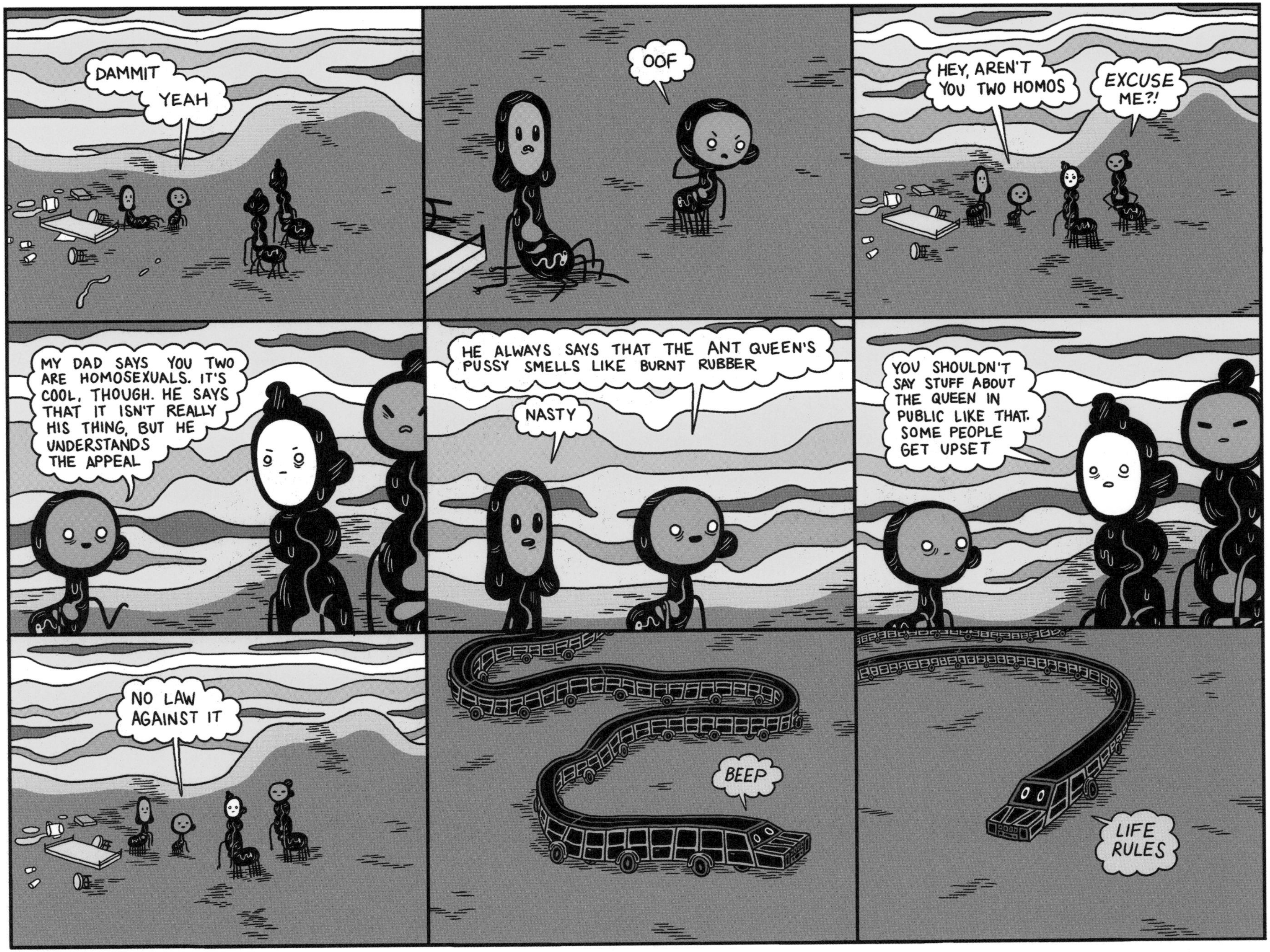
DAMMIT
YEAH
OOF
HEY, AREN'T YOU TWO HOMOS
EXCUSE ME?!
MY DAD SAYS YOU TWO ARE HOMOSEXUALS. IT'S COOL, THOUGH. HE SAYS THAT IT ISN'T REALLY HIS THING, BUT HE UNDERSTANDS THE APPEAL
HE ALWAYS SAYS THAT THE ANT QUEEN'S PUSSY SMELLS LIKE BURNT RUBBER
NASTY
YOU SHOULDN'T SAY STUFF ABOUT THE QUEEN IN PUBLIC LIKE THAT. SOME PEOPLE GET UPSET
NO LAW AGAINST IT
BEEP
LIFE RULES

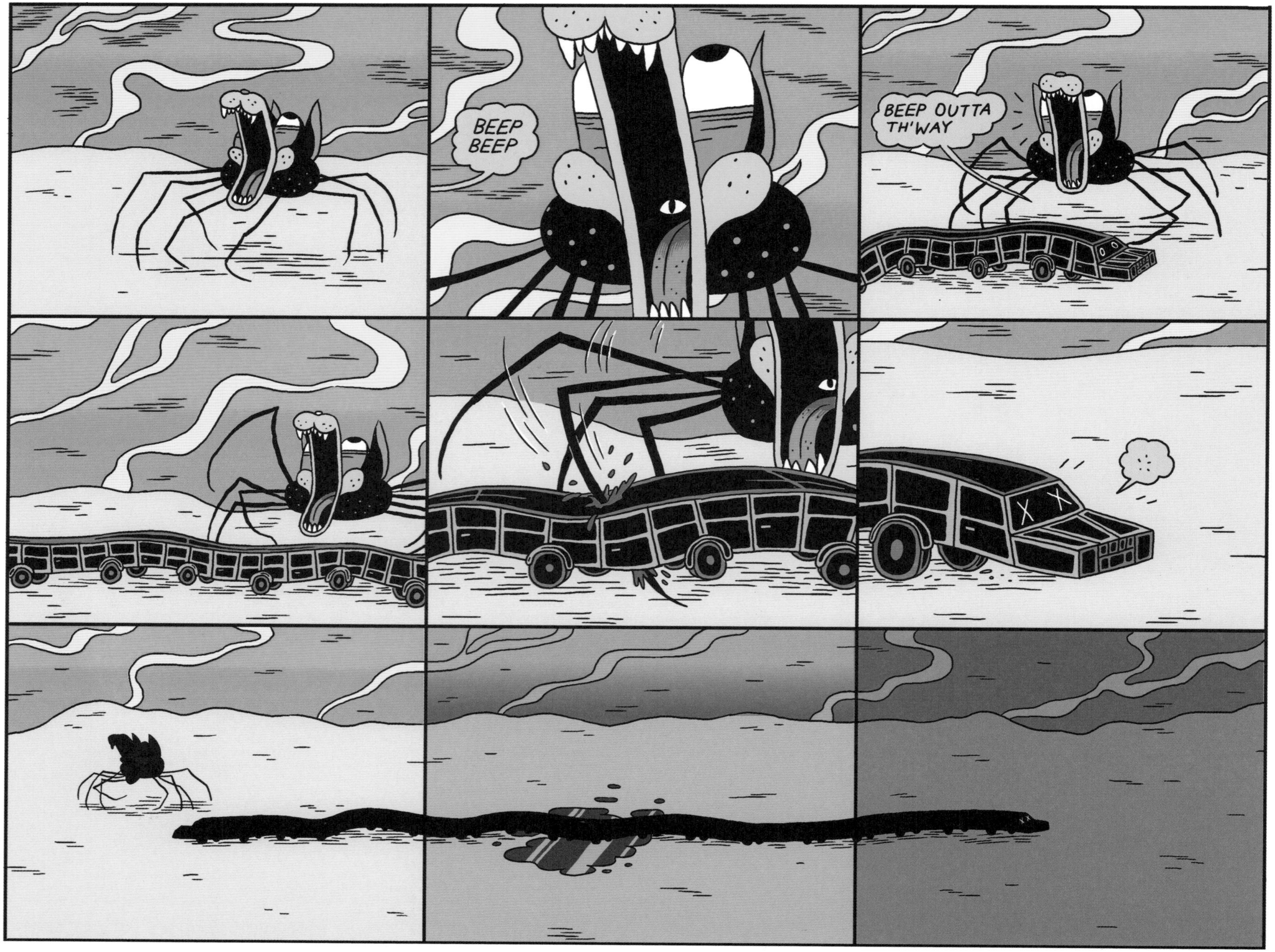
BEEP
BEEP
BEEP OUTTA
TH'WAY

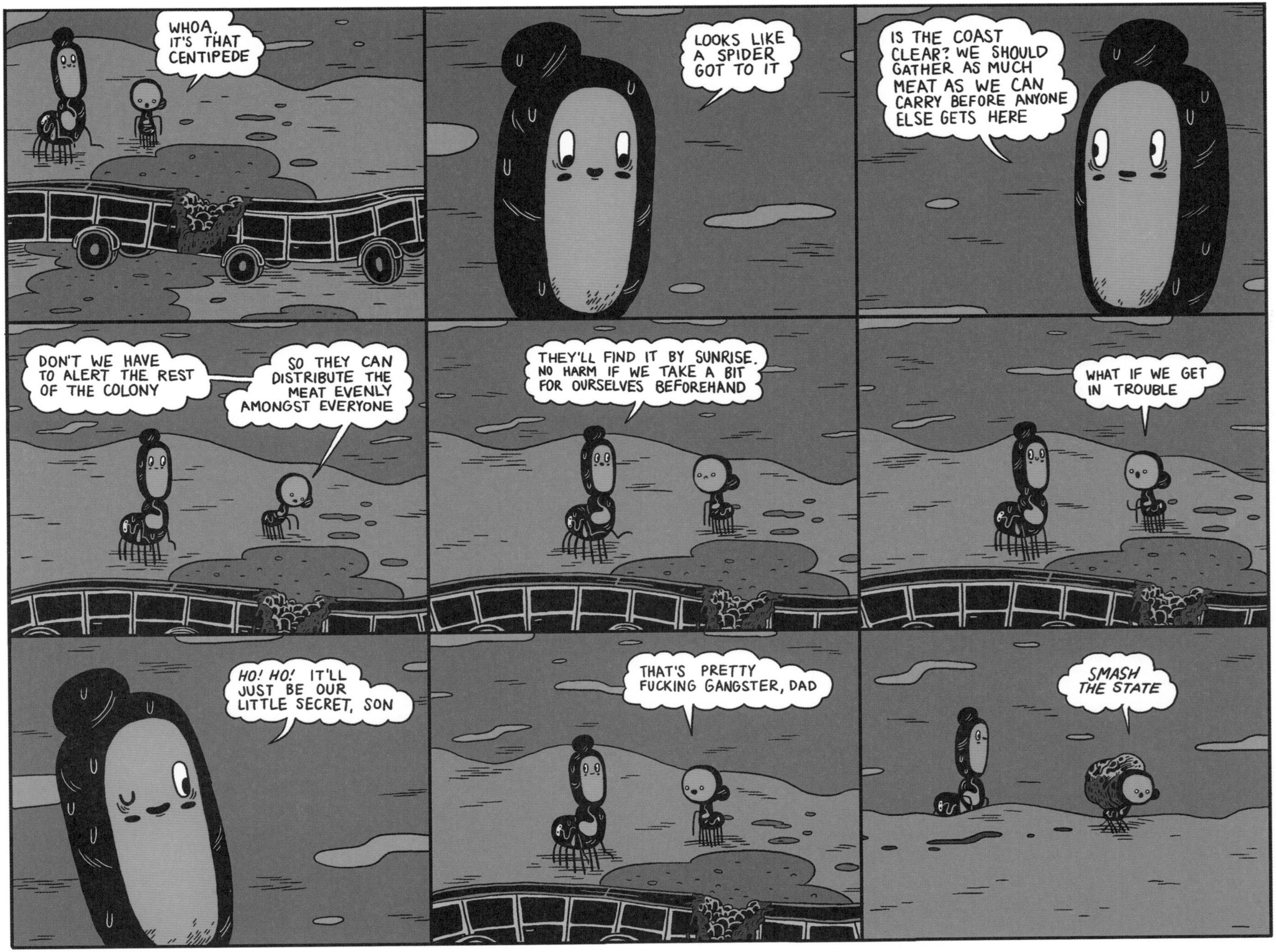
WHOA, IT'S THAT CENTIPEDE
LOOKS LIKE A SPIDER GOT TO IT
IS THE COAST CLEAR? WE SHOULD GATHER AS MUCH MEAT AS WE CAN CARRY BEFORE ANYONE ELSE GETS HERE
DON'T WE HAVE TO ALERT THE REST OF THE COLONY
SO THEY CAN DISTRIBUTE THE MEAT EVENLY AMONGST EVERYONE
THEY'LL FIND IT BY SUNRISE. NO HARM IF WE TAKE A BIT FOR OURSELVES BEFOREHAND
WHAT IF WE GET IN TROUBLE
HO! HO! IT'LL JUST BE OUR LITTLE SECRET, SON
THAT'S PRETTY FUCKING GANGSTER, DAD
SMASH THE STATE

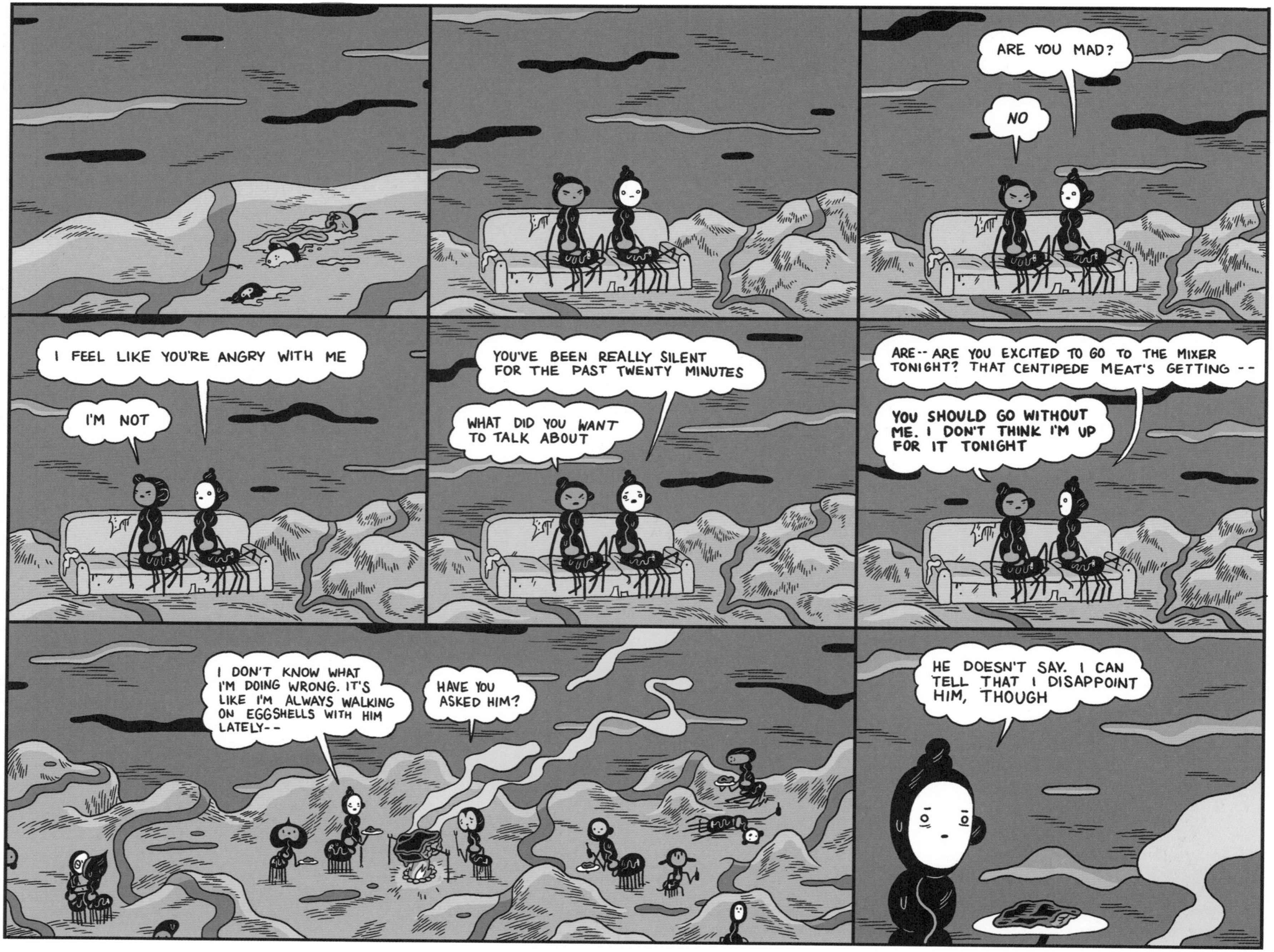
ARE YOU MAD?
NO
I FEEL LIKE YOU'RE ANGRY WITH ME
I'M NOT
YOU'VE BEEN REALLY SILENT FOR THE PAST TWENTY MINUTES
WHAT DID YOU WANT TO TALK ABOUT
ARE-- ARE YOU EXCITED TO GO TO THE MIXER TONIGHT? THAT CENTIPEDE MEAT'S GETTING --
YOU SHOULD GO WITHOUT ME. I DON'T THINK I'M UP FOR IT TONIGHT
I DON'T KNOW WHAT I'M DOING WRONG. IT'S LIKE I'M ALWAYS WALKING ON EGGSHELLS WITH HIM LATELY--
HAVE YOU ASKED HIM?
HE DOESN'T SAY. I CAN TELL THAT I DISAPPOINT HIM, THOUGH

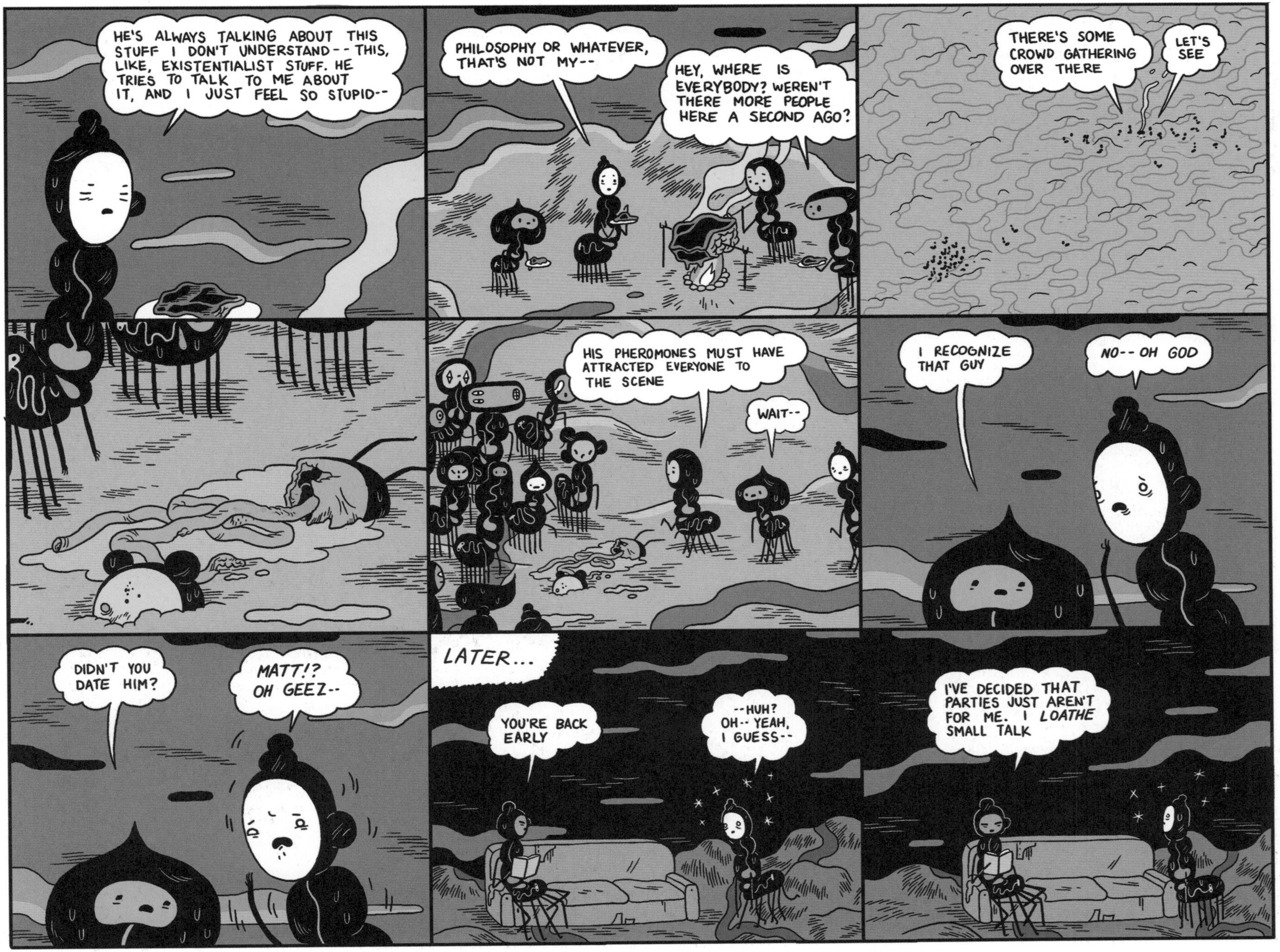
HE'S ALWAYS TALKING ABOUT THIS STUFF I DON'T UNDERSTAND--THIS, LIKE, EXISTENTIALIST STUFF. HE TRIES TO TALK TO ME ABOUT IT, AND I JUST FEEL SO STUPID--
PHILOSOPHY OR WHATEVER, THAT'S NOT MY--
HEY, WHERE IS EVERYBODY? WEREN'T THERE MORE PEOPLE HERE A SECOND AGO?
THERE'S SOME CROWD GATHERING OVER THERE
LET'S SEE
HIS PHEROMONES MUST HAVE ATTRACTED EVERYONE TO THE SCENE
WAIT--
I RECOGNIZE THAT GUY
NO--OH GOD
DIDN'T YOU DATE HIM?
MATT!? OH GEEZ--
LATER...
YOU'RE BACK EARLY
--HUH? OH--YEAH, I GUESS--
I'VE DECIDED THAT PARTIES JUST AREN'T FOR ME. I LOATHE SMALL TALK

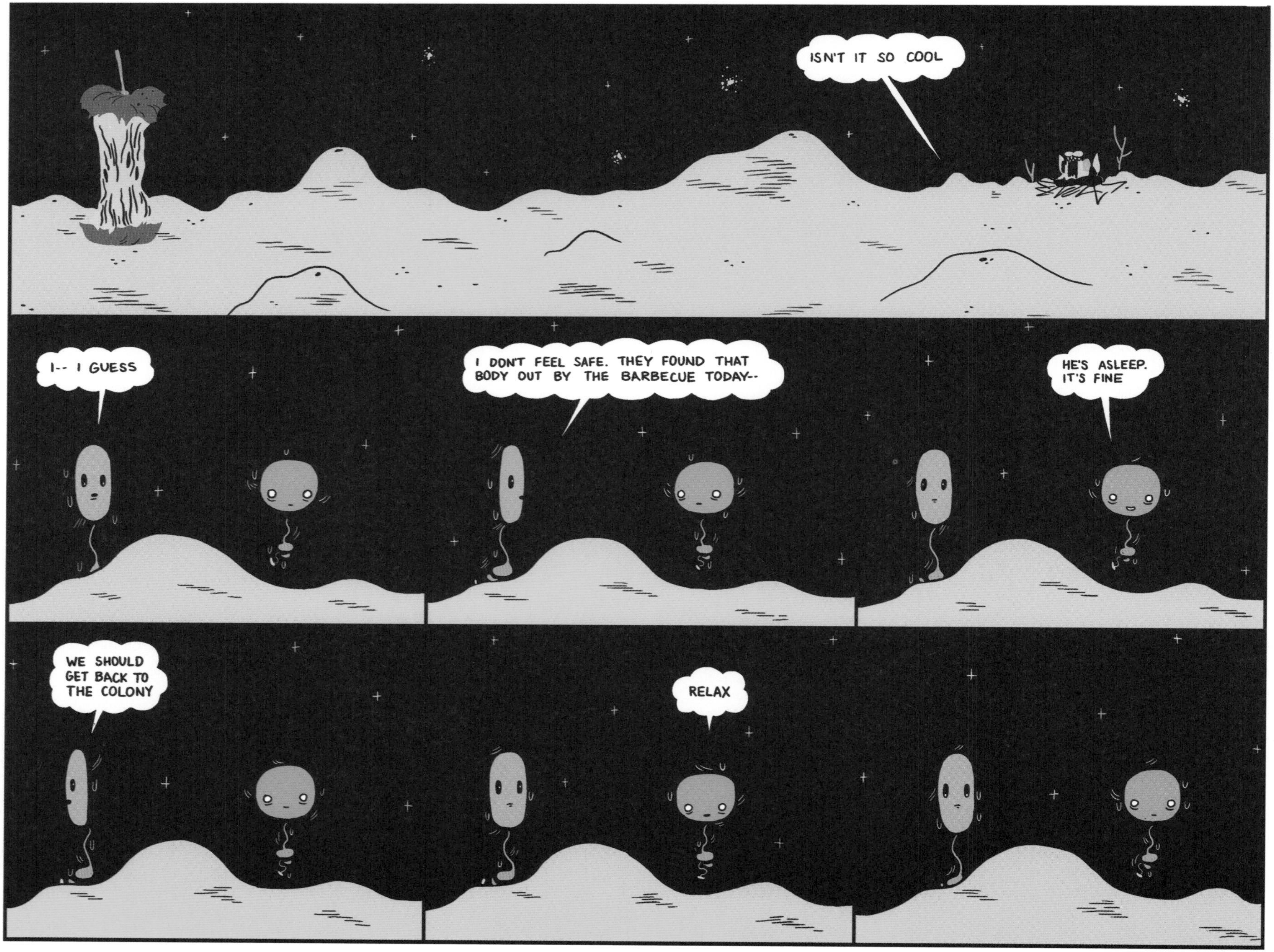
ISN'T IT SO COOL
I-- I GUESS
I DON'T FEEL SAFE. THEY FOUND THAT BODY OUT BY THE BARBECUE TODAY--
HE'S ASLEEP. IT'S FINE
WE SHOULD GET BACK TO THE COLONY
RELAX

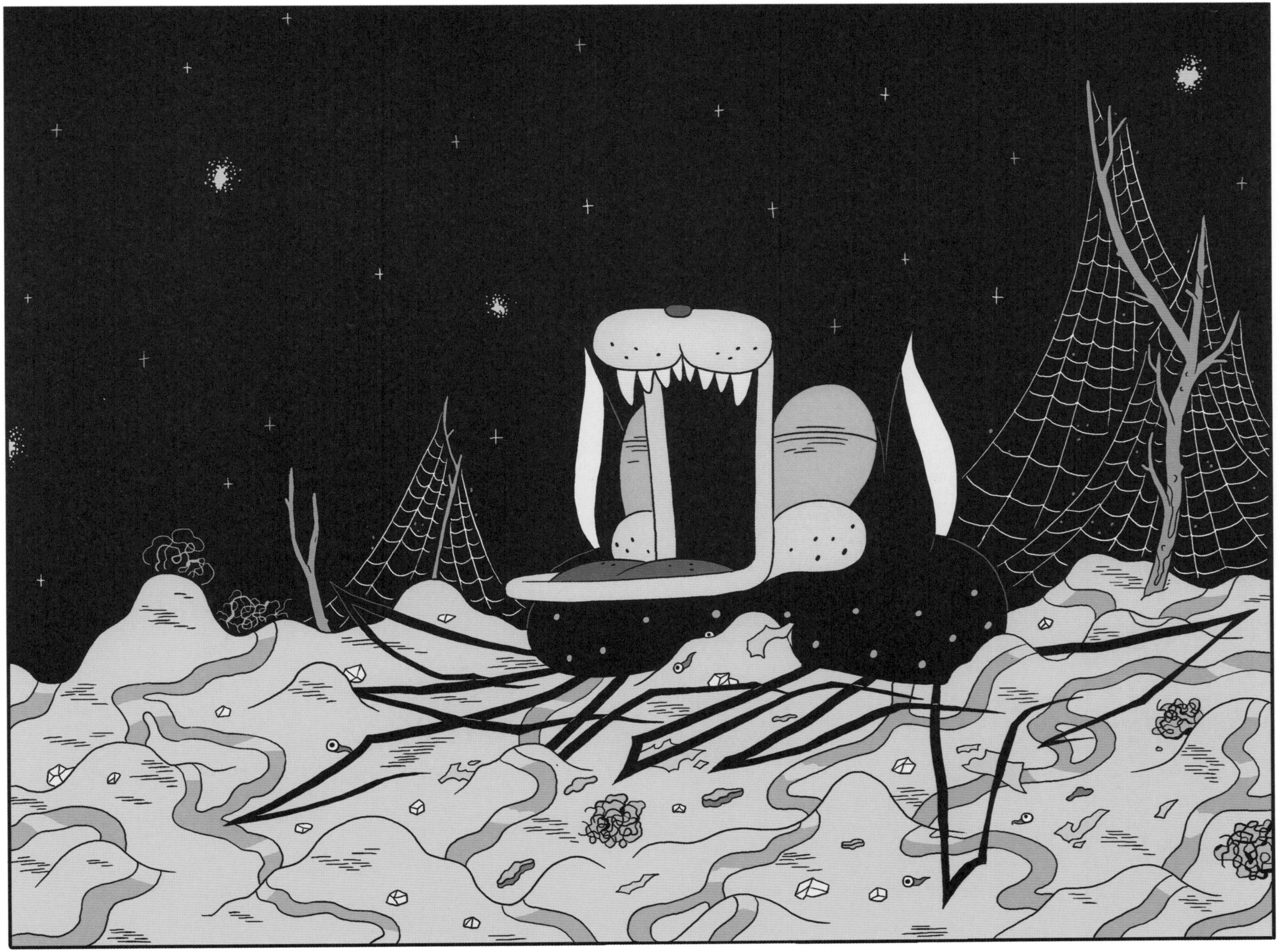

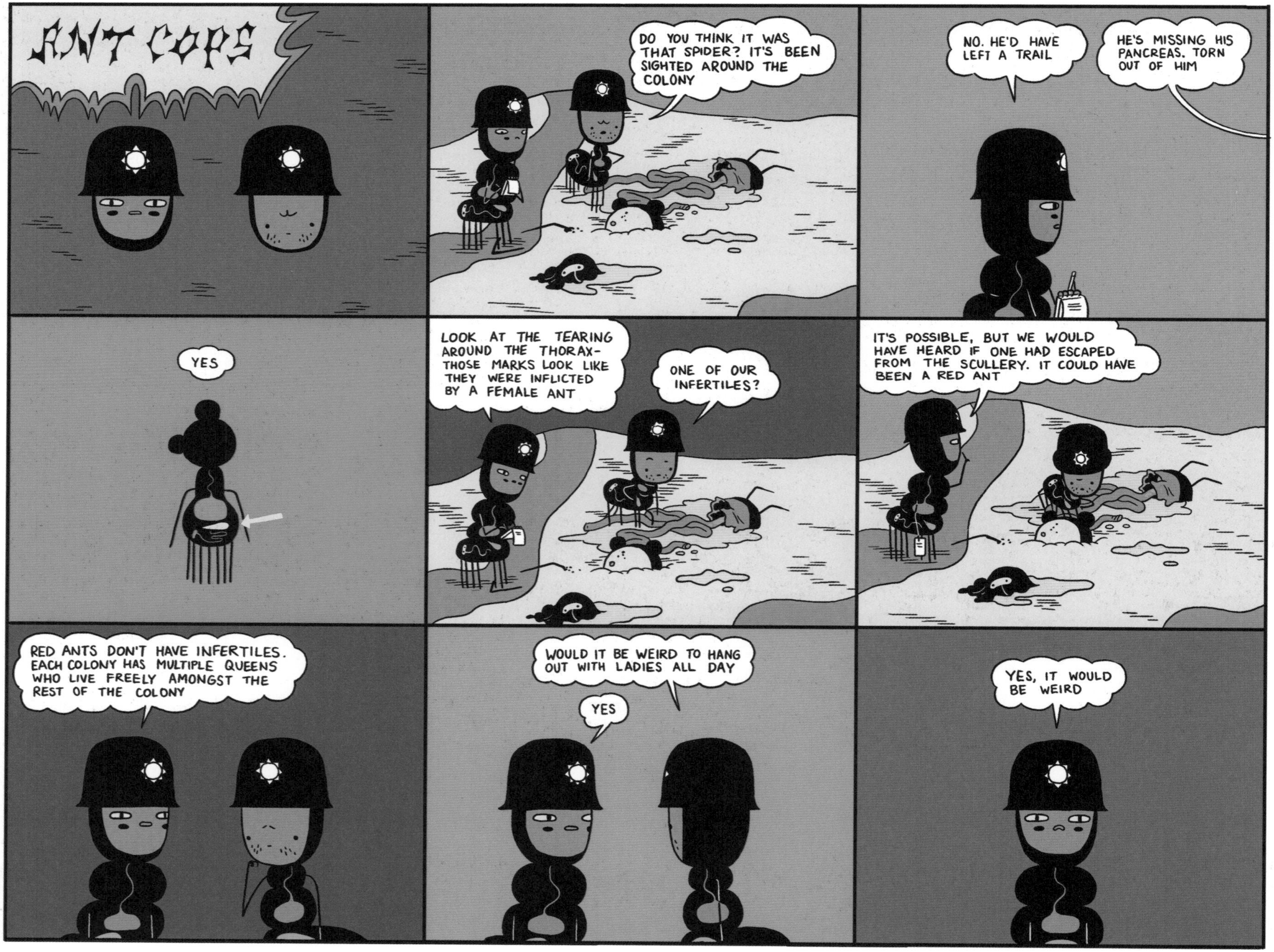
ANT COPS
DO YOU THINK IT WAS THAT SPIDER? IT'S BEEN SIGHTED AROUND THE COLONY
NO. HE'D HAVE LEFT A TRAIL
HE'S MISSING HIS PANCREAS. TORN OUT OF HIM
YES
LOOK AT THE TEARING AROUND THE THORAX- THOSE MARKS LOOK LIKE THEY WERE INFLICTED BY A FEMALE ANT
ONE OF OUR INFERTILES?
IT'S POSSIBLE, BUT WE WOULD HAVE HEARD IF ONE HAD ESCAPED FROM THE SCULLERY. IT COULD HAVE BEEN A RED ANT
RED ANTS DON'T HAVE INFERTILES. EACH COLONY HAS MULTIPLE QUEENS WHO LIVE FREELY AMONGST THE REST OF THE COLONY
WOULD IT BE WEIRD TO HANG OUT WITH LADIES ALL DAY
YES
YES, IT WOULD BE WEIRD

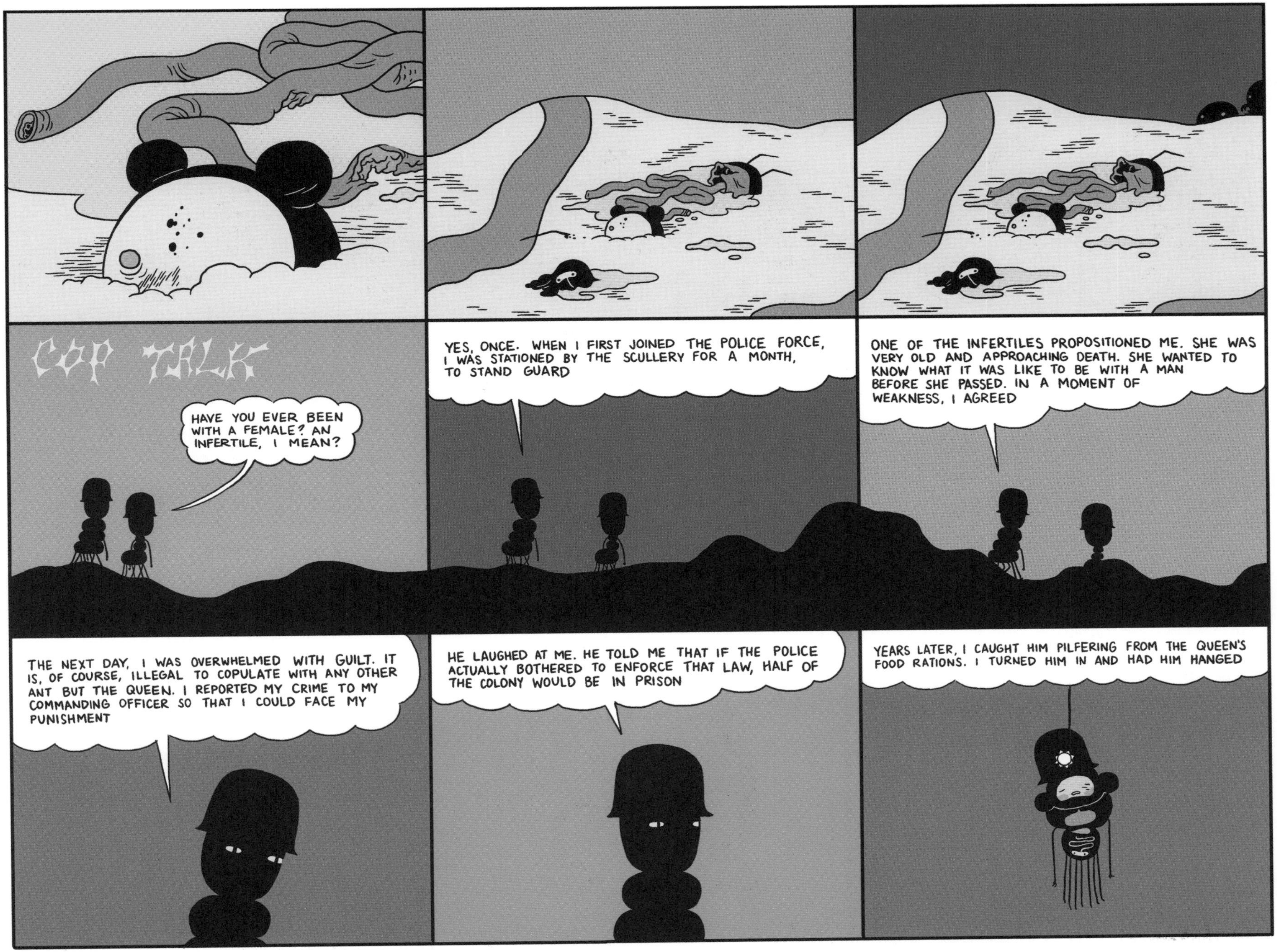
COP TALK
HAVE YOU EVER BEEN WITH A FEMALE? AN INFERTILE, I MEAN?
YES, ONCE. WHEN I FIRST JOINED THE POLICE FORCE, I WAS STATIONED BY THE SCULLERY FOR A MONTH, TO STAND GUARD
ONE OF THE INFERTILES PROPOSITIONED ME. SHE WAS VERY OLD AND APPROACHING DEATH. SHE WANTED TO KNOW WHAT IT WAS LIKE TO BE WITH A MAN BEFORE SHE PASSED. IN A MOMENT OF WEAKNESS, I AGREED
THE NEXT DAY, I WAS OVERWHELMED WITH GUILT. IT IS, OF COURSE, ILLEGAL TO COPULATE WITH ANY OTHER ANT BUT THE QUEEN. I REPORTED MY CRIME TO MY COMMANDING OFFICER SO THAT I COULD FACE MY PUNISHMENT
HE LAUGHED AT ME. HE TOLD ME THAT IF THE POLICE ACTUALLY BOTHERED TO ENFORCE THAT LAW, HALF OF THE COLONY WOULD BE IN PRISON
YEARS LATER, I CAUGHT HIM PILFERING FROM THE QUEEN'S FOOD RATIONS. I TURNED HIM IN AND HAD HIM HANGED

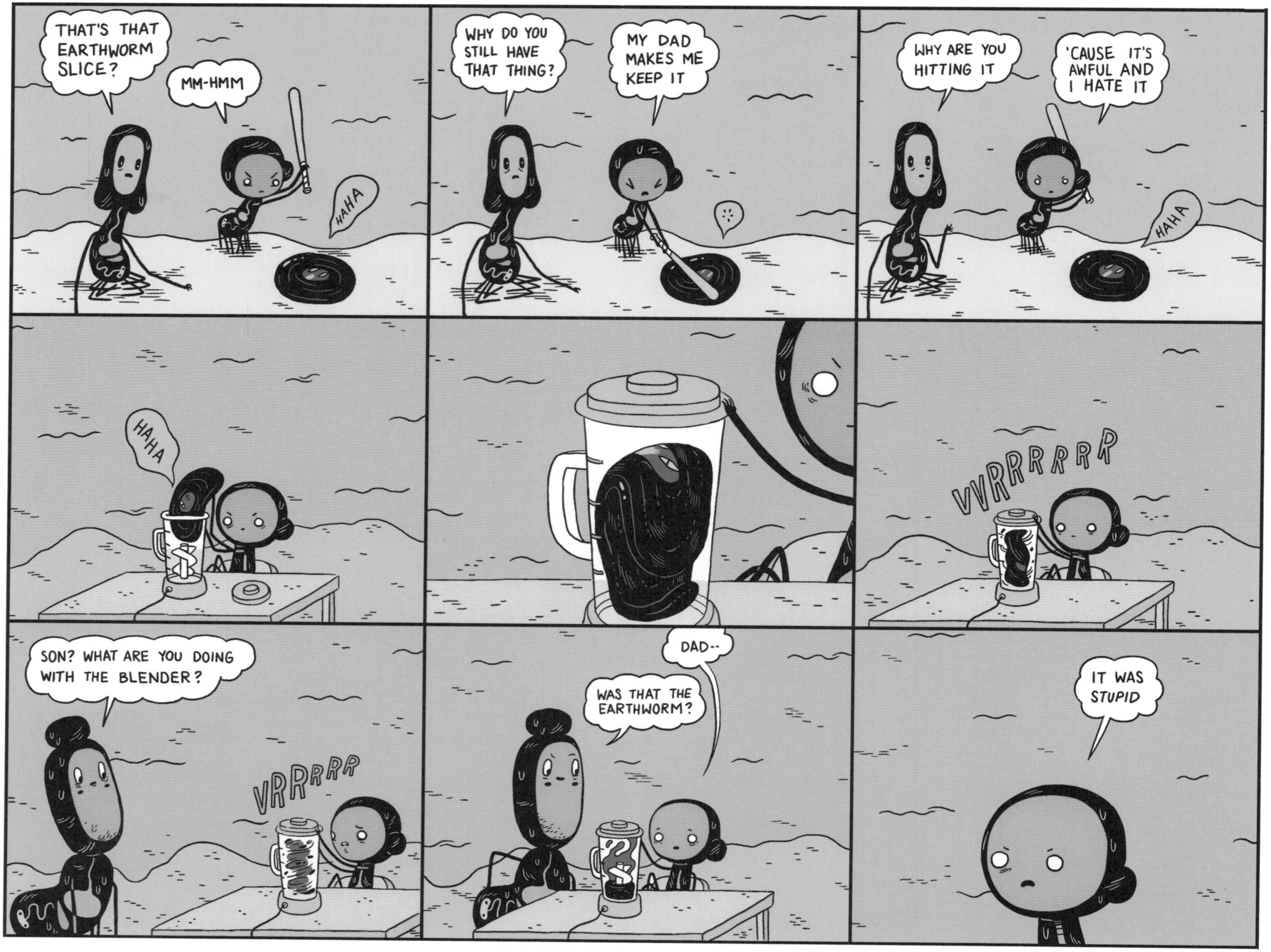
THAT'S THAT EARTHWORM SLICE?
MM-HMM
HAHA
WHY DO YOU STILL HAVE THAT THING?
MY DAD MAKES ME KEEP IT
WHY ARE YOU HITTING IT
'CAUSE IT'S AWFUL AND I HATE IT
HAHA
HAHA
VVRRRRRRR
SON? WHAT ARE YOU DOING WITH THE BLENDER?
VRRRRR
DAD--
WAS THAT THE EARTHWORM?
IT WAS STUPID

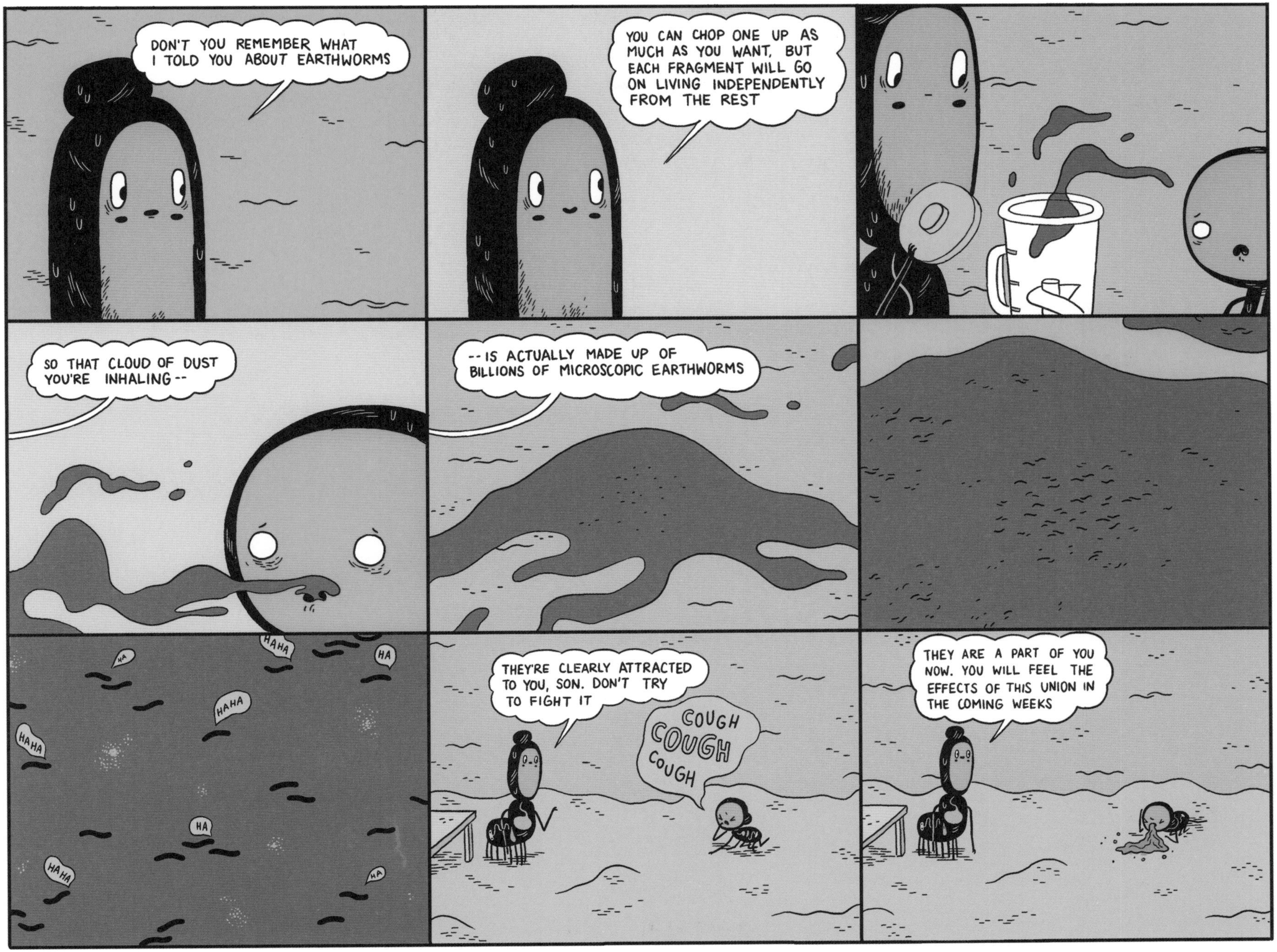
DON'T YOU REMEMBER WHAT I TOLD YOU ABOUT EARTHWORMS
YOU CAN CHOP ONE UP AS MUCH AS YOU WANT, BUT EACH FRAGMENT WILL GO ON LIVING INDEPENDENTLY FROM THE REST
SO THAT CLOUD OF DUST YOU'RE INHALING--
--IS ACTUALLY MADE UP OF BILLIONS OF MICROSCOPIC EARTHWORMS
HAHA
HA
HA
HAHA
HAHA
HA
HAHA
HA
THEY'RE CLEARLY ATTRACTED TO YOU, SON. DON'T TRY TO FIGHT IT
COUGH COUGH COUGH
THEY ARE A PART OF YOU NOW. YOU WILL FEEL THE EFFECTS OF THIS UNION IN THE COMING WEEKS

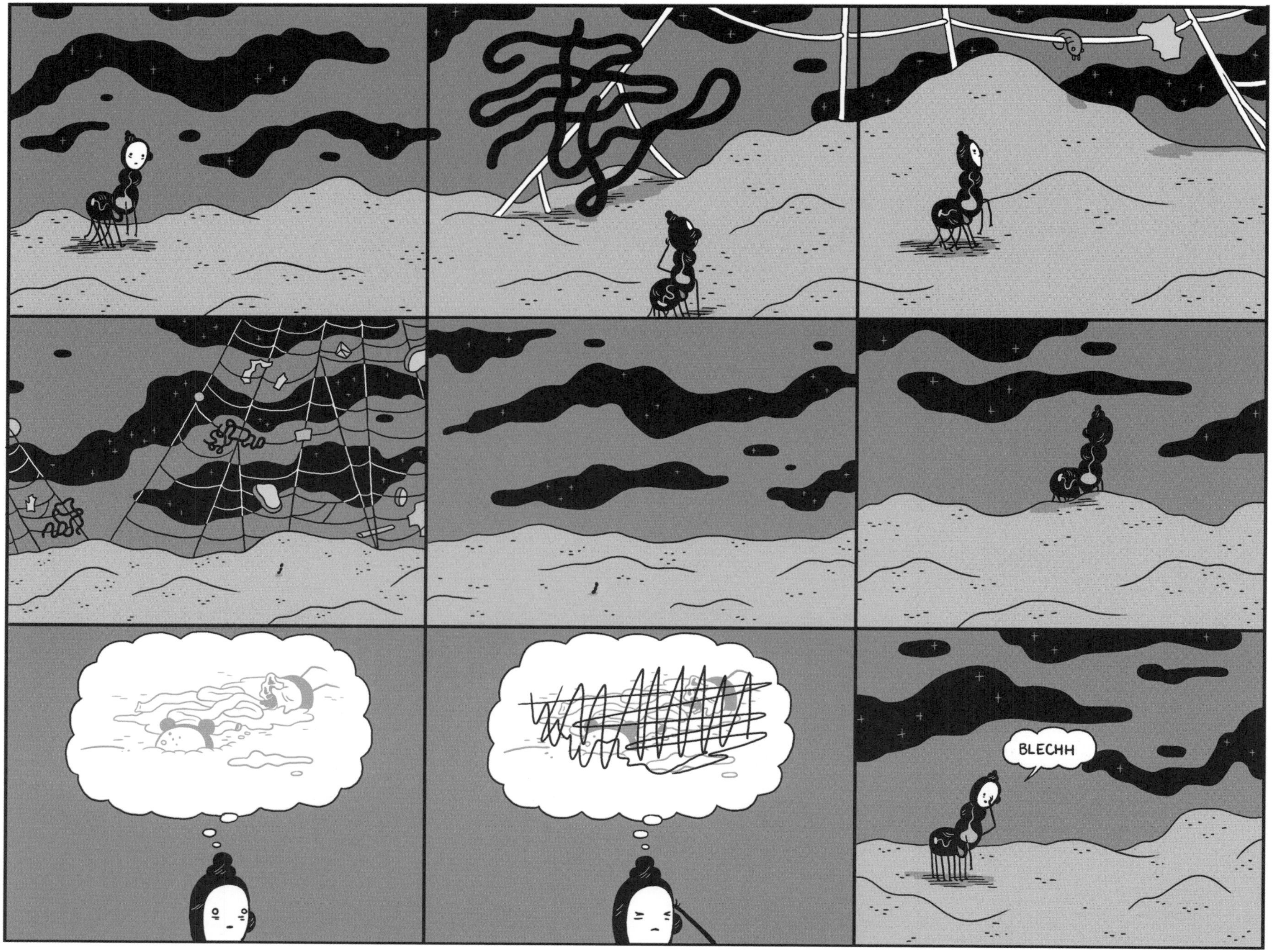
BLECHH

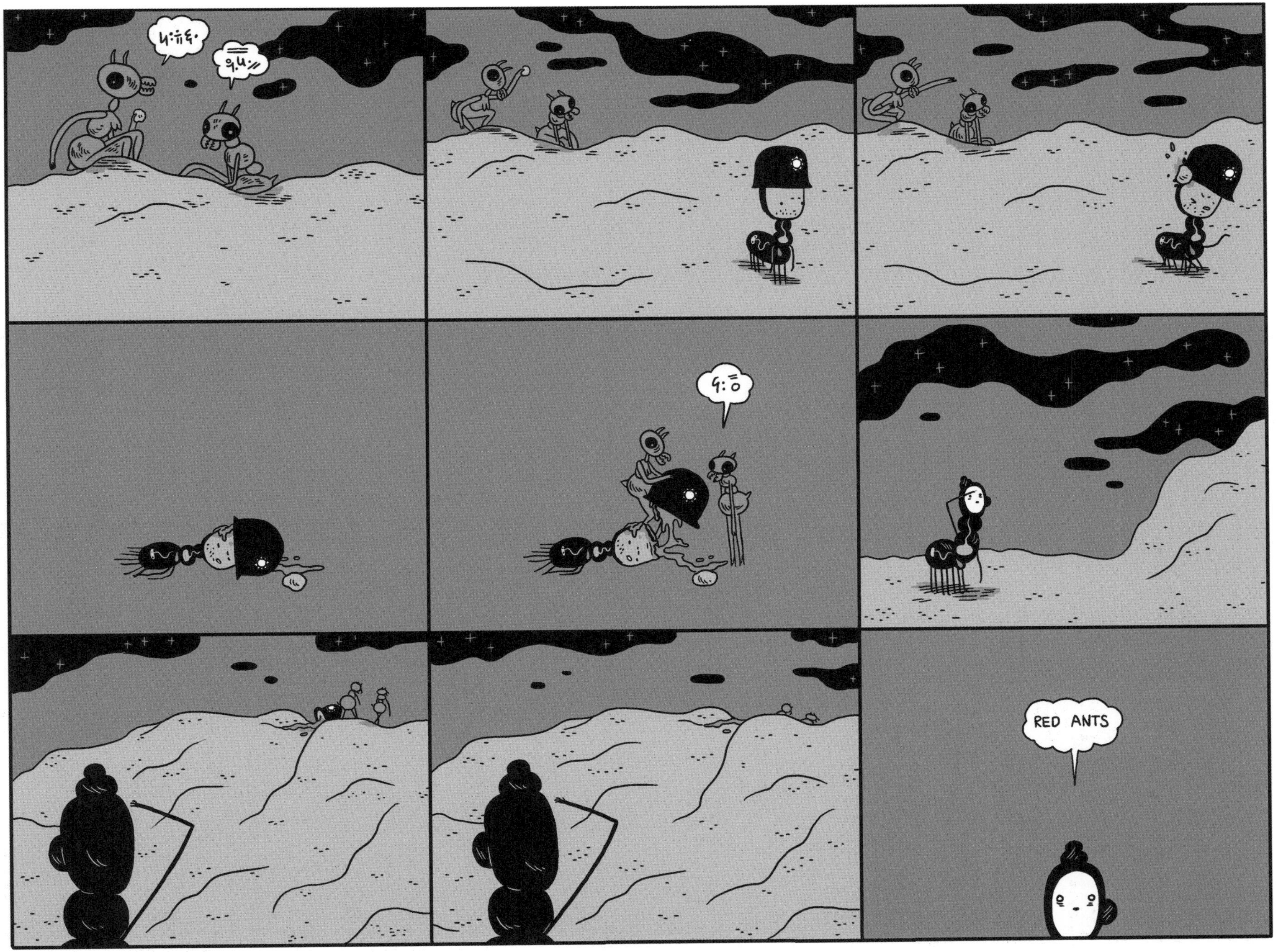
RED ANTS

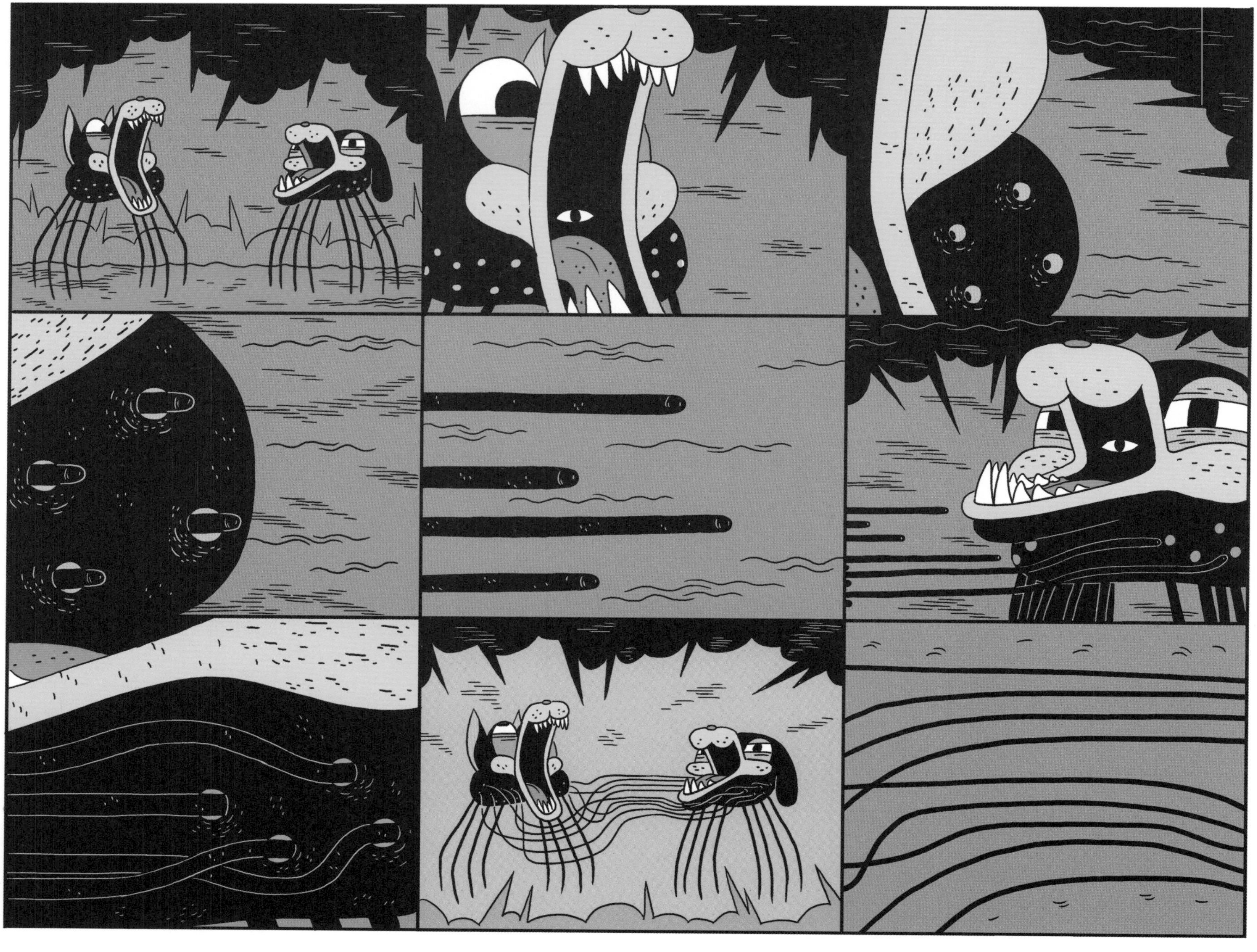

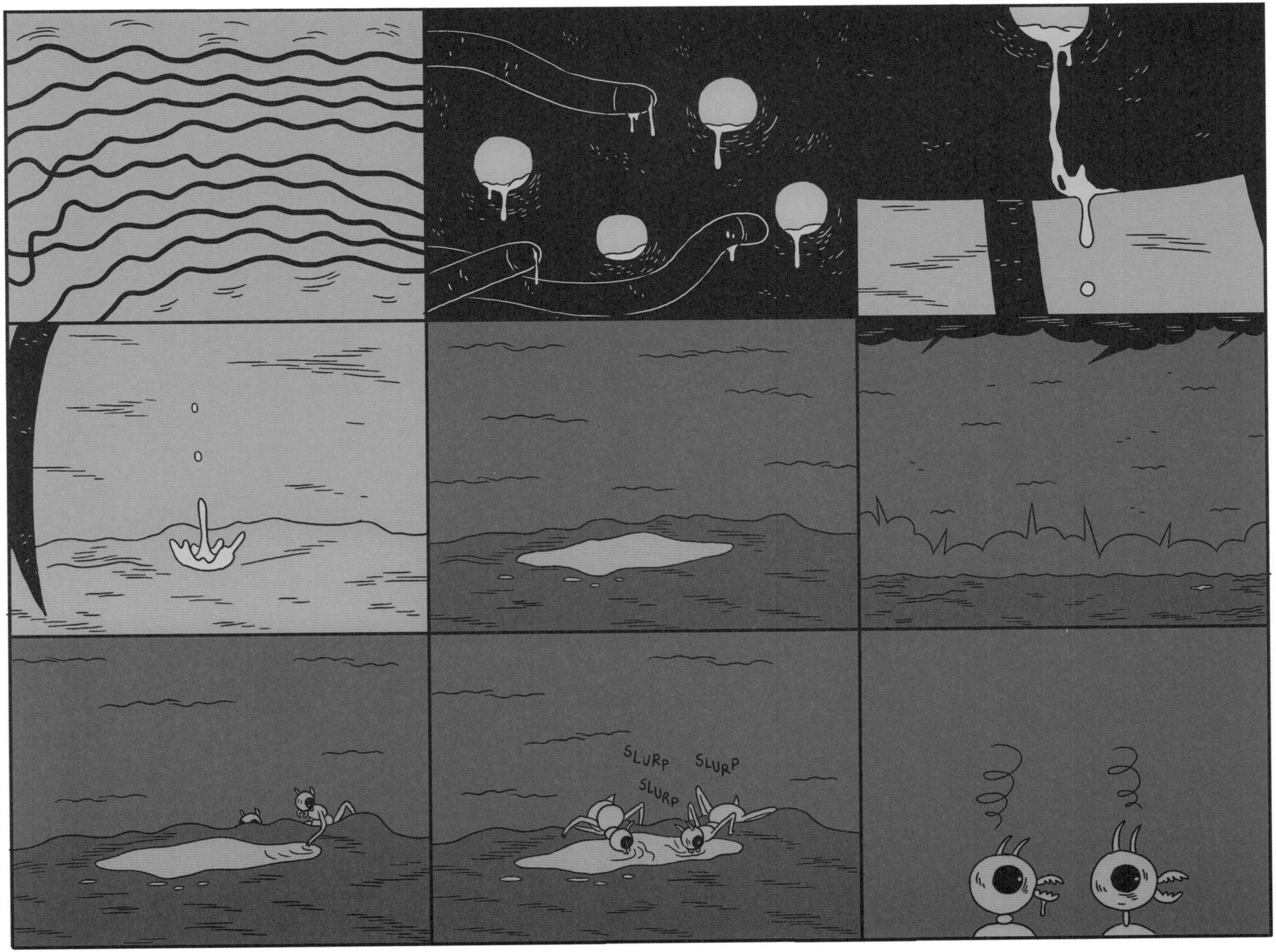
SLURP
SLURP
SLURP

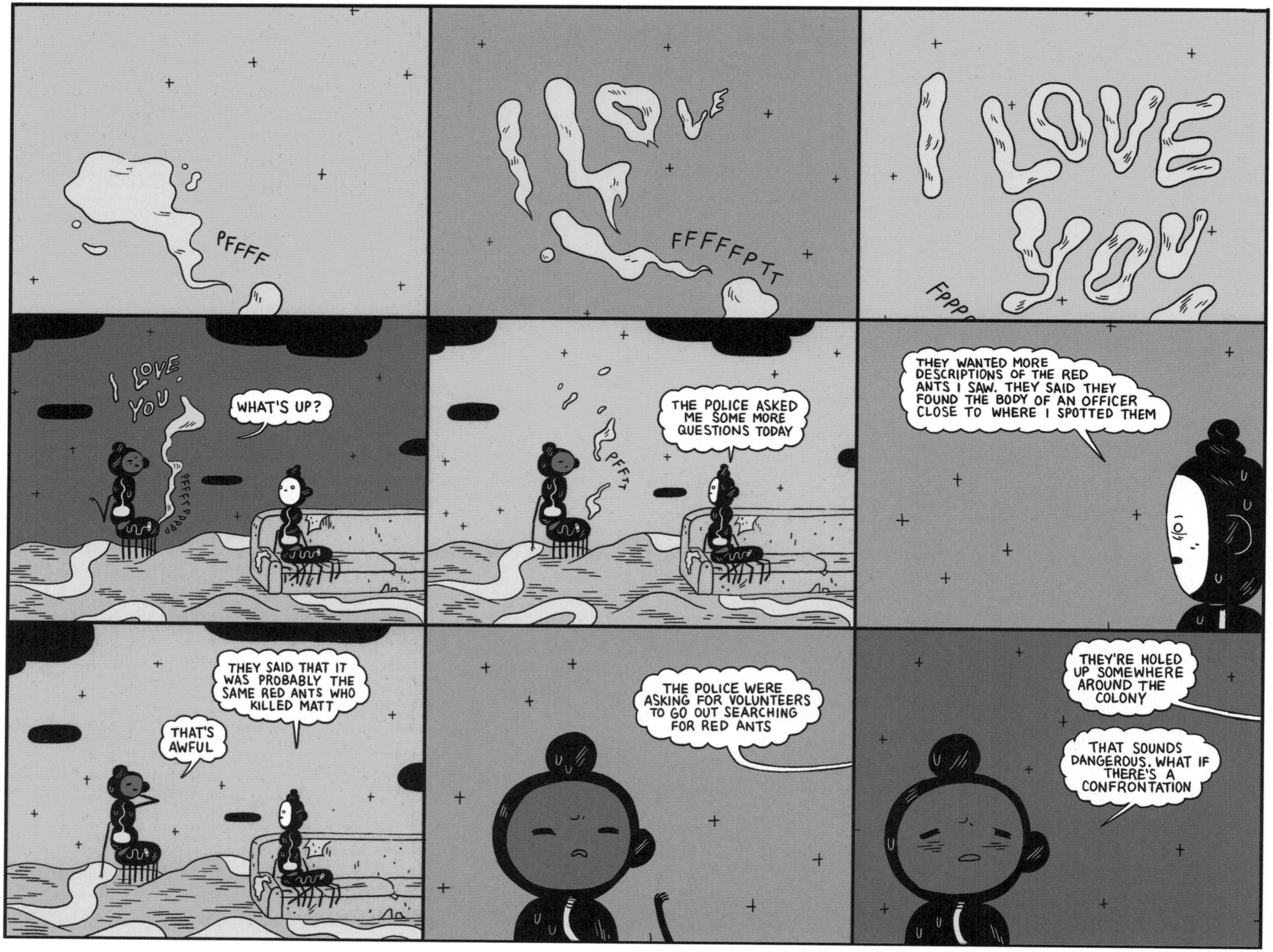
PFFFF
I LOVE
FFFFFPTT
I LOVE YOU
FPPP
I LOVE YOU
PFFTPPPP
WHAT'S UP?
PFFTT
THE POLICE ASKED ME SOME MORE QUESTIONS TODAY
THEY WANTED MORE DESCRIPTIONS OF THE RED ANTS I SAW. THEY SAID THEY FOUND THE BODY OF AN OFFICER CLOSE TO WHERE I SPOTTED THEM
THEY SAID THAT IT WAS PROBABLY THE SAME RED ANTS WHO KILLED MATT
THAT'S AWFUL
THE POLICE WERE ASKING FOR VOLUNTEERS TO GO OUT SEARCHING FOR RED ANTS
THEY'RE HOLED UP SOMEWHERE AROUND THE COLONY
THAT SOUNDS DANGEROUS. WHAT IF THERE'S A CONFRONTATION

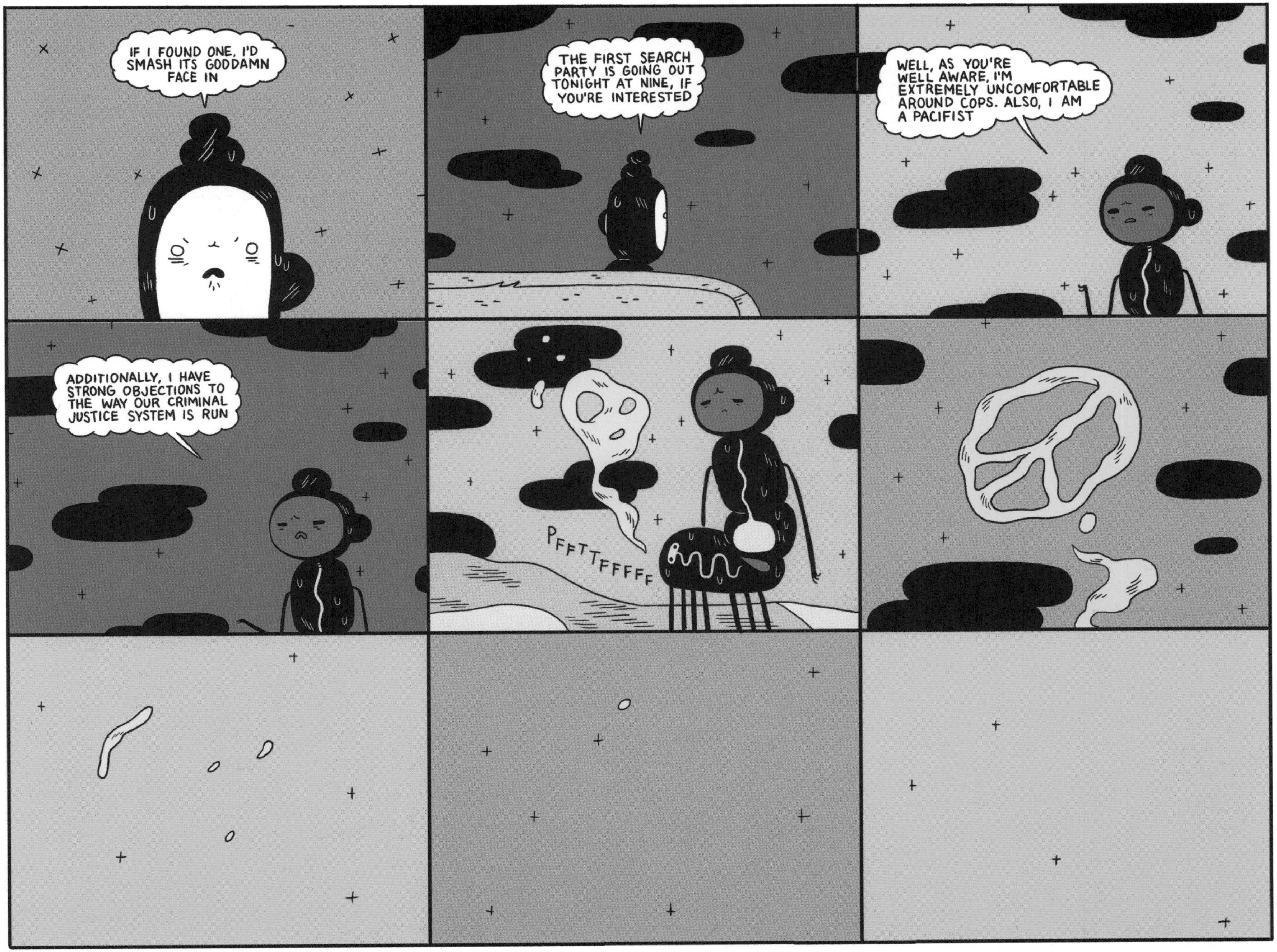
IF I FOUND ONE, I'D SMASH ITS GODDAMN FACE IN
THE FIRST SEARCH PARTY IS GOING OUT TONIGHT AT NINE, IF YOU'RE INTERESTED
WELL, AS YOU'RE WELL AWARE, I'M EXTREMELY UNCOMFORTABLE AROUND COPS. ALSO, I AM A PACIFIST
ADDITIONALLY, I HAVE STRONG OBJECTIONS TO THE WAY OUR CRIMINAL JUSTICE SYSTEM IS RUN
PFFTTFFFFF

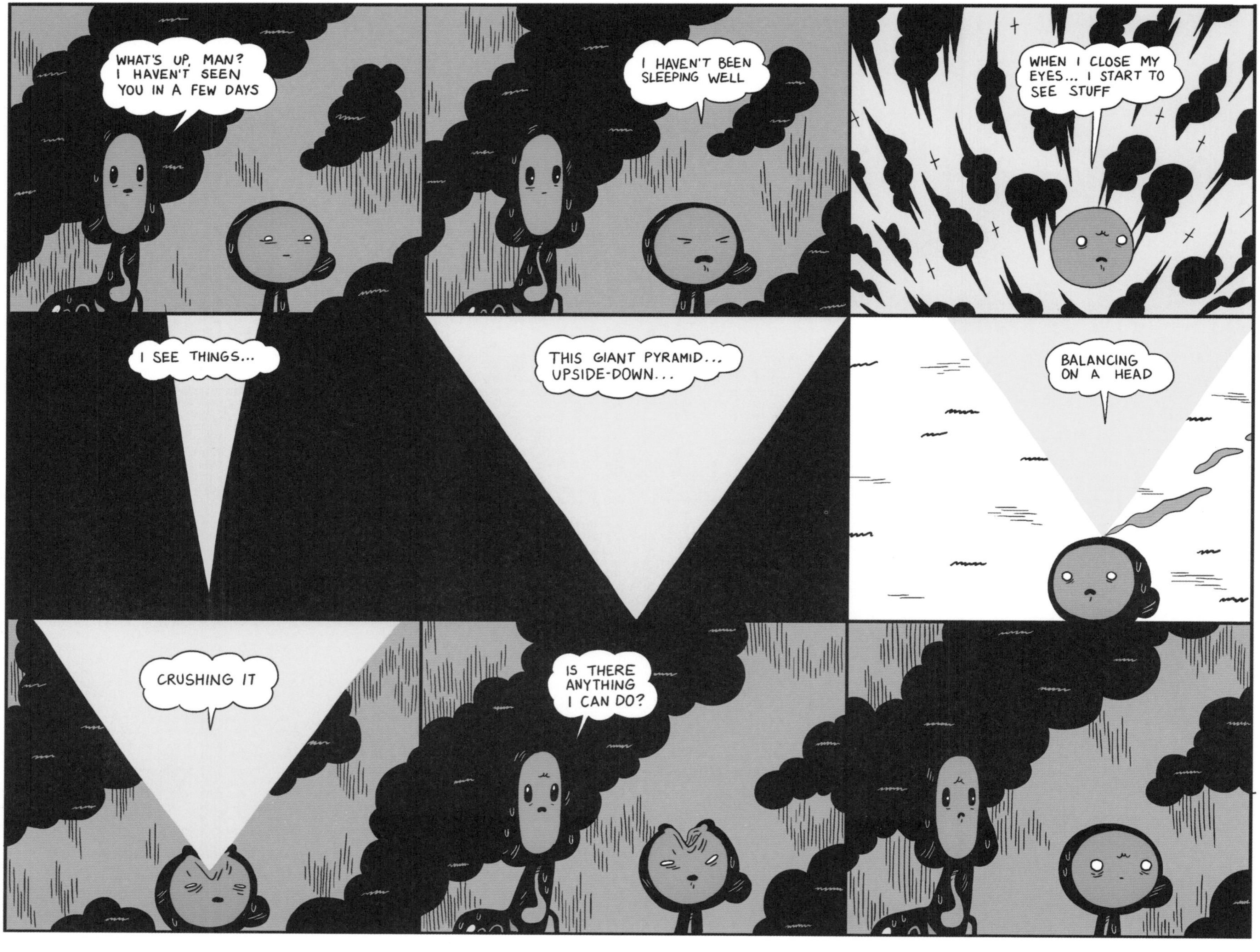
WHAT'S UP, MAN? I HAVEN'T SEEN YOU IN A FEW DAYS
I HAVEN'T BEEN SLEEPING WELL
WHEN I CLOSE MY EYES... I START TO SEE STUFF
I SEE THINGS...
THIS GIANT PYRAMID... UPSIDE-DOWN...
BALANCING ON A HEAD
CRUSHING IT
IS THERE ANYTHING I CAN DO?

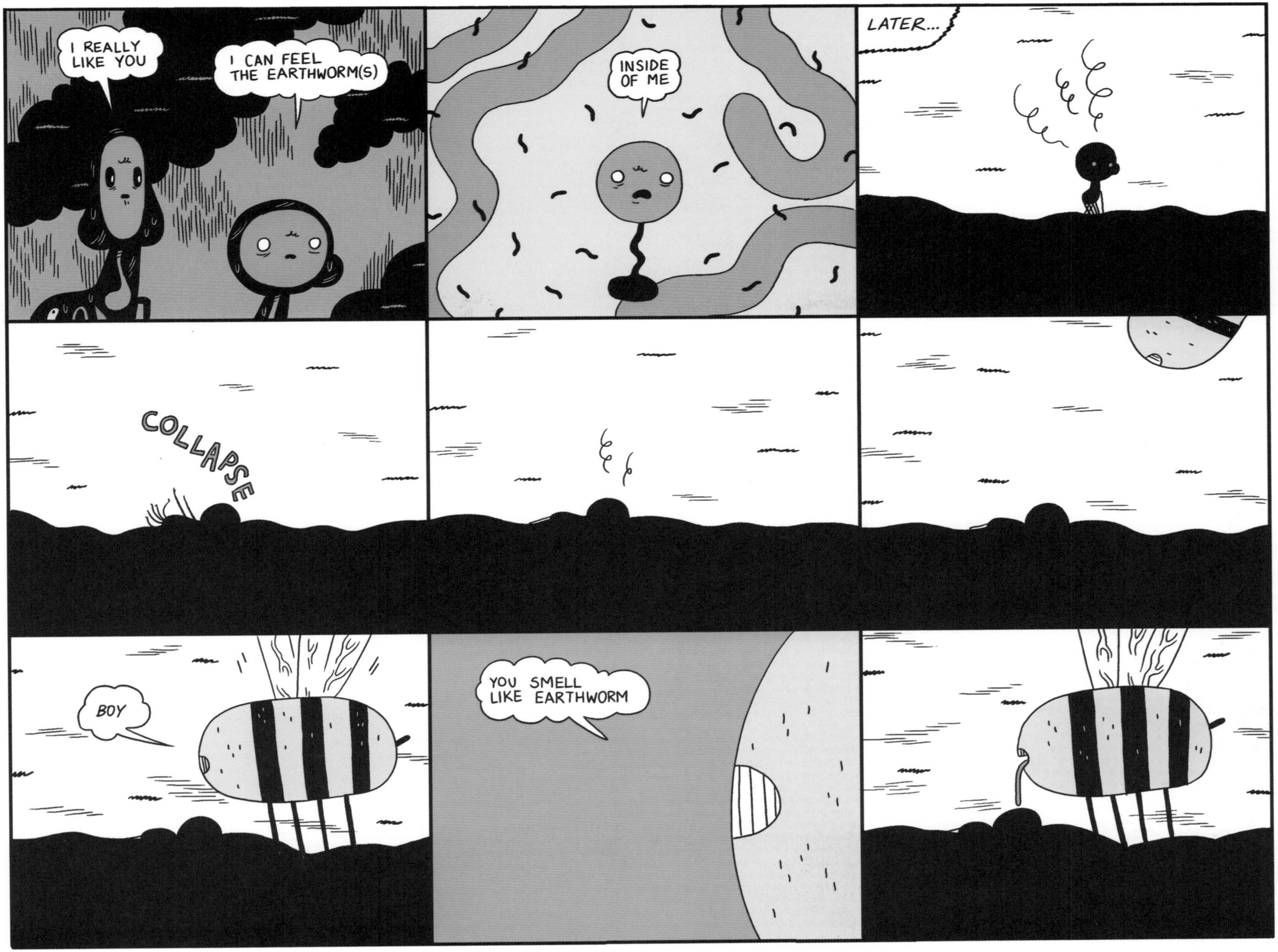
I REALLY LIKE YOU
I CAN FEEL THE EARTHWORM(S)
INSIDE OF ME
LATER...
COLLAPSE
BOY
YOU SMELL LIKE EARTHWORM

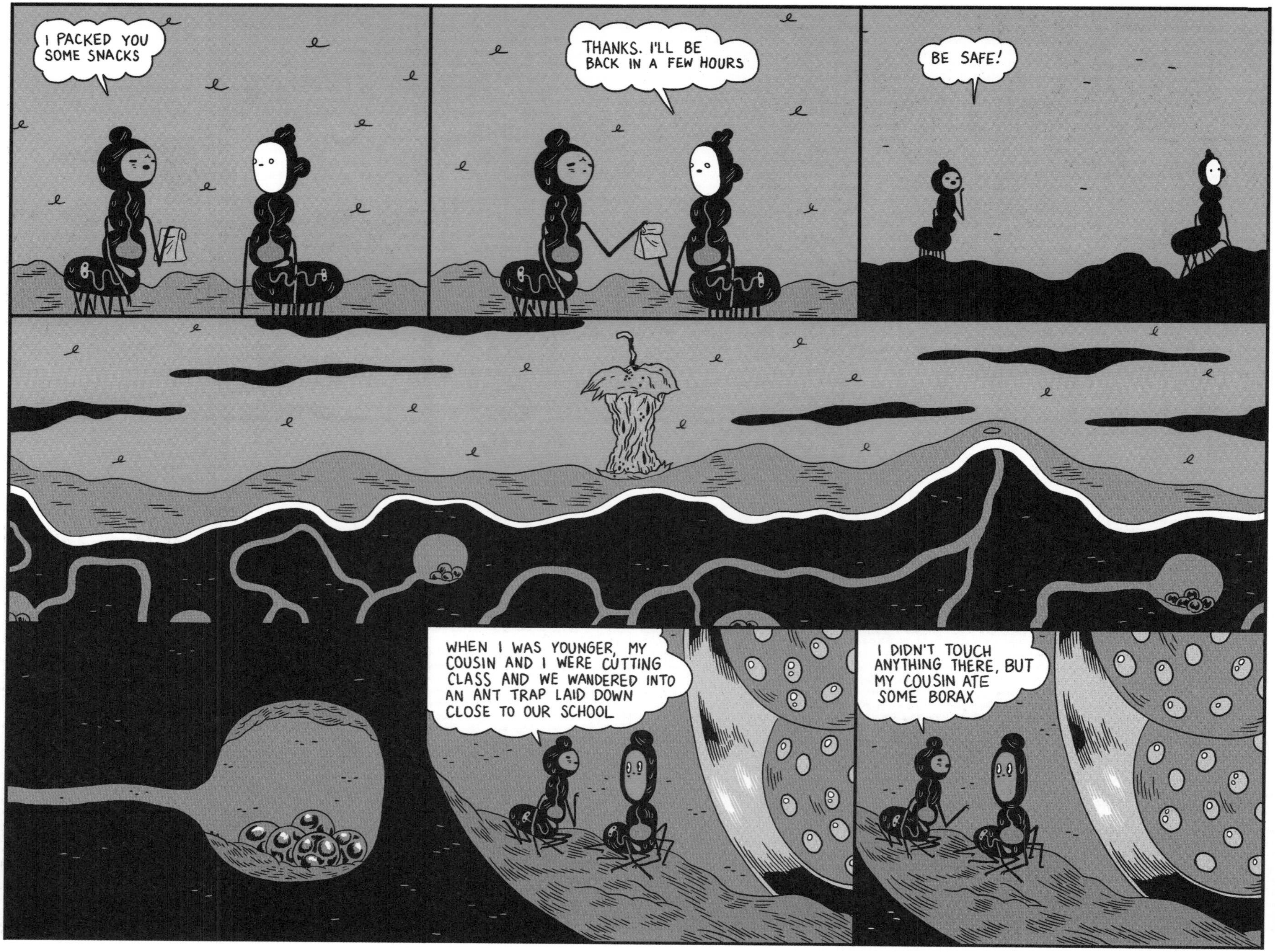

I PACKED YOU SOME SNACKS
THANKS. I'LL BE BACK IN A FEW HOURS
BE SAFE!
WHEN I WAS YOUNGER, MY COUSIN AND I WERE CUTTING CLASS AND WE WANDERED INTO AN ANT TRAP LAID DOWN CLOSE TO OUR SCHOOL
I DIDN'T TOUCH ANYTHING THERE, BUT MY COUSIN ATE SOME BORAX

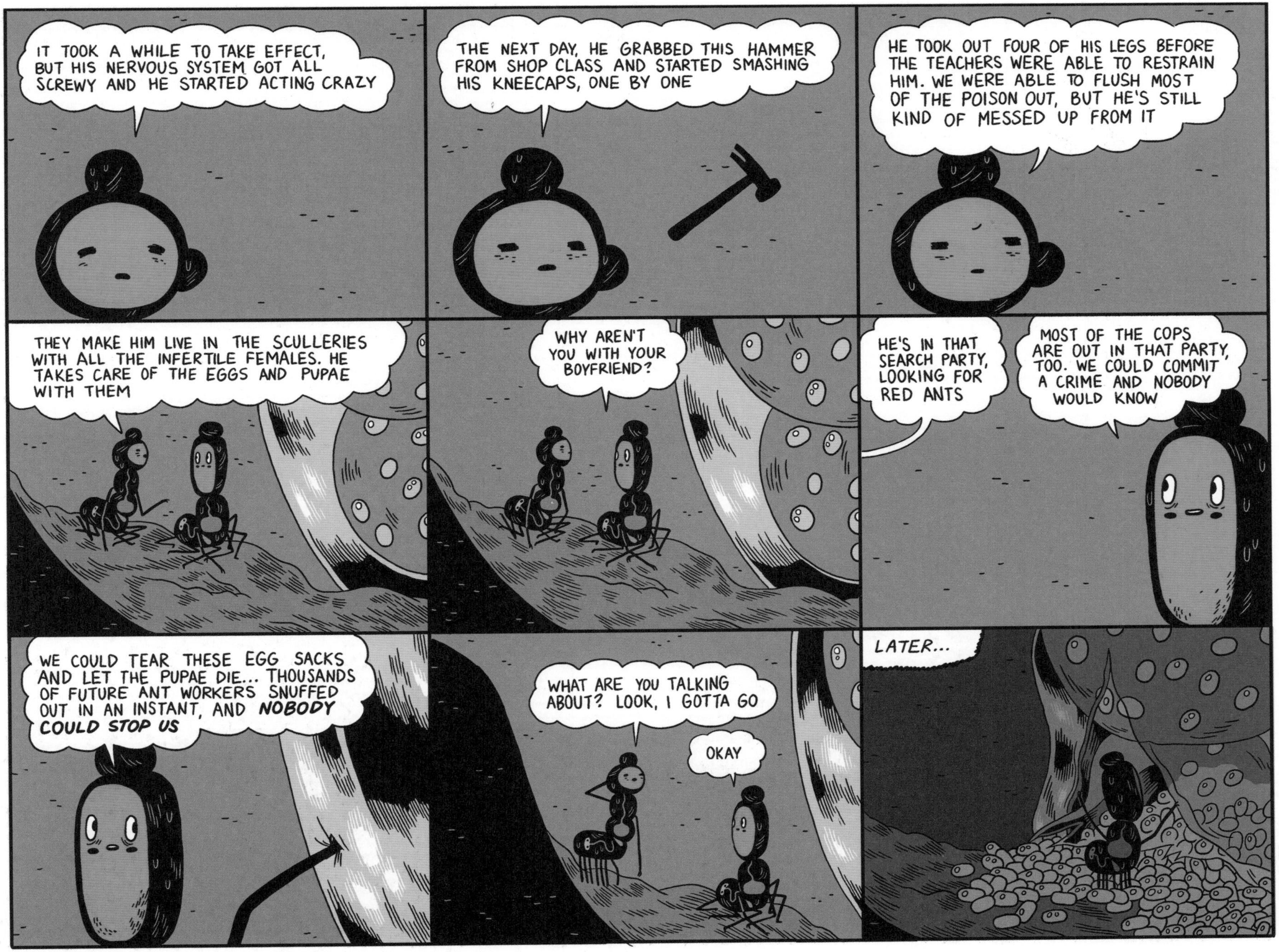

IT TOOK A WHILE TO TAKE EFFECT, BUT HIS NERVOUS SYSTEM GOT ALL SCREWY AND HE STARTED ACTING CRAZY
THE NEXT DAY, HE GRABBED THIS HAMMER FROM SHOP CLASS AND STARTED SMASHING HIS KNEECAPS, ONE BY ONE
HE TOOK OUT FOUR OF HIS LEGS BEFORE THE TEACHERS WERE ABLE TO RESTRAIN HIM. WE WERE ABLE TO FLUSH MOST OF THE POISON OUT, BUT HE'S STILL KIND OF MESSED UP FROM IT
THEY MAKE HIM LIVE IN THE SCULLERIES WITH ALL THE INFERTILE FEMALES. HE TAKES CARE OF THE EGGS AND PUPAE WITH THEM
WHY AREN'T YOU WITH YOUR BOYFRIEND?
HE'S IN THAT SEARCH PARTY, LOOKING FOR RED ANTS
MOST OF THE COPS ARE OUT IN THAT PARTY, TOO. WE COULD COMMIT A CRIME AND NOBODY WOULD KNOW
WE COULD TEAR THESE EGG SACKS AND LET THE PUPAE DIE... THOUSANDS OF FUTURE ANT WORKERS SNUFFED OUT IN AN INSTANT, AND **NOBODY COULD STOP US**
WHAT ARE YOU TALKING ABOUT? LOOK, I GOTTA GO
OKAY
LATER...

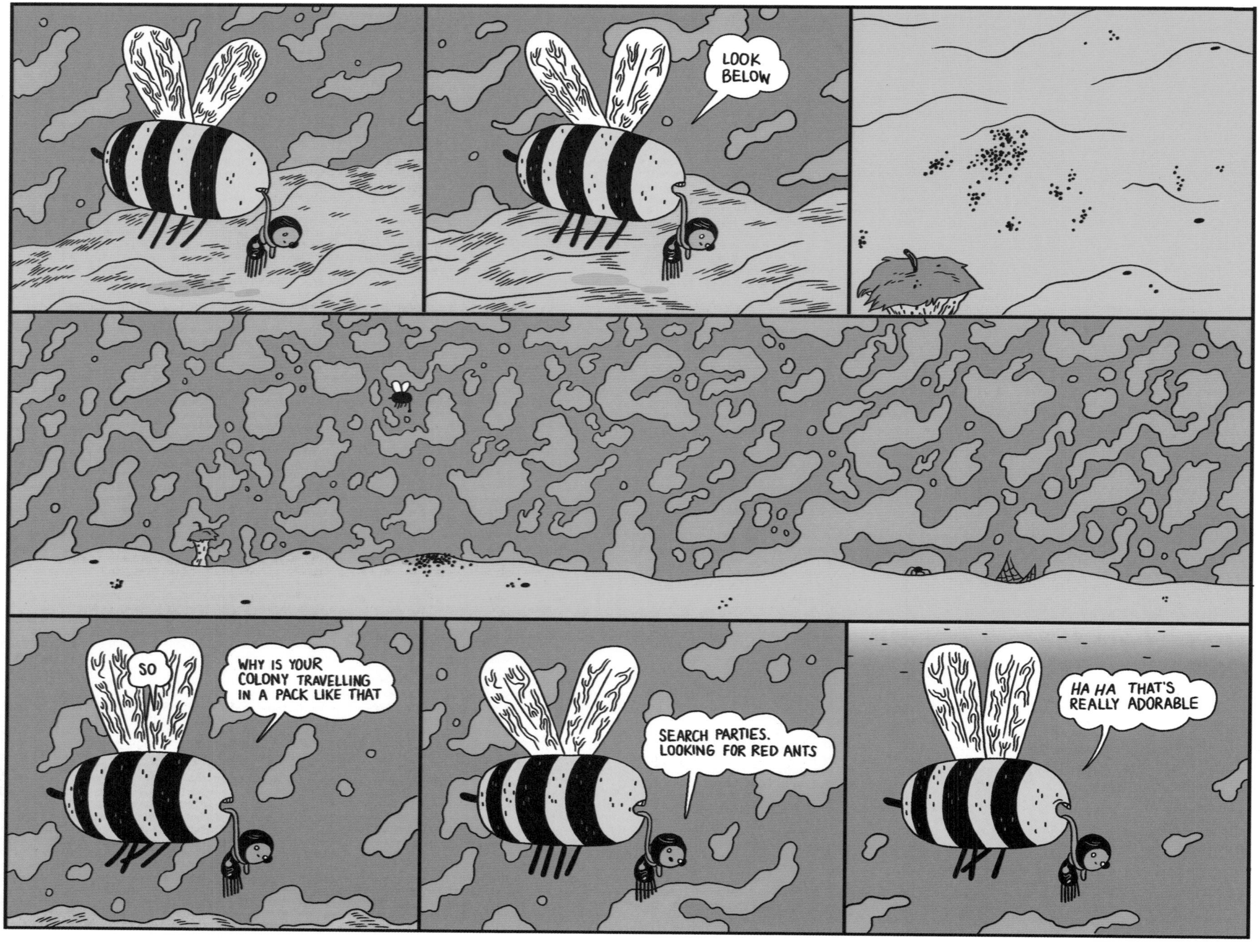
LOOK BELOW
SO
WHY IS YOUR COLONY TRAVELLING IN A PACK LIKE THAT
SEARCH PARTIES. LOOKING FOR RED ANTS
HA HA THAT'S REALLY ADORABLE

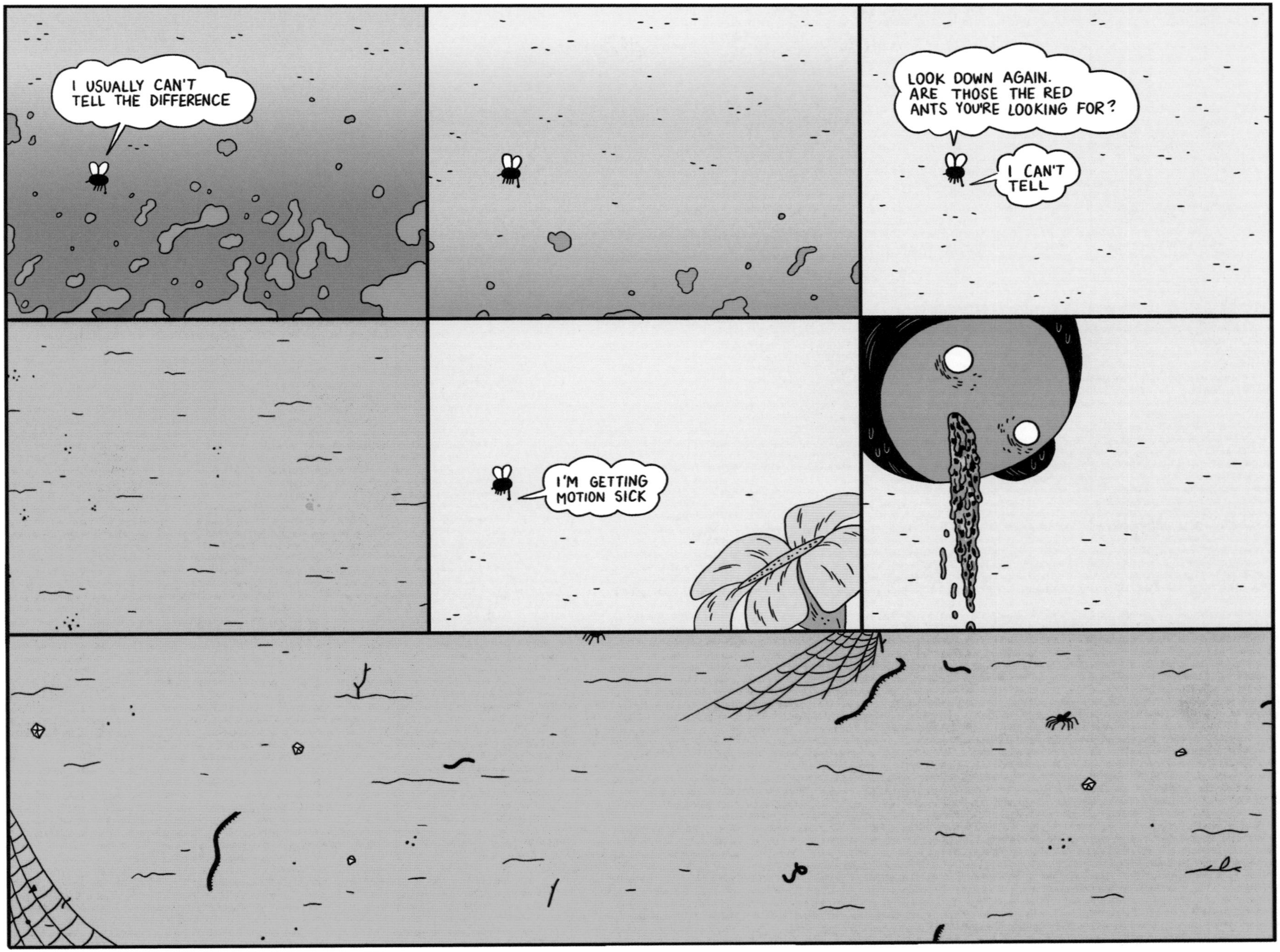
I USUALLY CAN'T TELL THE DIFFERENCE
LOOK DOWN AGAIN. ARE THOSE THE RED ANTS YOU'RE LOOKING FOR?
I CAN'T TELL
I'M GETTING MOTION SICK

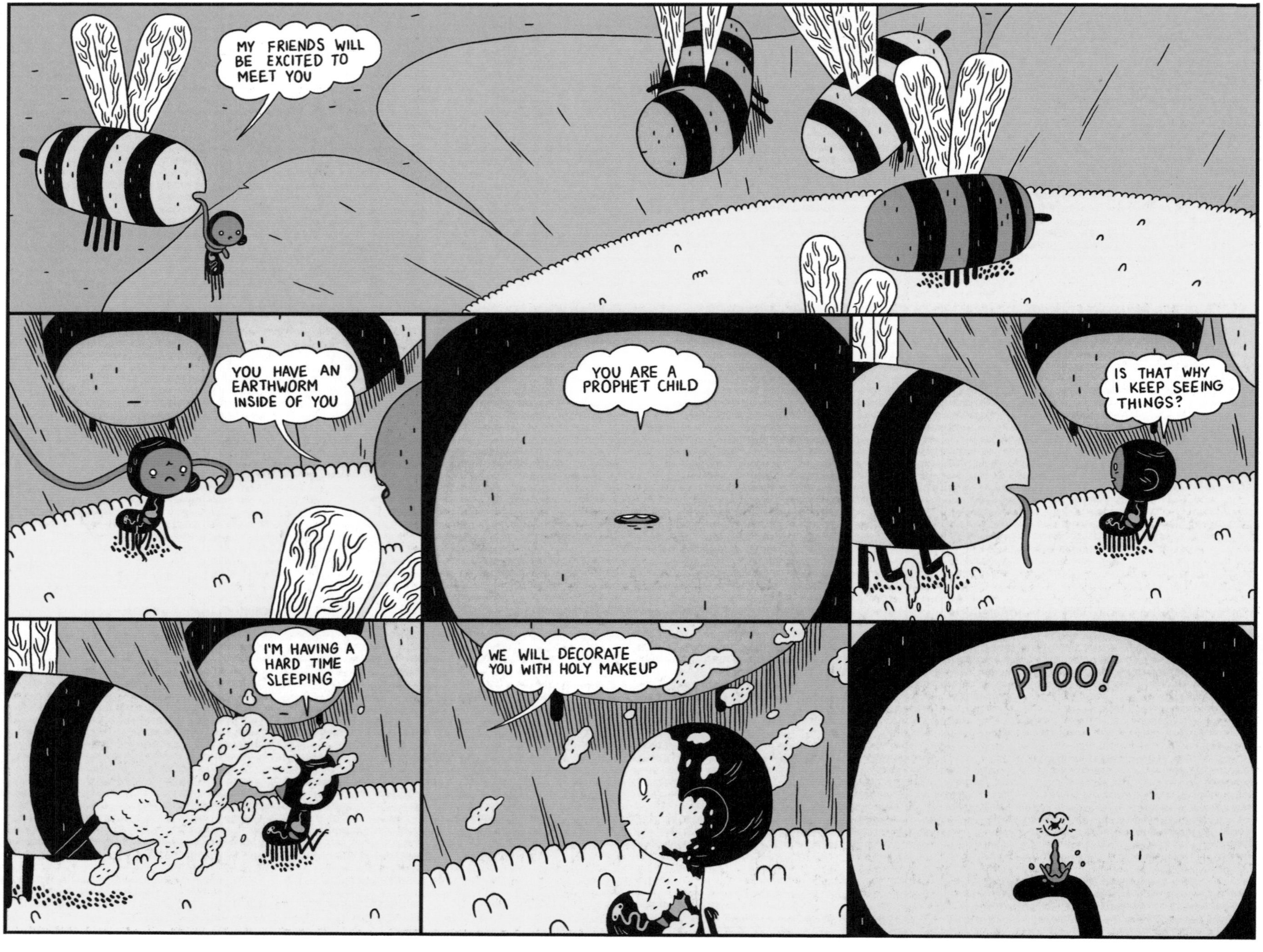
MY FRIENDS WILL BE EXCITED TO MEET YOU
YOU HAVE AN EARTHWORM INSIDE OF YOU
YOU ARE A PROPHET CHILD
IS THAT WHY I KEEP SEEING THINGS?
I'M HAVING A HARD TIME SLEEPING
WE WILL DECORATE YOU WITH HOLY MAKEUP
PTOO!

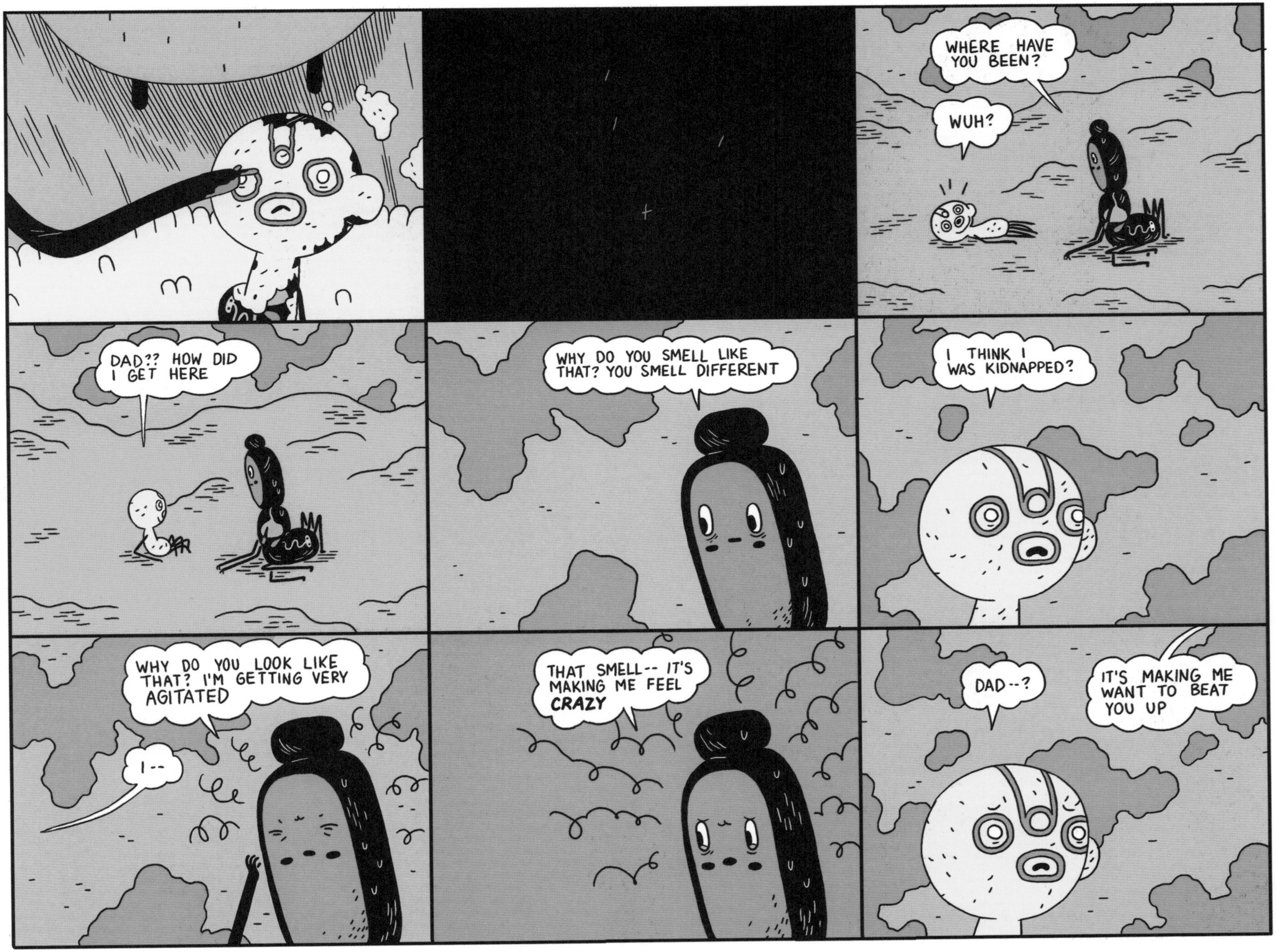
WHERE HAVE YOU BEEN?
WUH?
DAD?? HOW DID I GET HERE
WHY DO YOU SMELL LIKE THAT? YOU SMELL DIFFERENT
I THINK I WAS KIDNAPPED?
WHY DO YOU LOOK LIKE THAT? I'M GETTING VERY AGITATED
I--
THAT SMELL-- IT'S MAKING ME FEEL CRAZY
DAD--?
IT'S MAKING ME WANT TO BEAT YOU UP

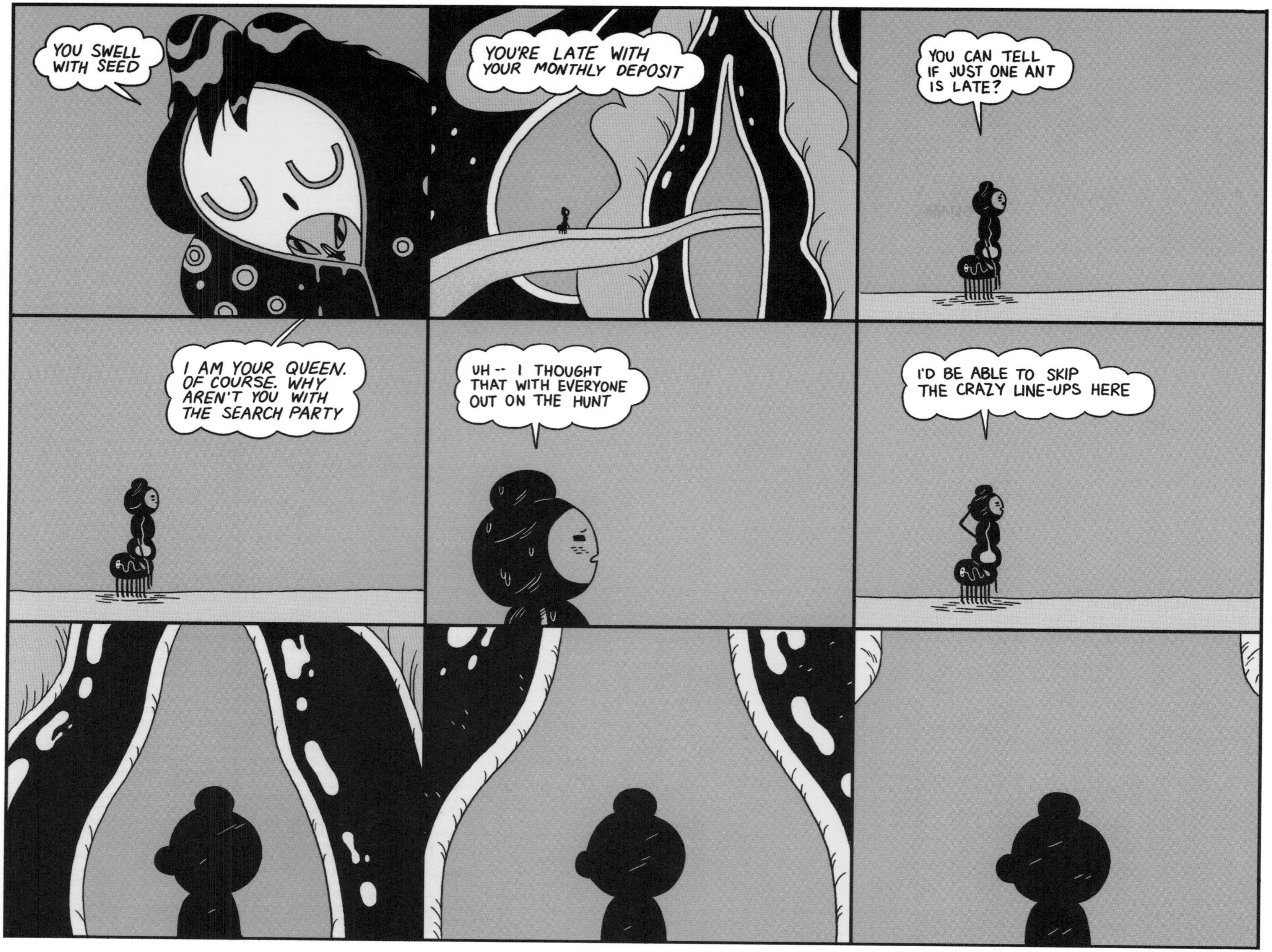
YOU SWELL WITH SEED
YOU'RE LATE WITH YOUR MONTHLY DEPOSIT
YOU CAN TELL IF JUST ONE ANT IS LATE?
I AM YOUR QUEEN. OF COURSE. WHY AREN'T YOU WITH THE SEARCH PARTY
UH -- I THOUGHT THAT WITH EVERYONE OUT ON THE HUNT
I'D BE ABLE TO SKIP THE CRAZY LINE-UPS HERE

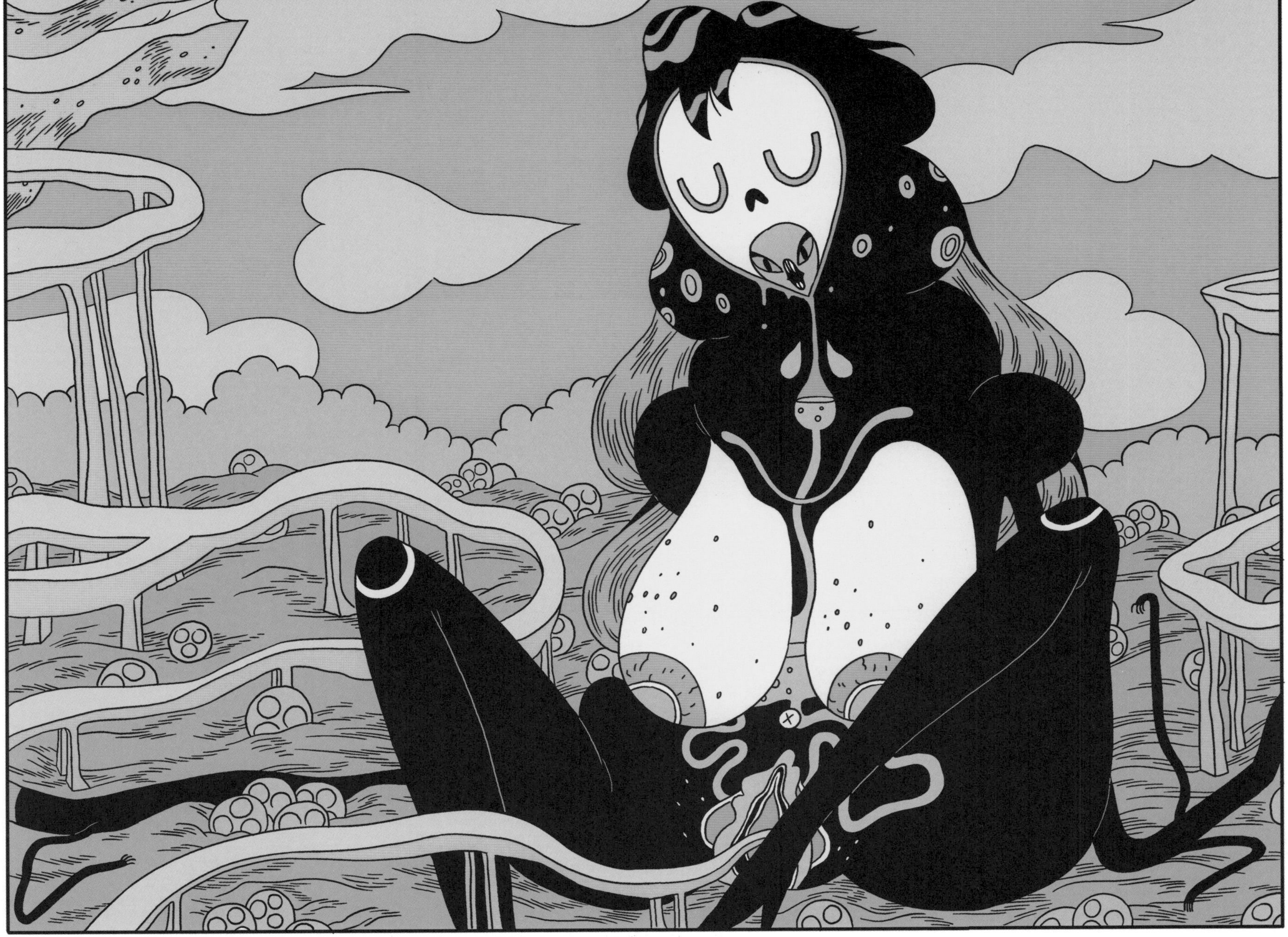

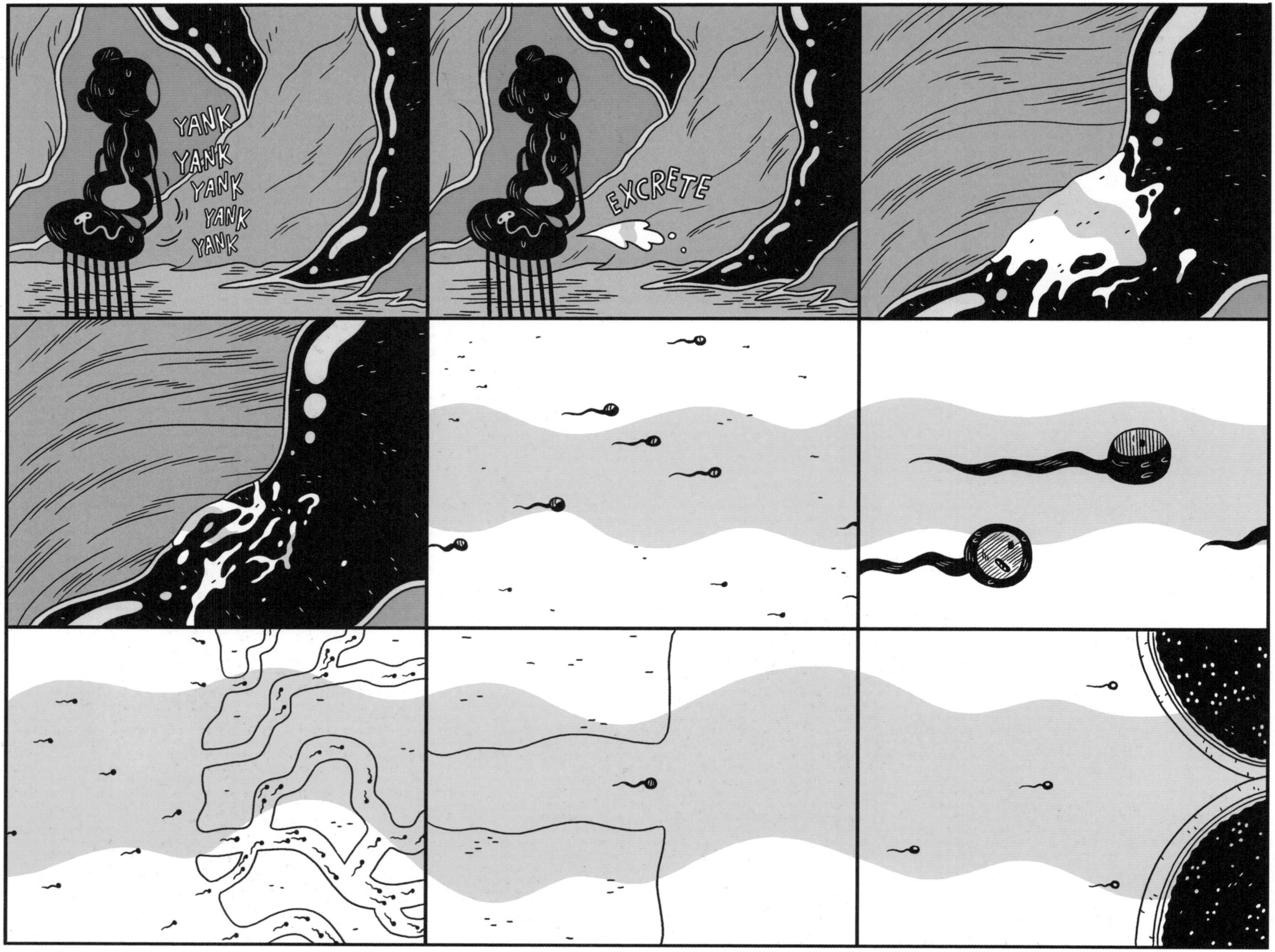
YANK
YANK
YANK
YANK
YANK
EXCRETE

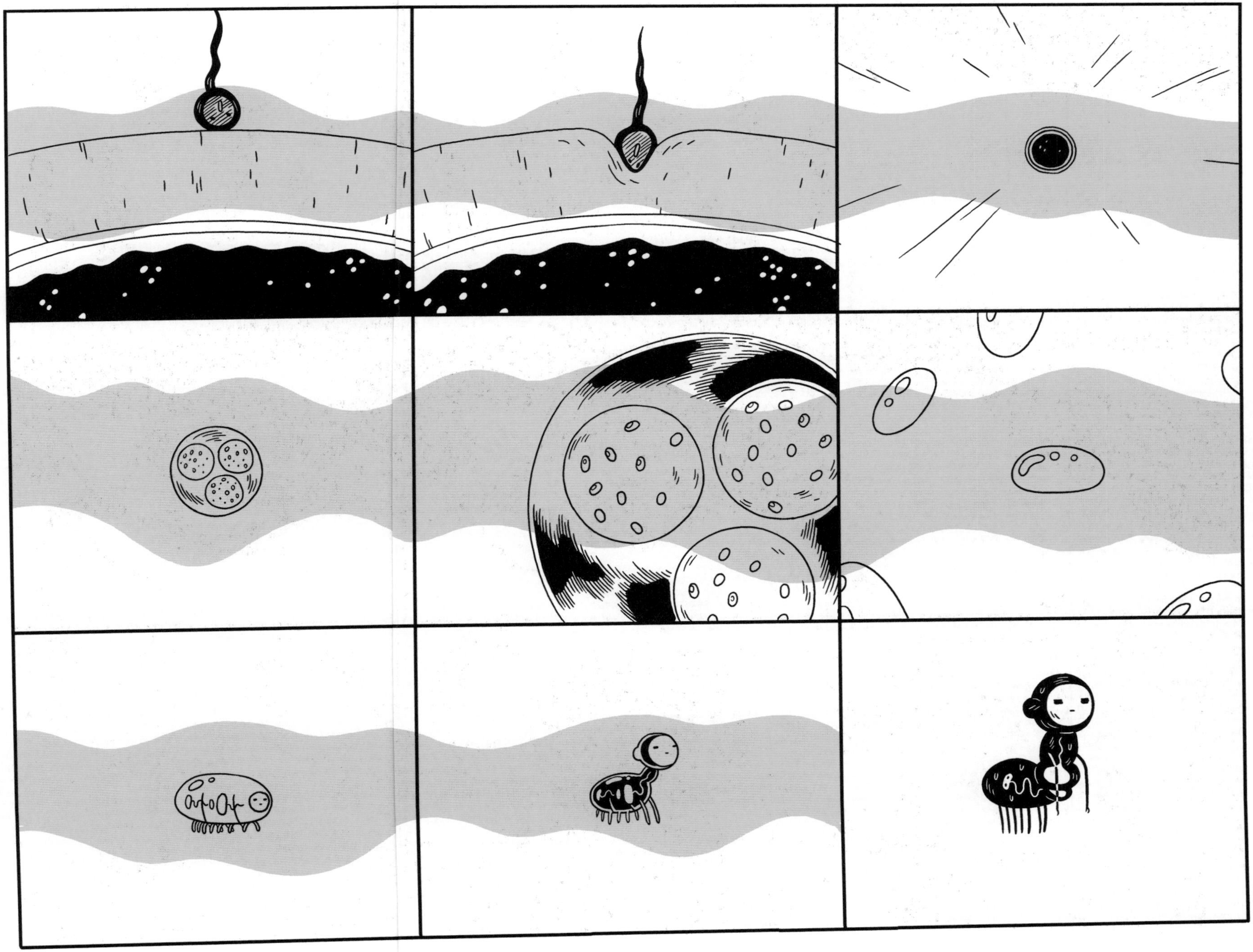

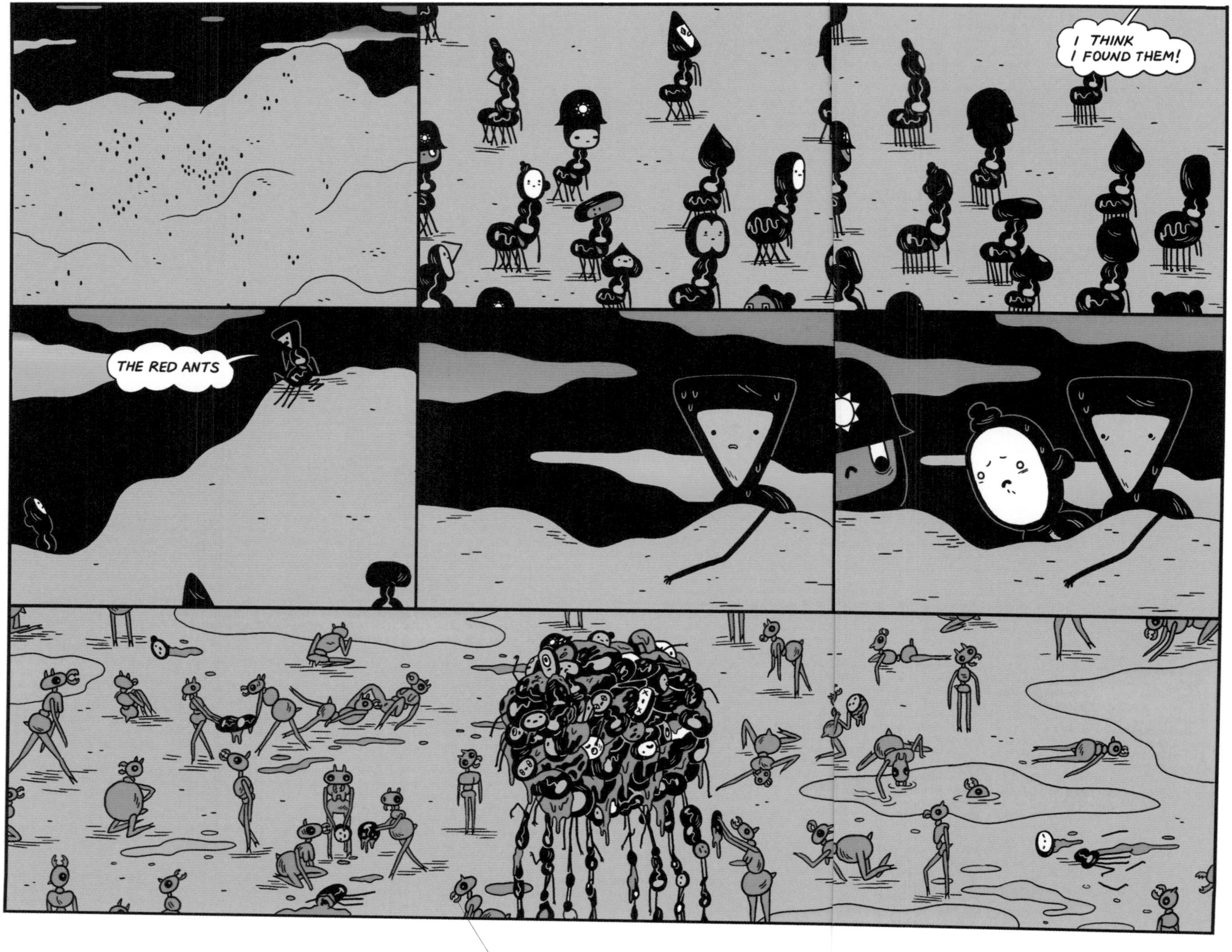
I THINK
I FOUND THEM!
THE RED ANTS

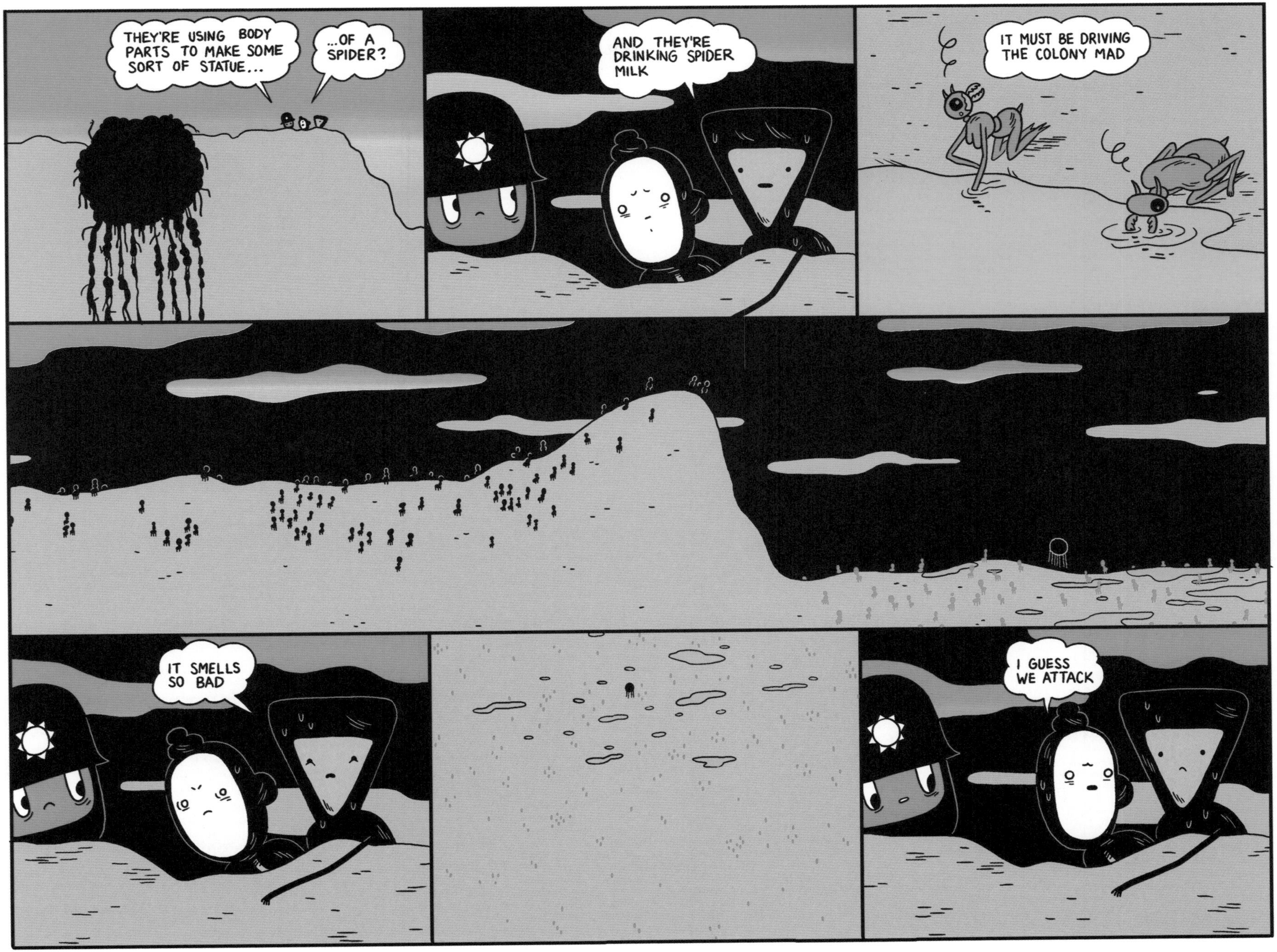
THEY'RE USING BODY PARTS TO MAKE SOME SORT OF STATUE...
...OF A SPIDER?
AND THEY'RE DRINKING SPIDER MILK
IT MUST BE DRIVING THE COLONY MAD
IT SMELLS SO BAD
I GUESS WE ATTACK

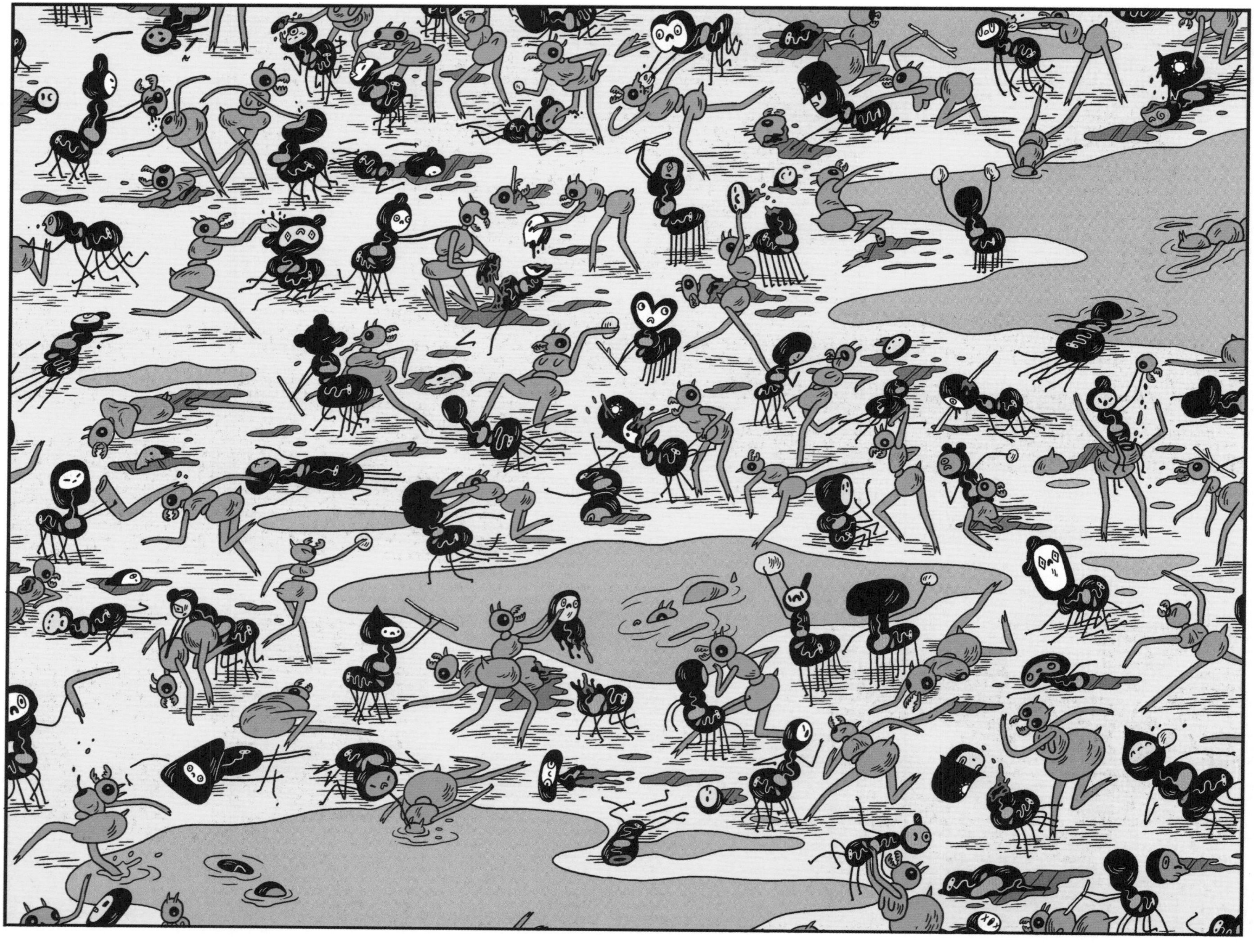

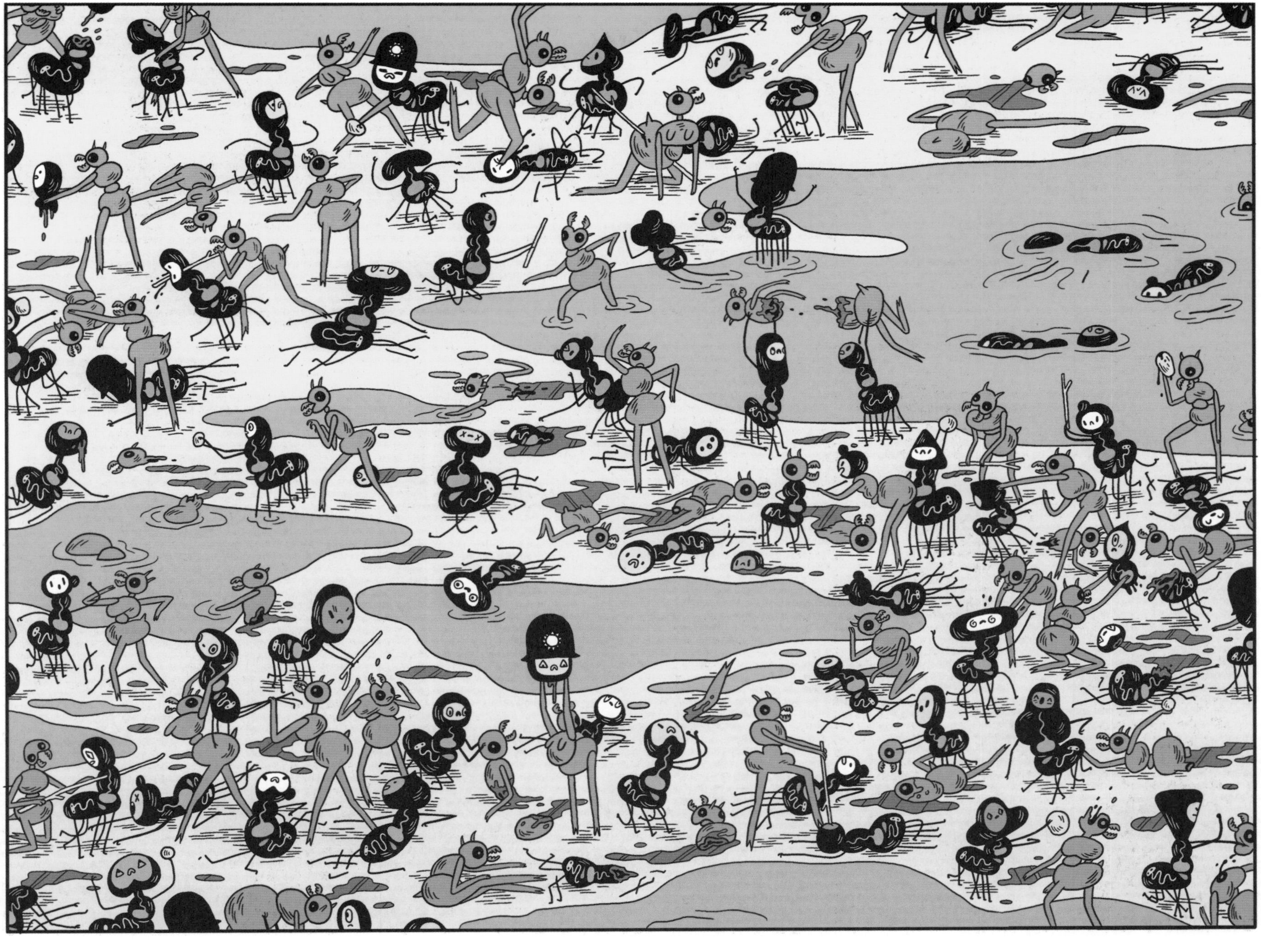

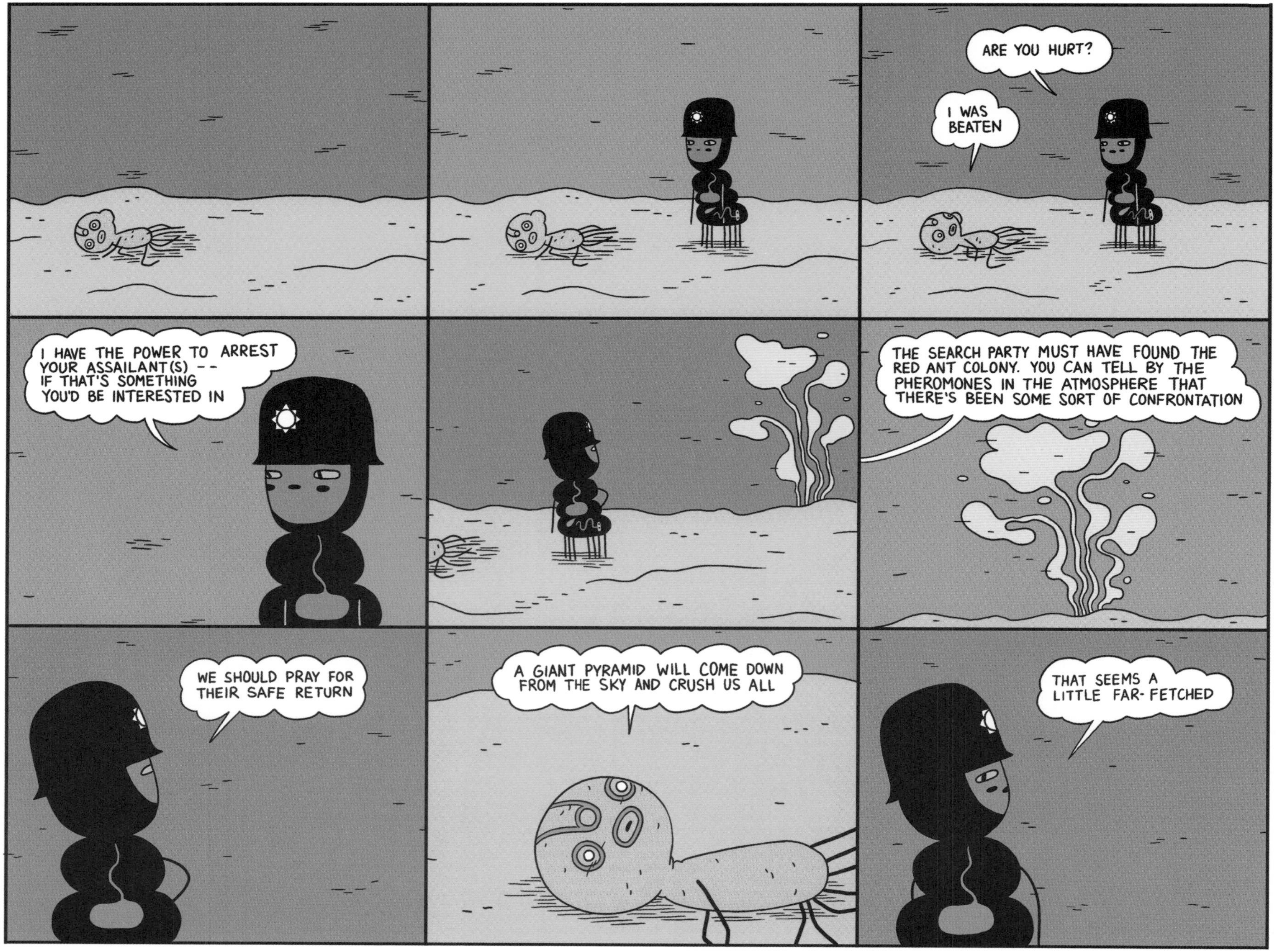
ARE YOU HURT?
I WAS BEATEN
I HAVE THE POWER TO ARREST YOUR ASSAILANT(S) -- IF THAT'S SOMETHING YOU'D BE INTERESTED IN
THE SEARCH PARTY MUST HAVE FOUND THE RED ANT COLONY. YOU CAN TELL BY THE PHEROMONES IN THE ATMOSPHERE THAT THERE'S BEEN SOME SORT OF CONFRONTATION
WE SHOULD PRAY FOR THEIR SAFE RETURN
A GIANT PYRAMID WILL COME DOWN FROM THE SKY AND CRUSH US ALL
THAT SEEMS A LITTLE FAR-FETCHED

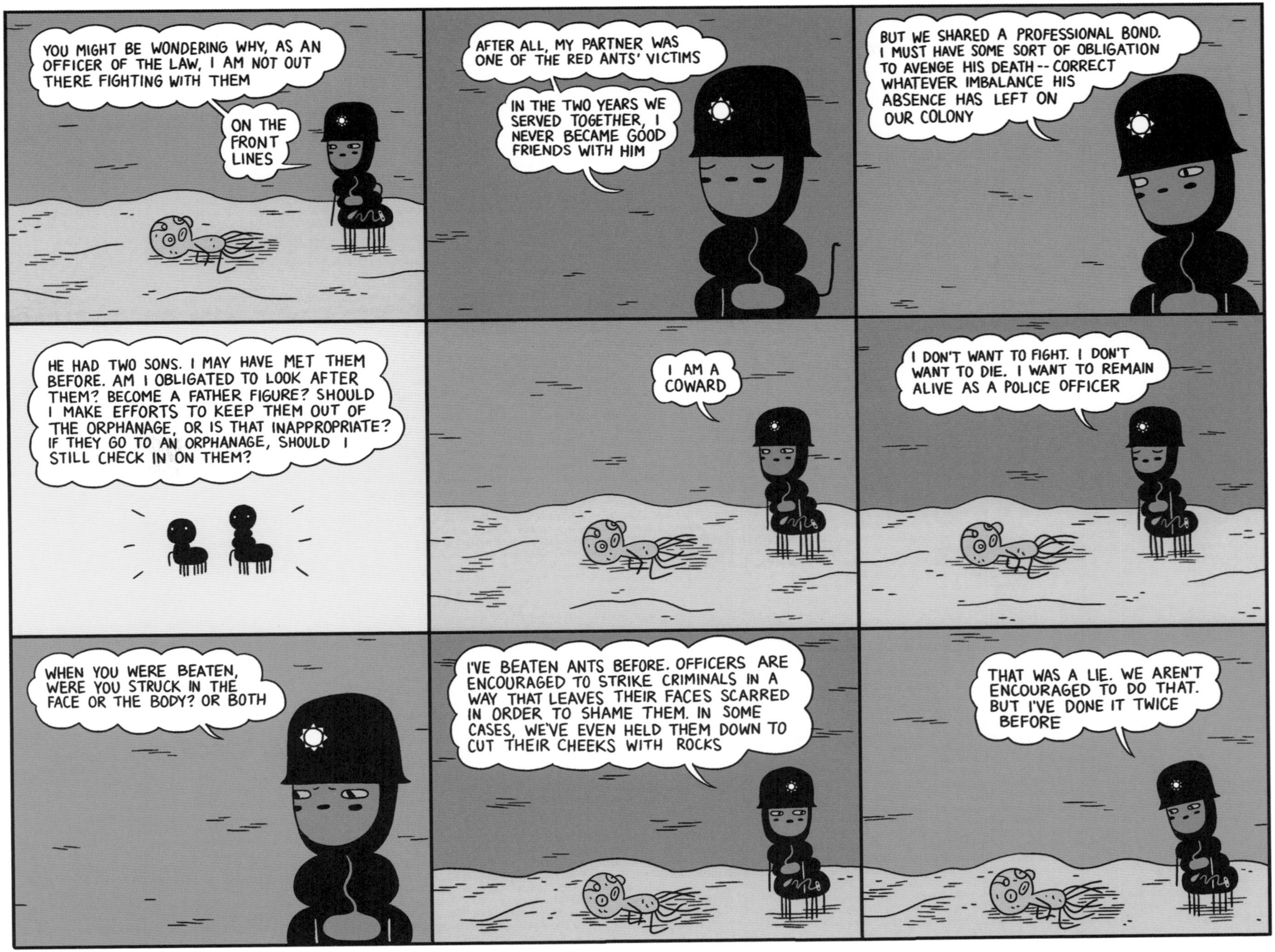
YOU MIGHT BE WONDERING WHY, AS AN OFFICER OF THE LAW, I AM NOT OUT THERE FIGHTING WITH THEM
ON THE FRONT LINES
AFTER ALL, MY PARTNER WAS ONE OF THE RED ANTS' VICTIMS
IN THE TWO YEARS WE SERVED TOGETHER, I NEVER BECAME GOOD FRIENDS WITH HIM
BUT WE SHARED A PROFESSIONAL BOND. I MUST HAVE SOME SORT OF OBLIGATION TO AVENGE HIS DEATH -- CORRECT WHATEVER IMBALANCE HIS ABSENCE HAS LEFT ON OUR COLONY
HE HAD TWO SONS. I MAY HAVE MET THEM BEFORE. AM I OBLIGATED TO LOOK AFTER THEM? BECOME A FATHER FIGURE? SHOULD I MAKE EFFORTS TO KEEP THEM OUT OF THE ORPHANAGE, OR IS THAT INAPPROPRIATE? IF THEY GO TO AN ORPHANAGE, SHOULD I STILL CHECK IN ON THEM?
I AM A COWARD
I DON'T WANT TO FIGHT. I DON'T WANT TO DIE. I WANT TO REMAIN ALIVE AS A POLICE OFFICER
WHEN YOU WERE BEATEN, WERE YOU STRUCK IN THE FACE OR THE BODY? OR BOTH
I'VE BEATEN ANTS BEFORE. OFFICERS ARE ENCOURAGED TO STRIKE CRIMINALS IN A WAY THAT LEAVES THEIR FACES SCARRED IN ORDER TO SHAME THEM. IN SOME CASES, WE'VE EVEN HELD THEM DOWN TO CUT THEIR CHEEKS WITH ROCKS
THAT WAS A LIE. WE AREN'T ENCOURAGED TO DO THAT. BUT I'VE DONE IT TWICE BEFORE

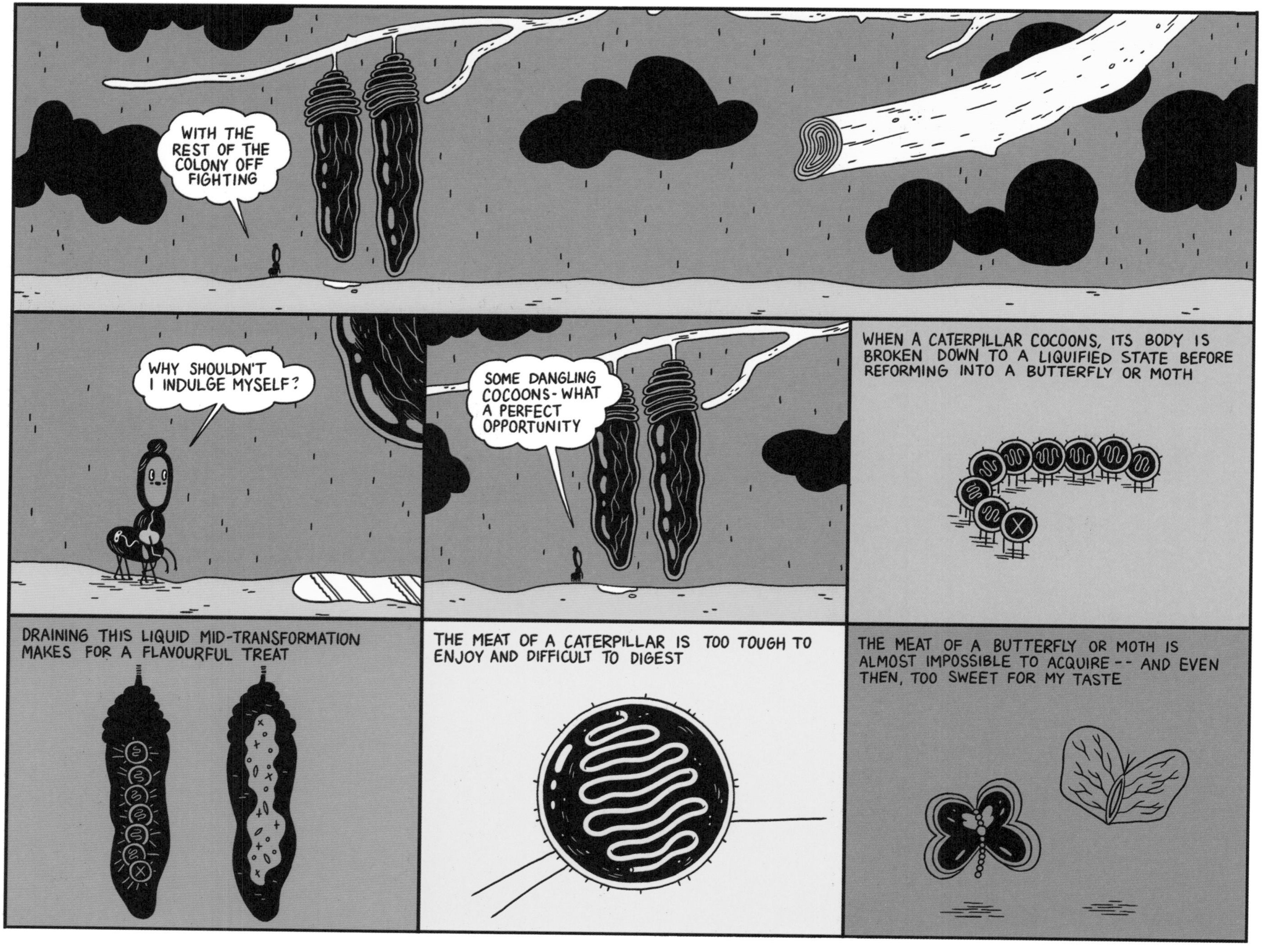
WITH THE REST OF THE COLONY OFF FIGHTING
WHY SHOULDN'T I INDULGE MYSELF?
SOME DANGLING COCOONS- WHAT A PERFECT OPPORTUNITY
WHEN A CATERPILLAR COCOONS, ITS BODY IS BROKEN DOWN TO A LIQUIFIED STATE BEFORE REFORMING INTO A BUTTERFLY OR MOTH
DRAINING THIS LIQUID MID-TRANSFORMATION MAKES FOR A FLAVOURFUL TREAT
THE MEAT OF A CATERPILLAR IS TOO TOUGH TO ENJOY AND DIFFICULT TO DIGEST
THE MEAT OF A BUTTERFLY OR MOTH IS ALMOST IMPOSSIBLE TO ACQUIRE-- AND EVEN THEN, TOO SWEET FOR MY TASTE

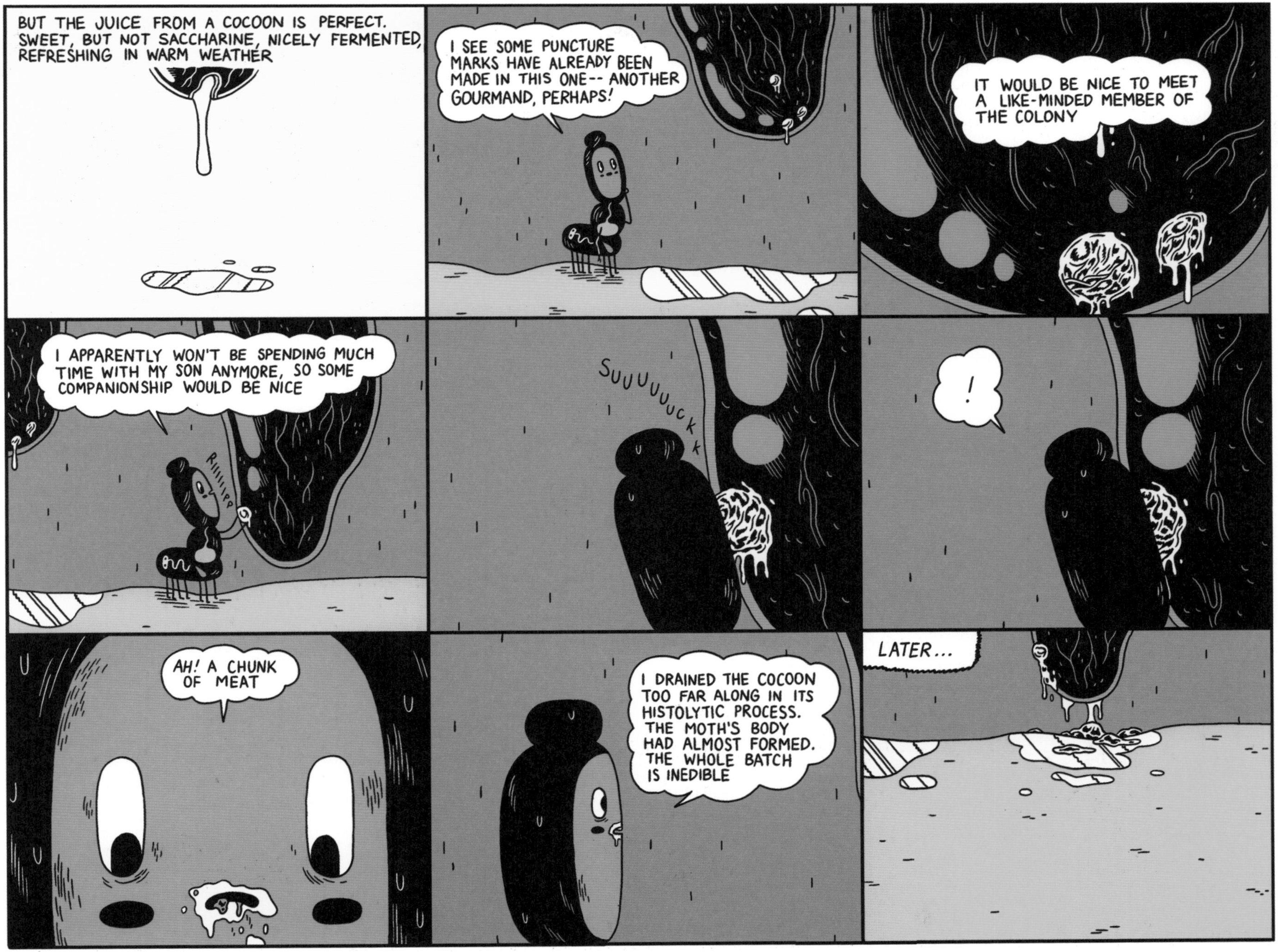
BUT THE JUICE FROM A COCOON IS PERFECT. SWEET, BUT NOT SACCHARINE, NICELY FERMENTED, REFRESHING IN WARM WEATHER
I SEE SOME PUNCTURE MARKS HAVE ALREADY BEEN MADE IN THIS ONE-- ANOTHER GOURMAND, PERHAPS!
IT WOULD BE NICE TO MEET A LIKE-MINDED MEMBER OF THE COLONY
I APPARENTLY WON'T BE SPENDING MUCH TIME WITH MY SON ANYMORE, SO SOME COMPANIONSHIP WOULD BE NICE
RIIIIIPP
SUUUUUUCKK
!
AH! A CHUNK OF MEAT
I DRAINED THE COCOON TOO FAR ALONG IN ITS HISTOLYTIC PROCESS. THE MOTH'S BODY HAD ALMOST FORMED. THE WHOLE BATCH IS INEDIBLE
LATER...

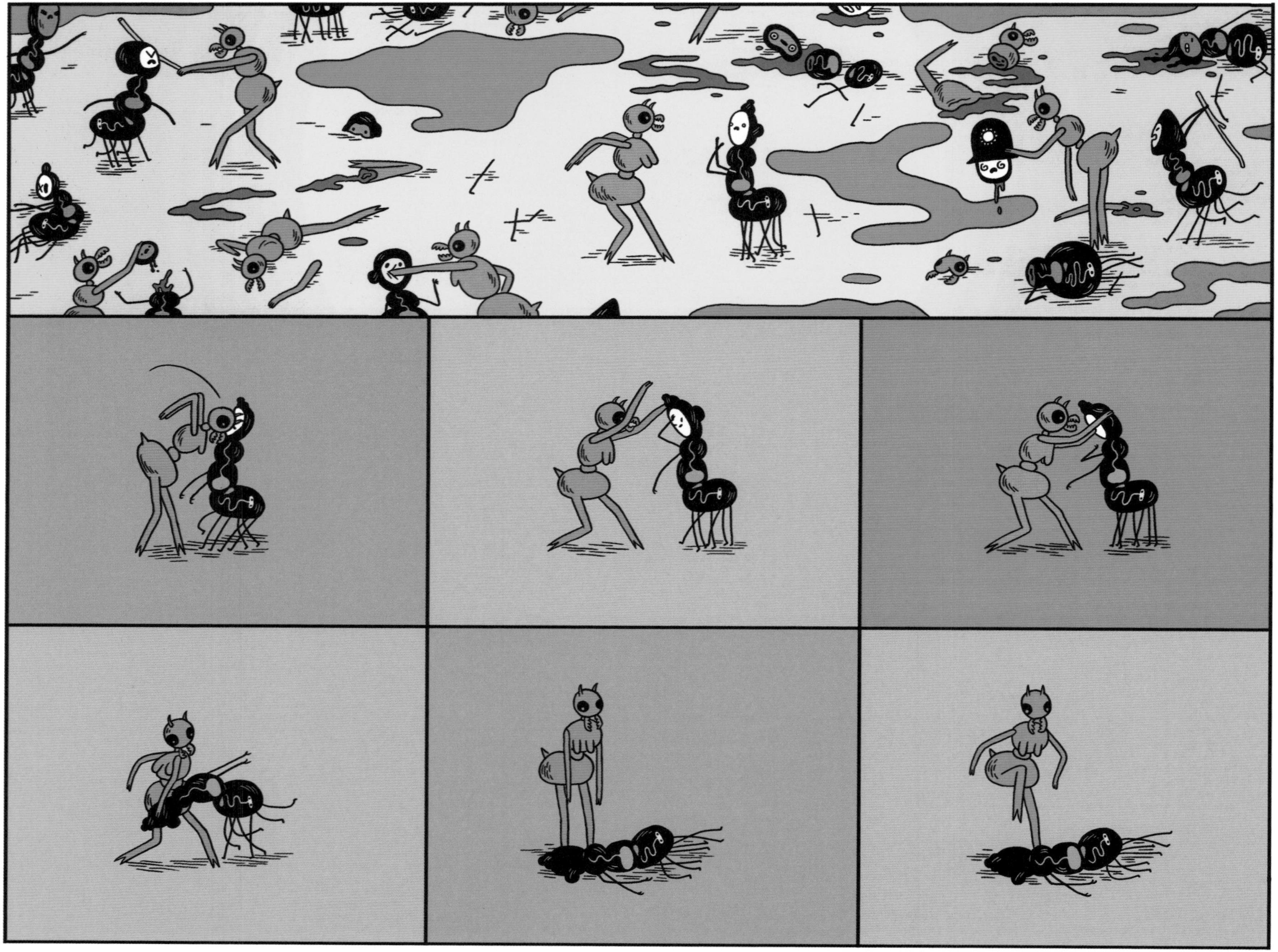

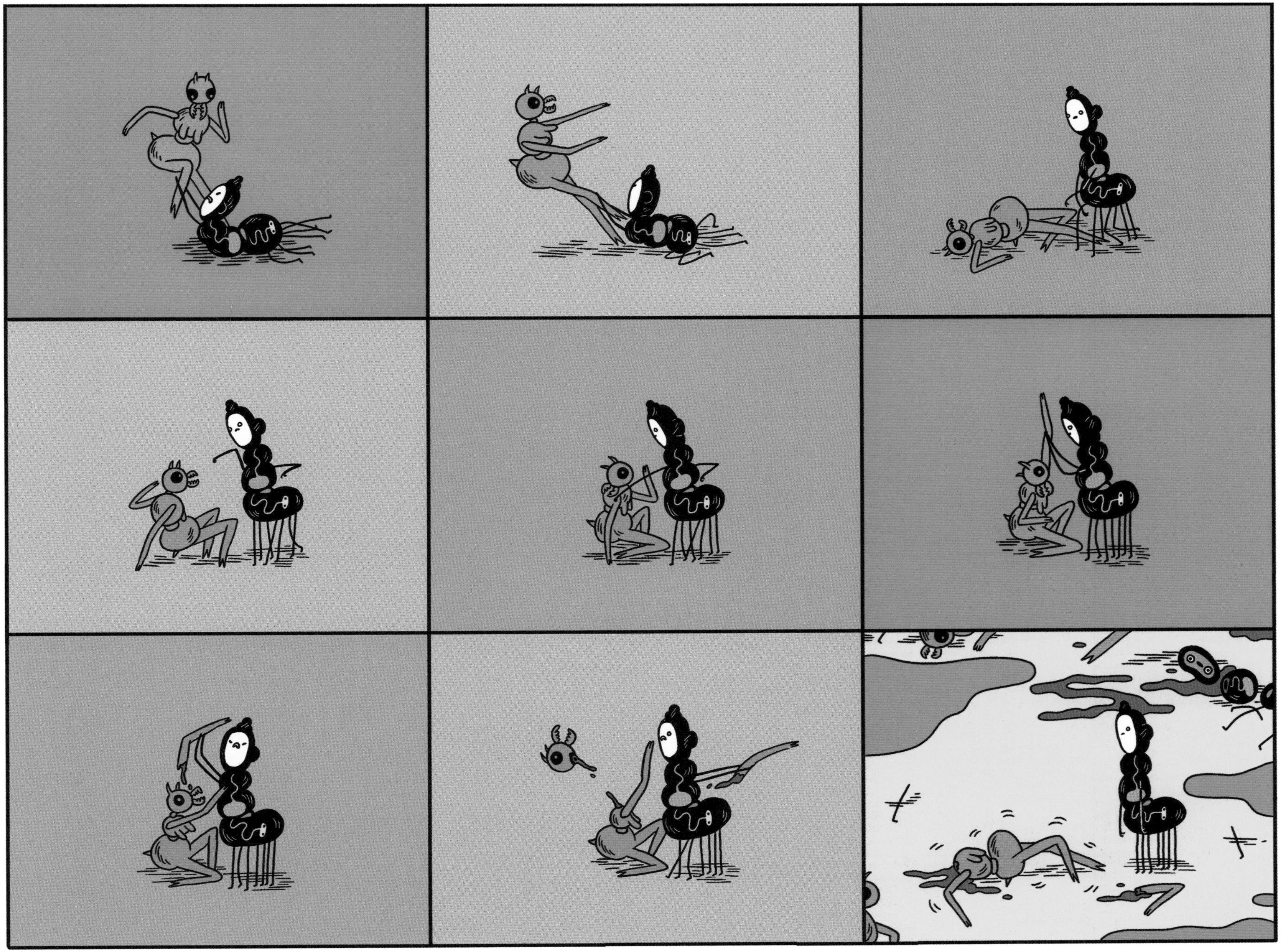

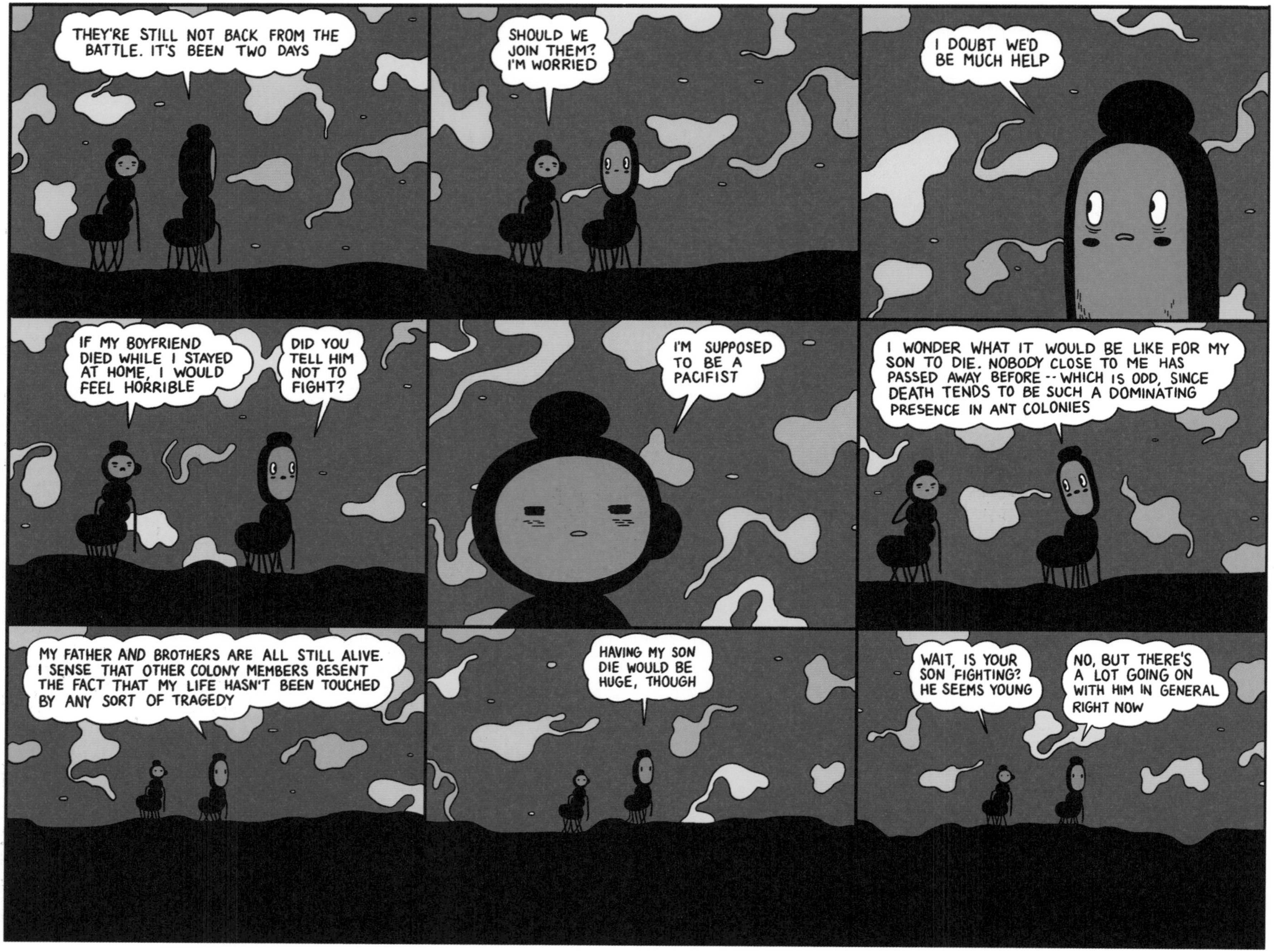
THEY'RE STILL NOT BACK FROM THE BATTLE. IT'S BEEN TWO DAYS
SHOULD WE JOIN THEM? I'M WORRIED
I DOUBT WE'D BE MUCH HELP
IF MY BOYFRIEND DIED WHILE I STAYED AT HOME, I WOULD FEEL HORRIBLE
DID YOU TELL HIM NOT TO FIGHT?
I'M SUPPOSED TO BE A PACIFIST
I WONDER WHAT IT WOULD BE LIKE FOR MY SON TO DIE. NOBODY CLOSE TO ME HAS PASSED AWAY BEFORE -- WHICH IS ODD, SINCE DEATH TENDS TO BE SUCH A DOMINATING PRESENCE IN ANT COLONIES
MY FATHER AND BROTHERS ARE ALL STILL ALIVE. I SENSE THAT OTHER COLONY MEMBERS RESENT THE FACT THAT MY LIFE HASN'T BEEN TOUCHED BY ANY SORT OF TRAGEDY
HAVING MY SON DIE WOULD BE HUGE, THOUGH
WAIT, IS YOUR SON FIGHTING? HE SEEMS YOUNG
NO, BUT THERE'S A LOT GOING ON WITH HIM IN GENERAL RIGHT NOW

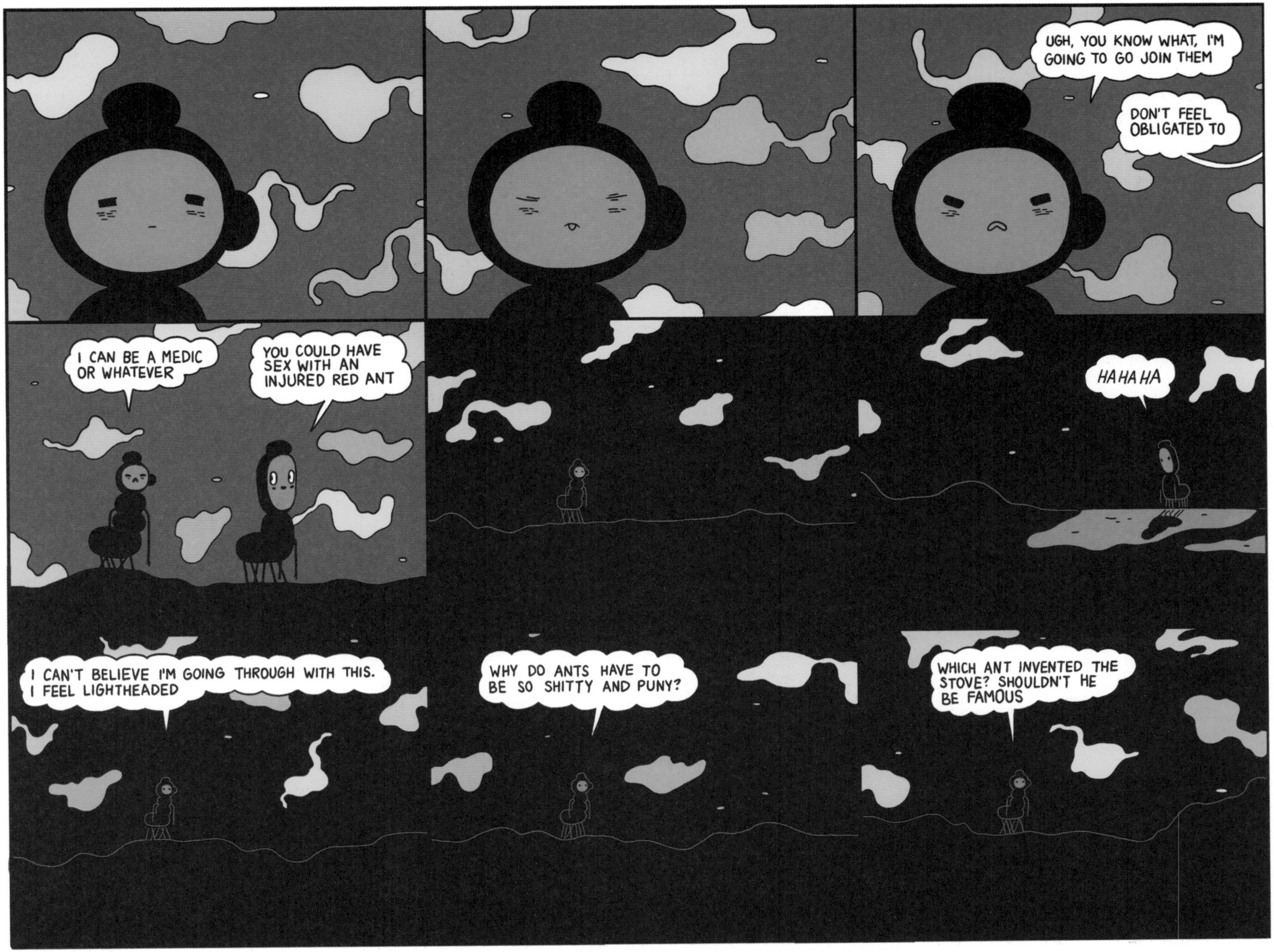
UGH, YOU KNOW WHAT, I'M GOING TO GO JOIN THEM
DON'T FEEL OBLIGATED TO
I CAN BE A MEDIC OR WHATEVER
YOU COULD HAVE SEX WITH AN INJURED RED ANT
HAHAHA
I CAN'T BELIEVE I'M GOING THROUGH WITH THIS. I FEEL LIGHTHEADED
WHY DO ANTS HAVE TO BE SO SHITTY AND PUNY?
WHICH ANT INVENTED THE STOVE? SHOULDN'T HE BE FAMOUS

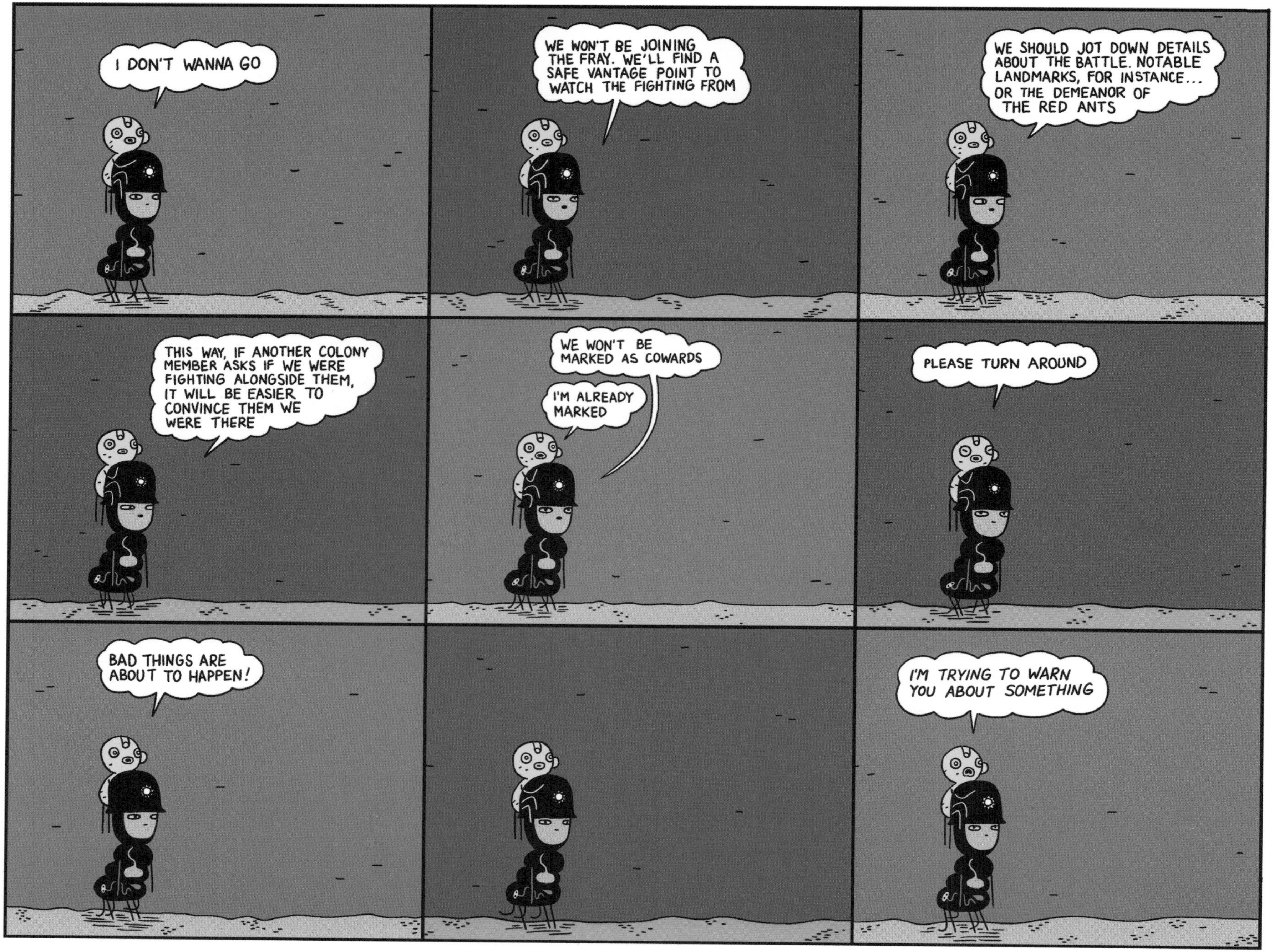
I DON'T WANNA GO
WE WON'T BE JOINING THE FRAY. WE'LL FIND A SAFE VANTAGE POINT TO WATCH THE FIGHTING FROM
WE SHOULD JOT DOWN DETAILS ABOUT THE BATTLE. NOTABLE LANDMARKS, FOR INSTANCE... OR THE DEMEANOR OF THE RED ANTS
THIS WAY, IF ANOTHER COLONY MEMBER ASKS IF WE WERE FIGHTING ALONGSIDE THEM, IT WILL BE EASIER TO CONVINCE THEM WE WERE THERE
WE WON'T BE MARKED AS COWARDS
I'M ALREADY MARKED
PLEASE TURN AROUND
BAD THINGS ARE ABOUT TO HAPPEN!
I'M TRYING TO WARN YOU ABOUT SOMETHING

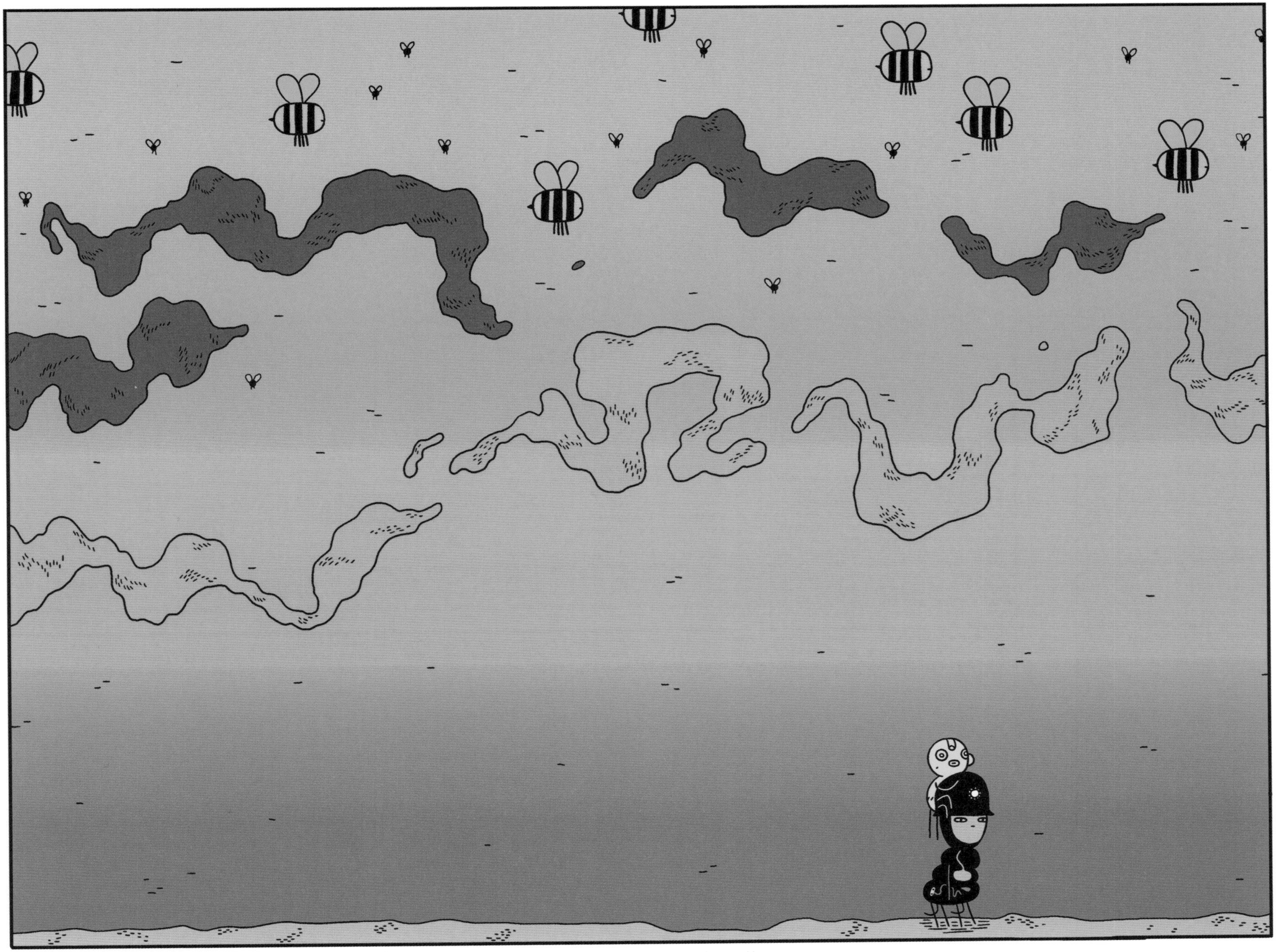

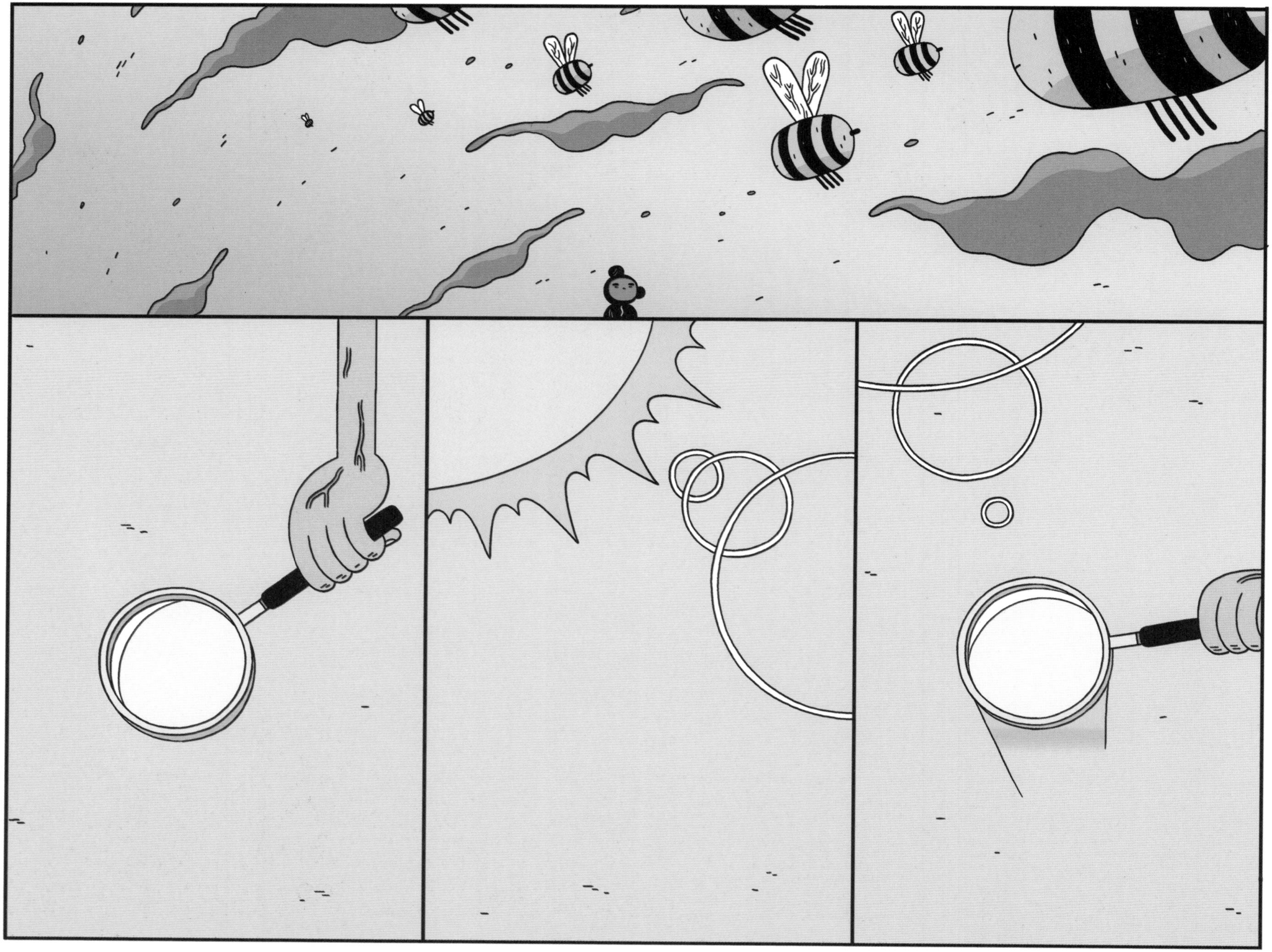

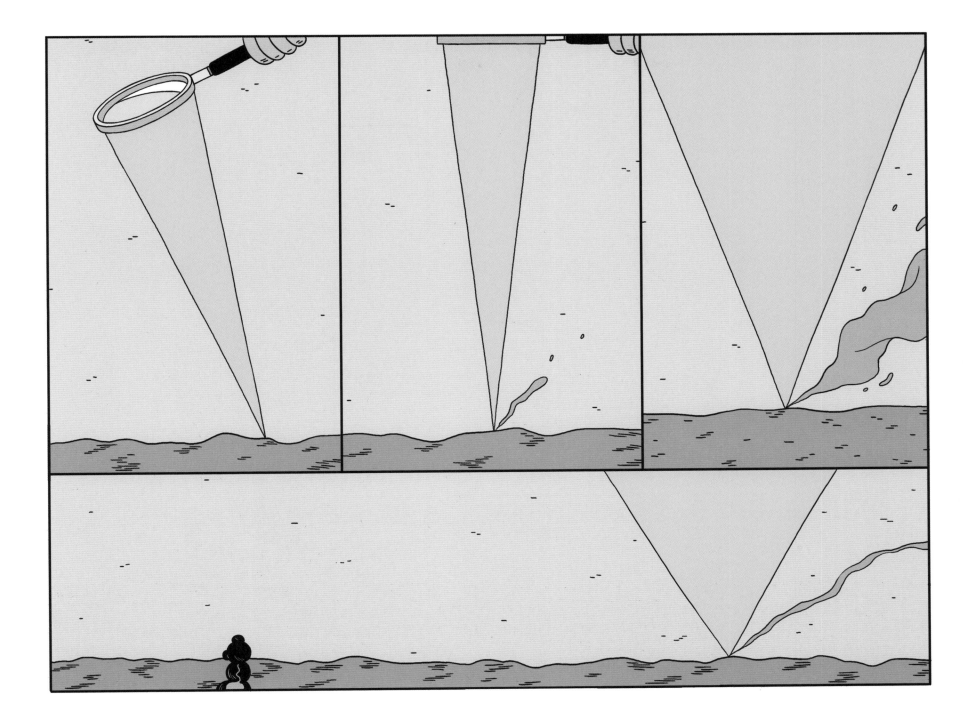

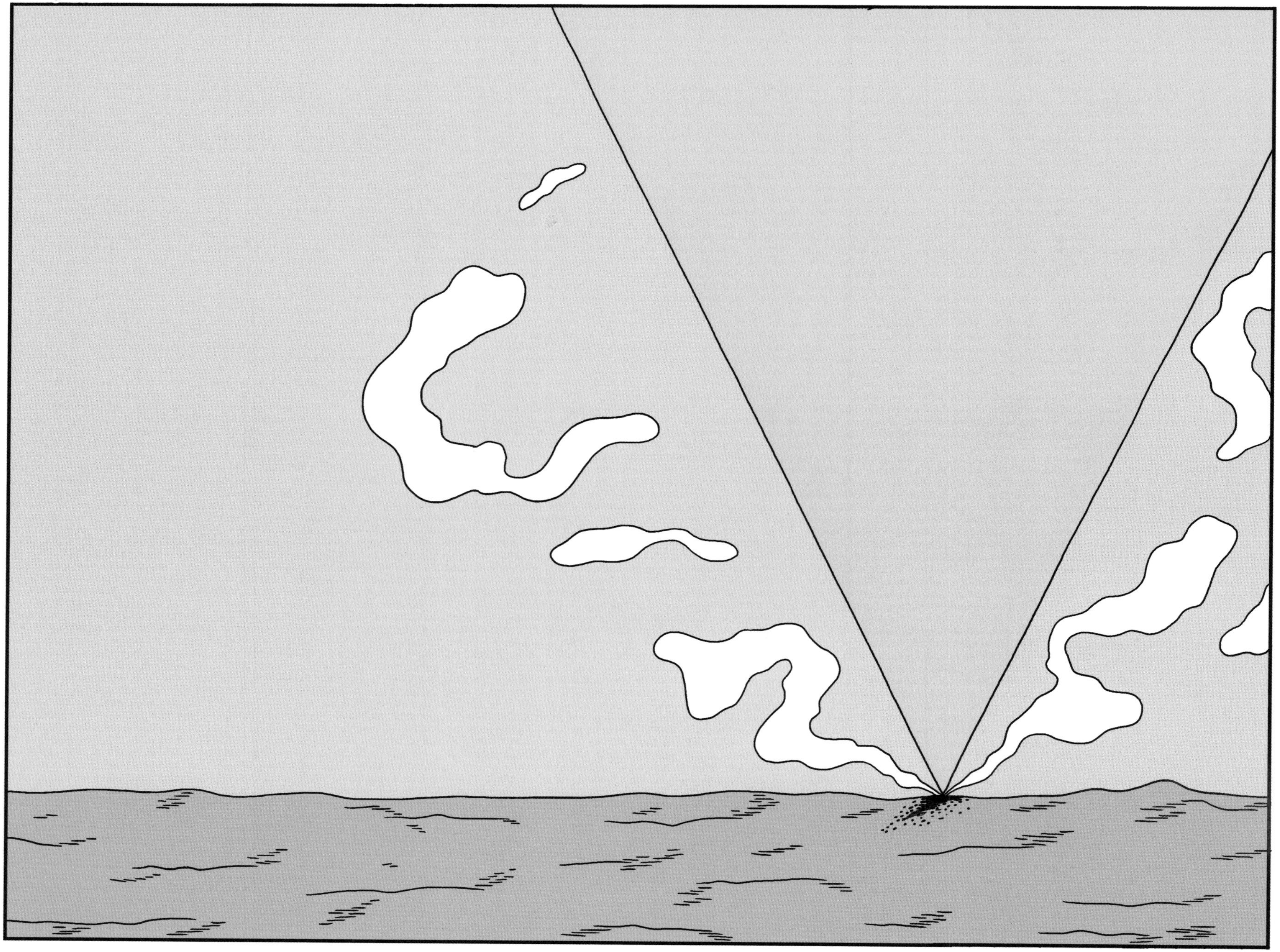

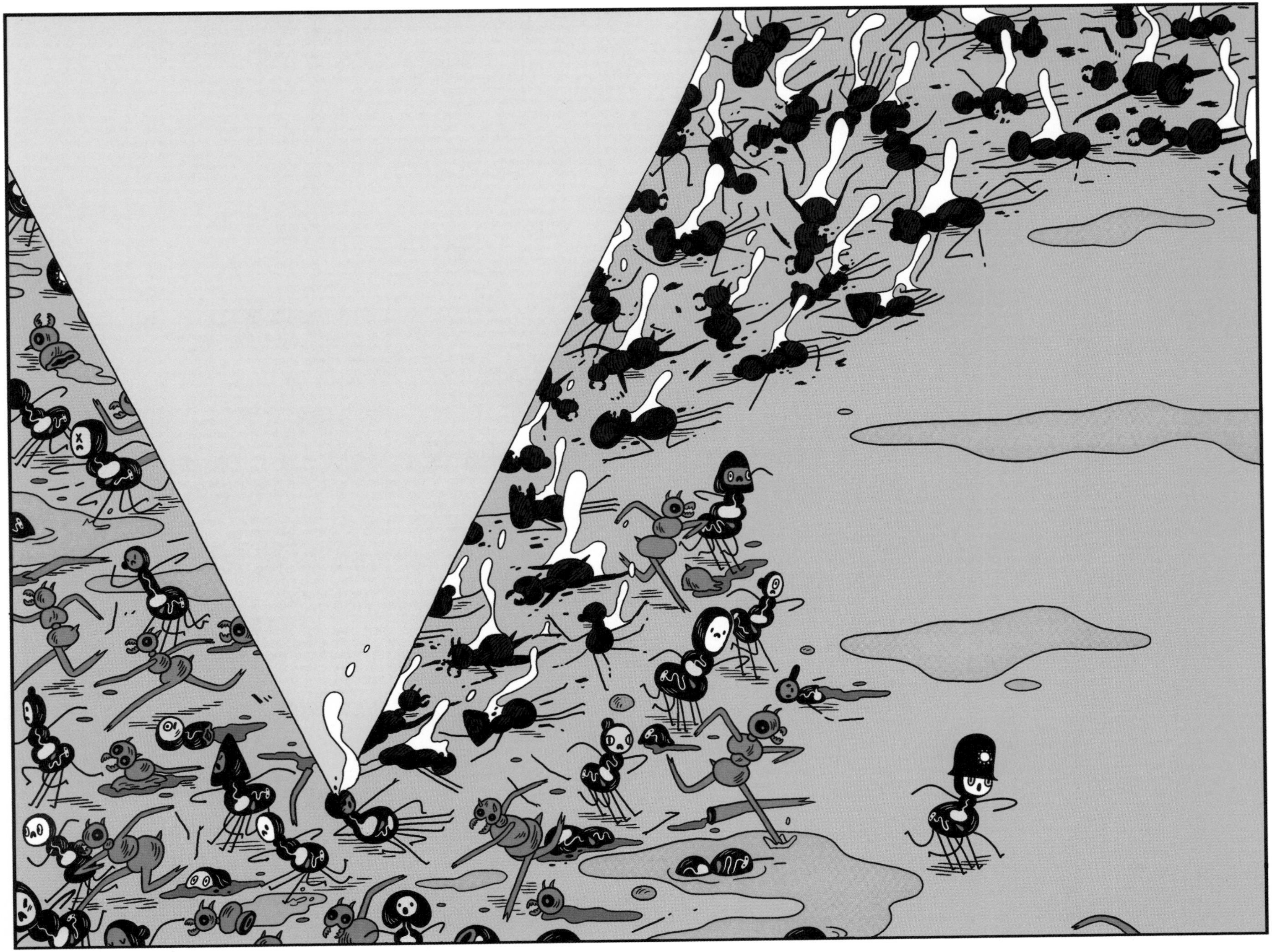

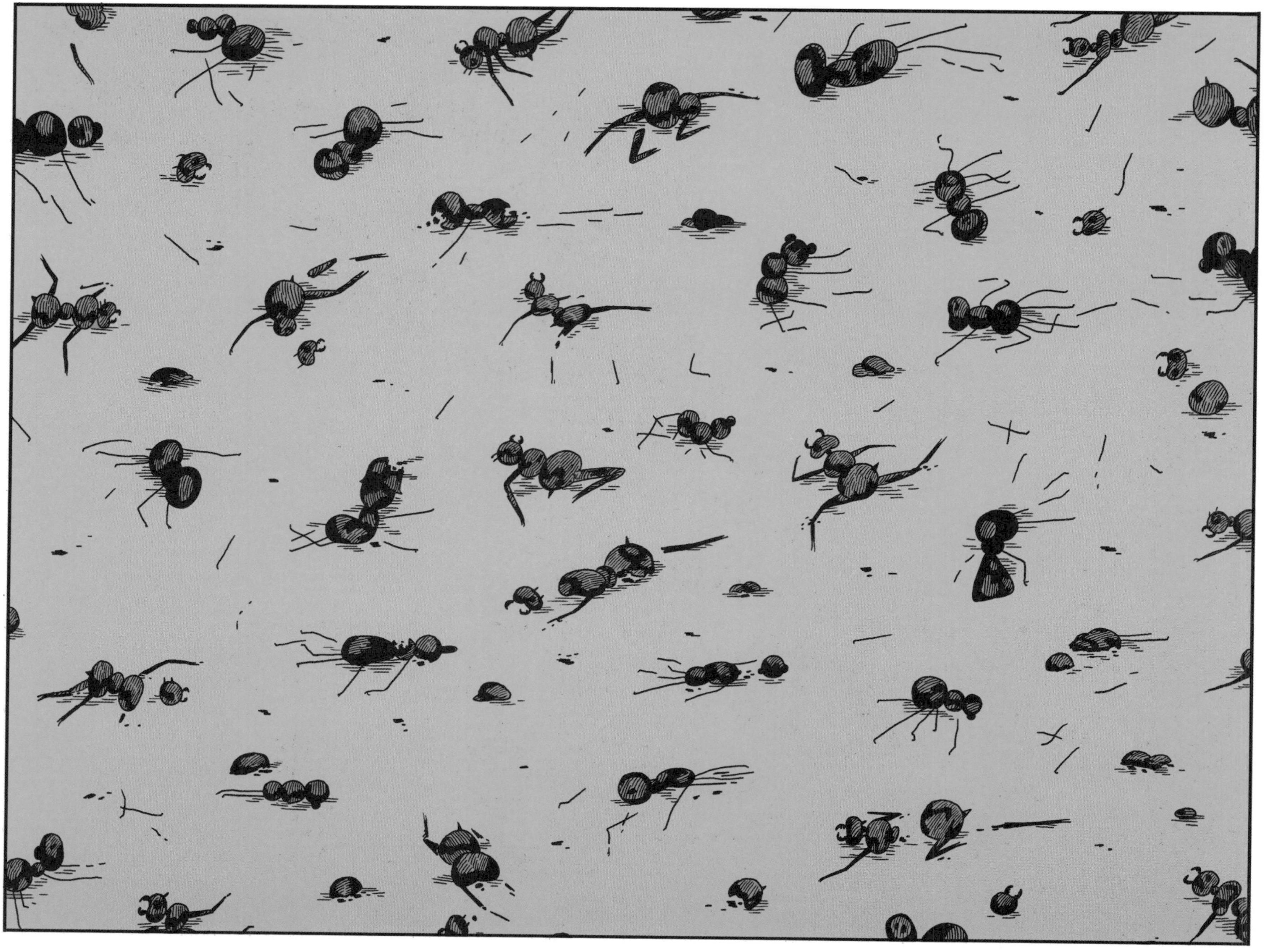

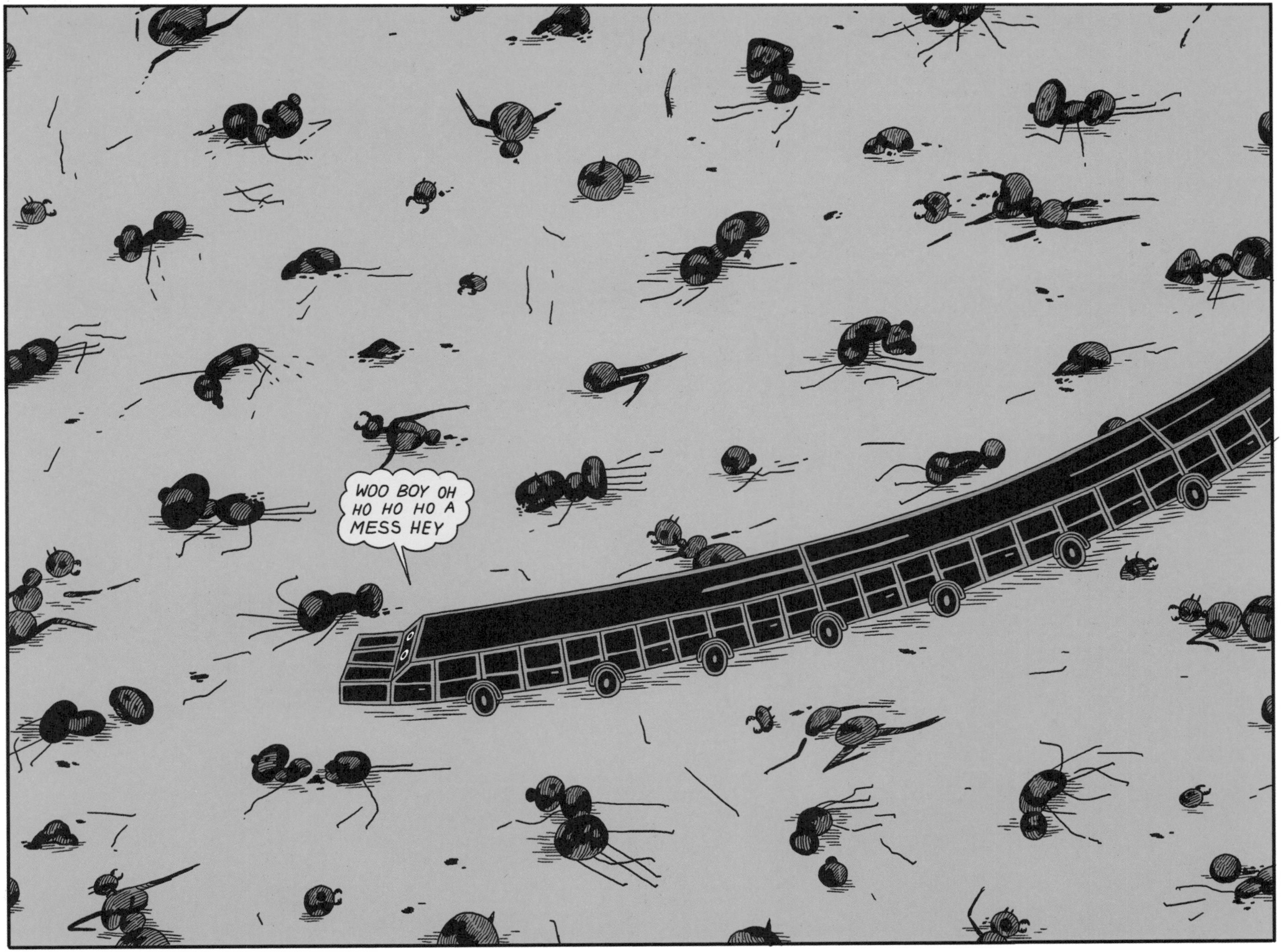
WOO BOY OH HO HO HO A MESS HEY

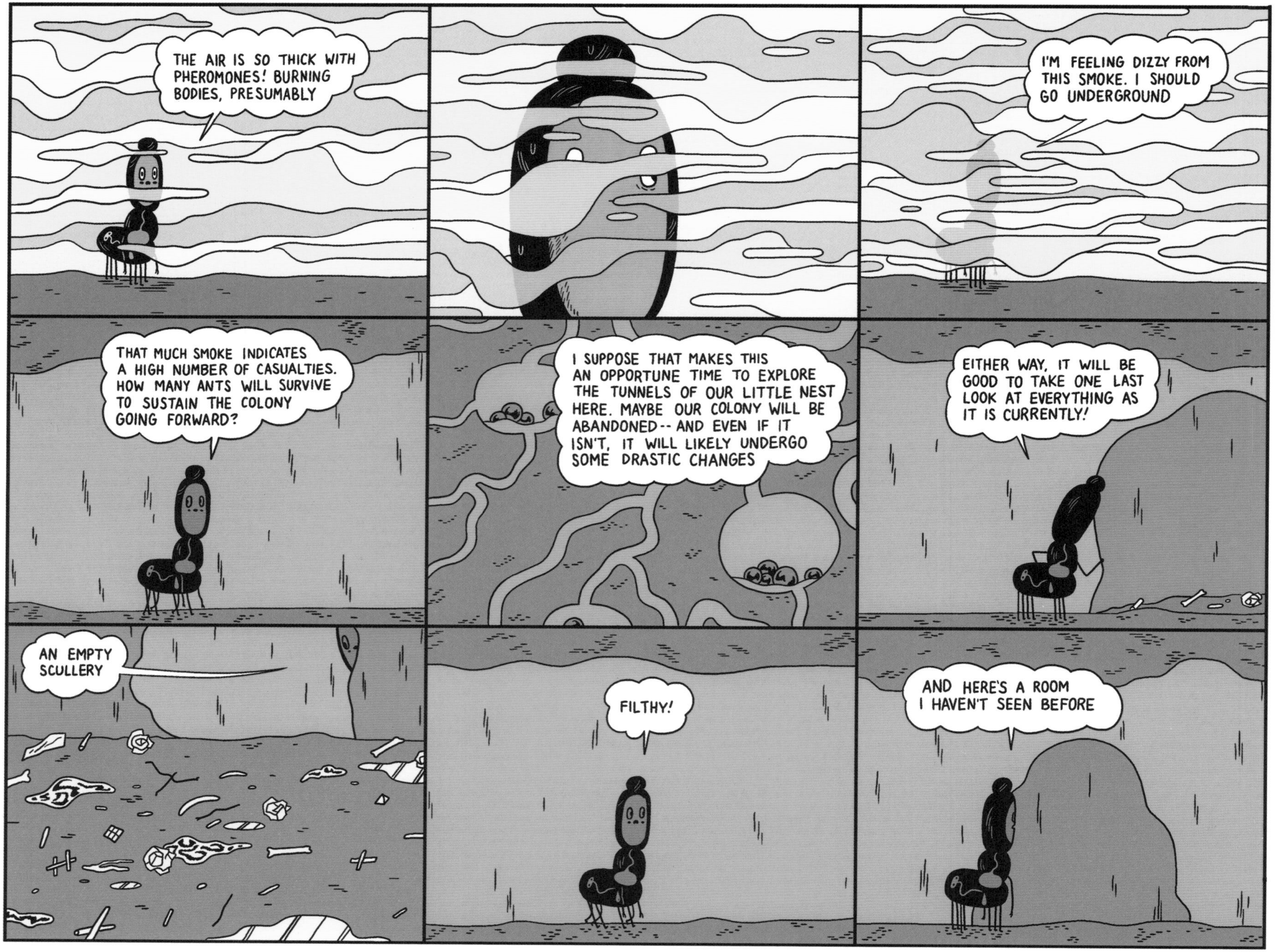
THE AIR IS SO THICK WITH PHEROMONES! BURNING BODIES, PRESUMABLY
I'M FEELING DIZZY FROM THIS SMOKE. I SHOULD GO UNDERGROUND
THAT MUCH SMOKE INDICATES A HIGH NUMBER OF CASUALTIES. HOW MANY ANTS WILL SURVIVE TO SUSTAIN THE COLONY GOING FORWARD?
I SUPPOSE THAT MAKES THIS AN OPPORTUNE TIME TO EXPLORE THE TUNNELS OF OUR LITTLE NEST HERE. MAYBE OUR COLONY WILL BE ABANDONED-- AND EVEN IF IT ISN'T, IT WILL LIKELY UNDERGO SOME DRASTIC CHANGES
EITHER WAY, IT WILL BE GOOD TO TAKE ONE LAST LOOK AT EVERYTHING AS IT IS CURRENTLY!
AN EMPTY SCULLERY
FILTHY!
AND HERE'S A ROOM I HAVEN'T SEEN BEFORE

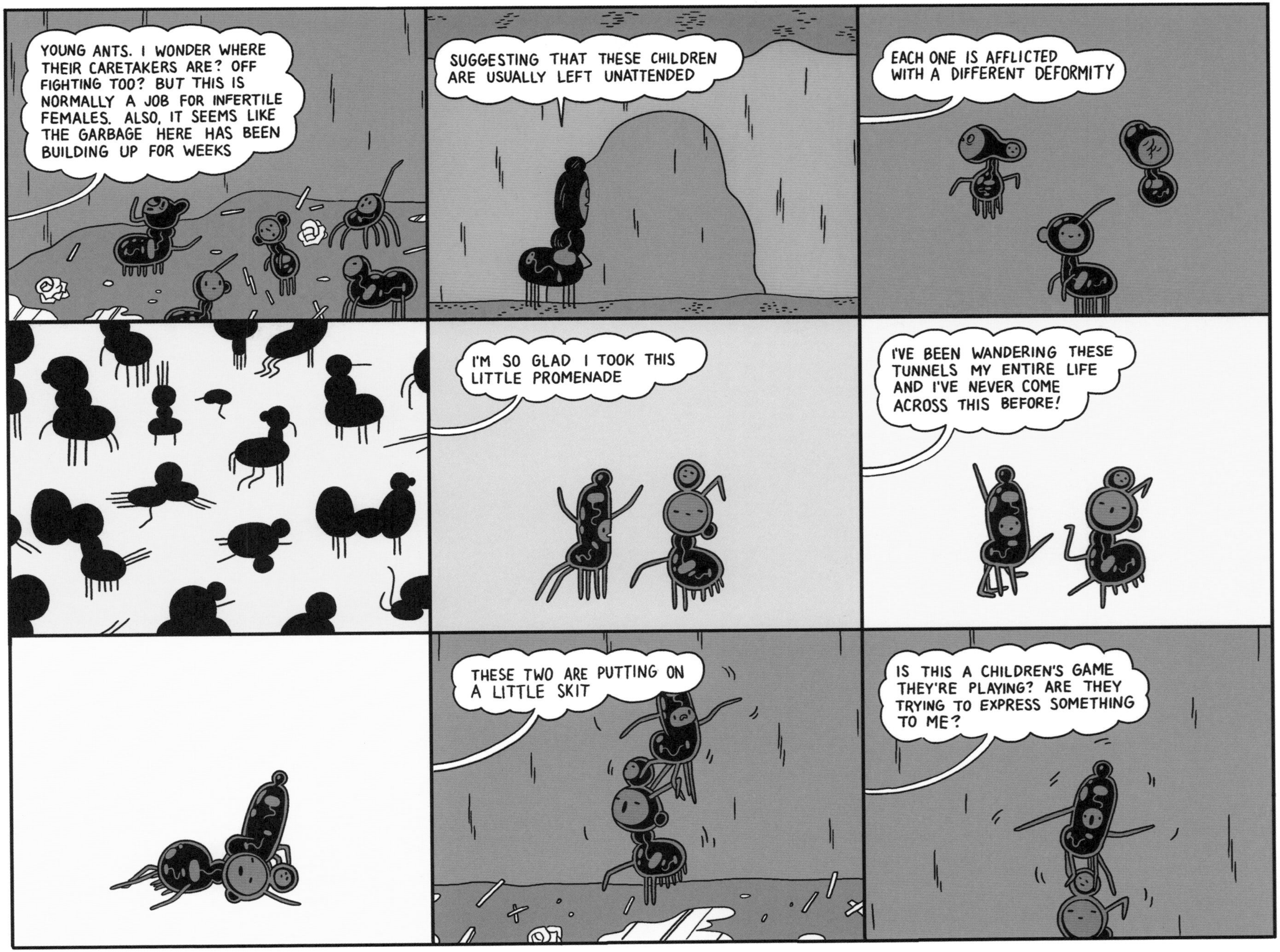
YOUNG ANTS. I WONDER WHERE THEIR CARETAKERS ARE? OFF FIGHTING TOO? BUT THIS IS NORMALLY A JOB FOR INFERTILE FEMALES. ALSO, IT SEEMS LIKE THE GARBAGE HERE HAS BEEN BUILDING UP FOR WEEKS
SUGGESTING THAT THESE CHILDREN ARE USUALLY LEFT UNATTENDED
EACH ONE IS AFFLICTED WITH A DIFFERENT DEFORMITY
I'M SO GLAD I TOOK THIS LITTLE PROMENADE
I'VE BEEN WANDERING THESE TUNNELS MY ENTIRE LIFE AND I'VE NEVER COME ACROSS THIS BEFORE!
THESE TWO ARE PUTTING ON A LITTLE SKIT
IS THIS A CHILDREN'S GAME THEY'RE PLAYING? ARE THEY TRYING TO EXPRESS SOMETHING TO ME?

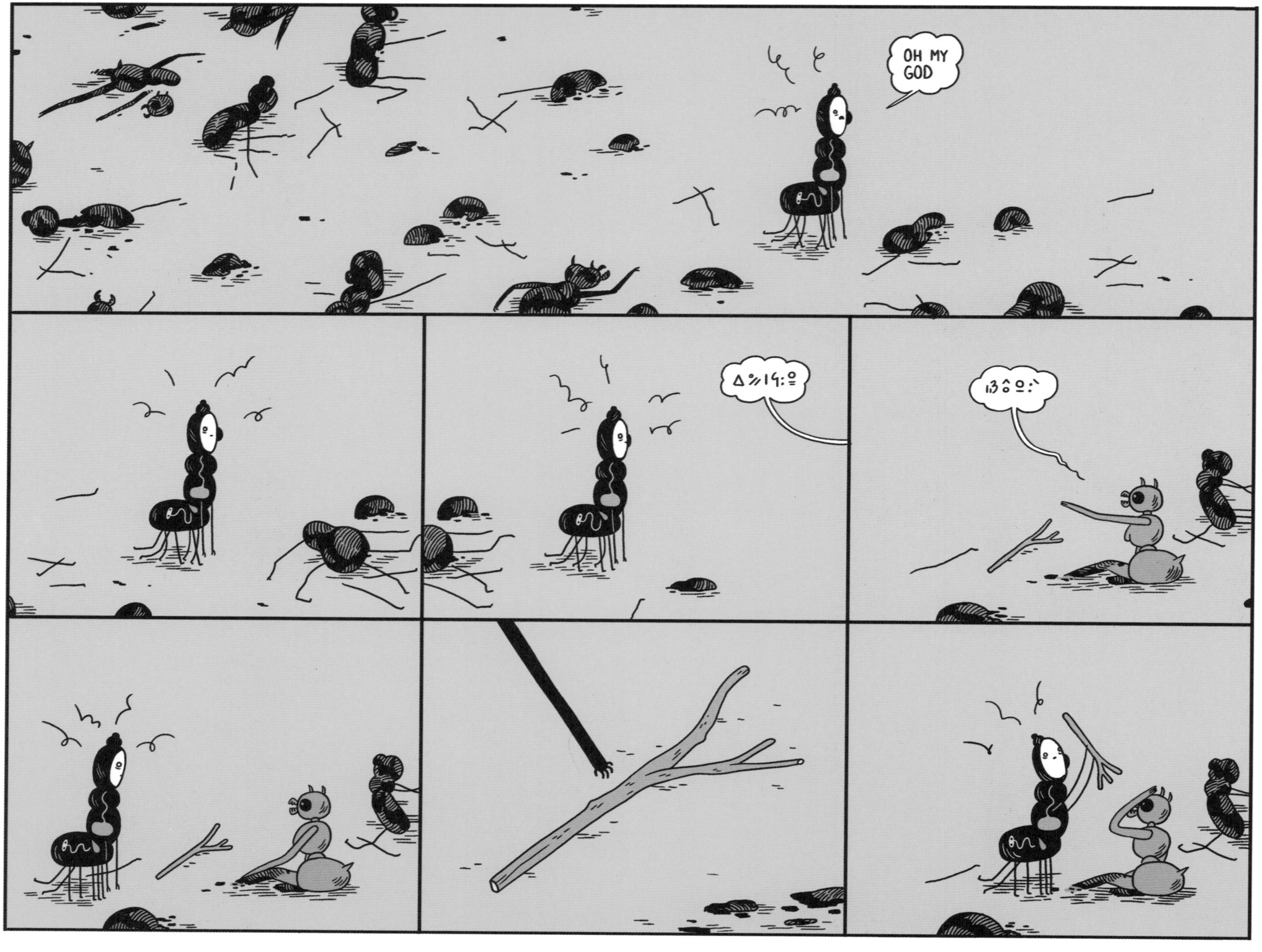
OH MY GOD

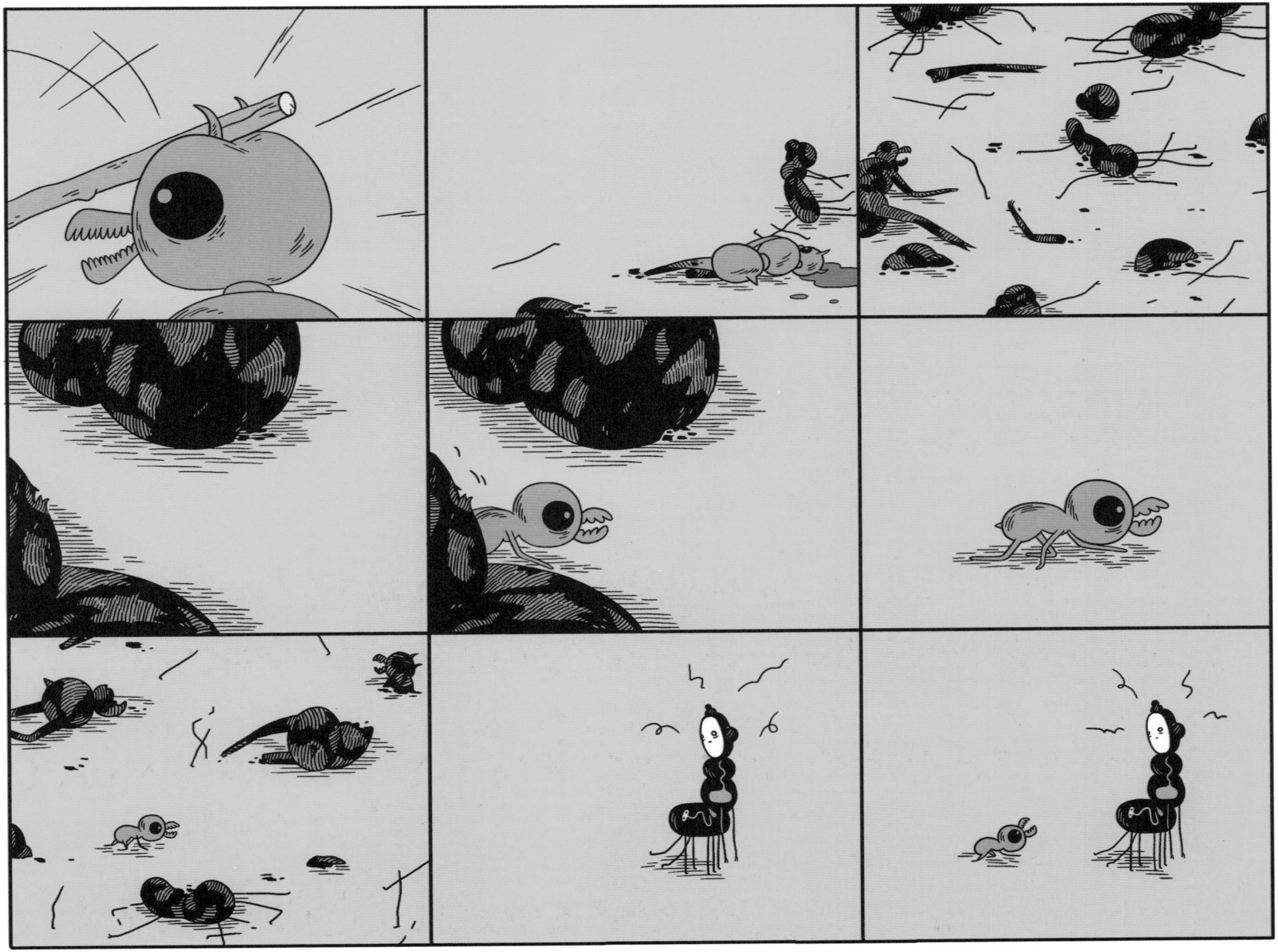

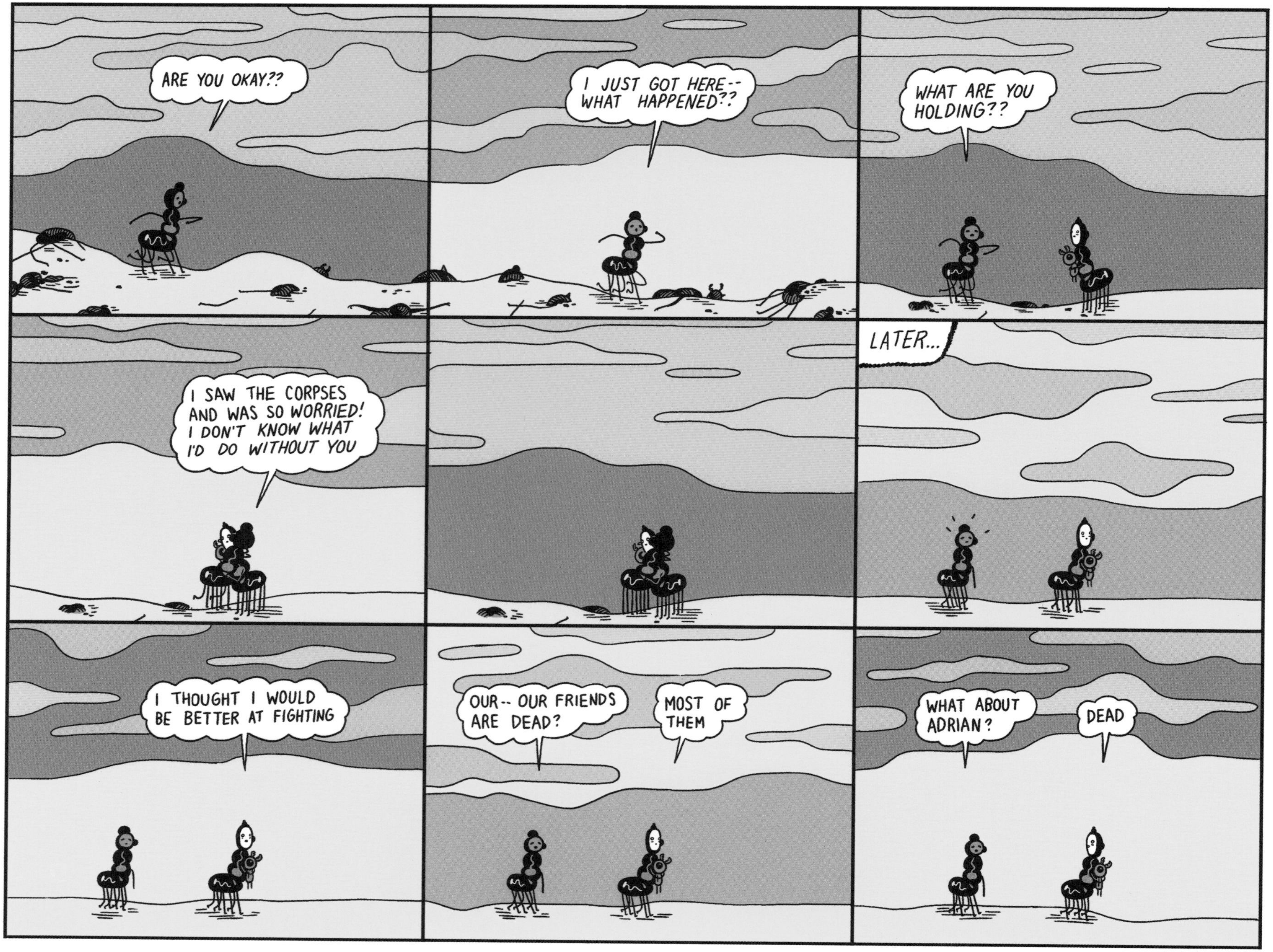
ARE YOU OKAY??
I JUST GOT HERE-- WHAT HAPPENED??
WHAT ARE YOU HOLDING??
I SAW THE CORPSES AND WAS SO WORRIED! I DON'T KNOW WHAT I'D DO WITHOUT YOU
LATER...
I THOUGHT I WOULD BE BETTER AT FIGHTING
OUR-- OUR FRIENDS ARE DEAD?
MOST OF THEM
WHAT ABOUT ADRIAN?
DEAD

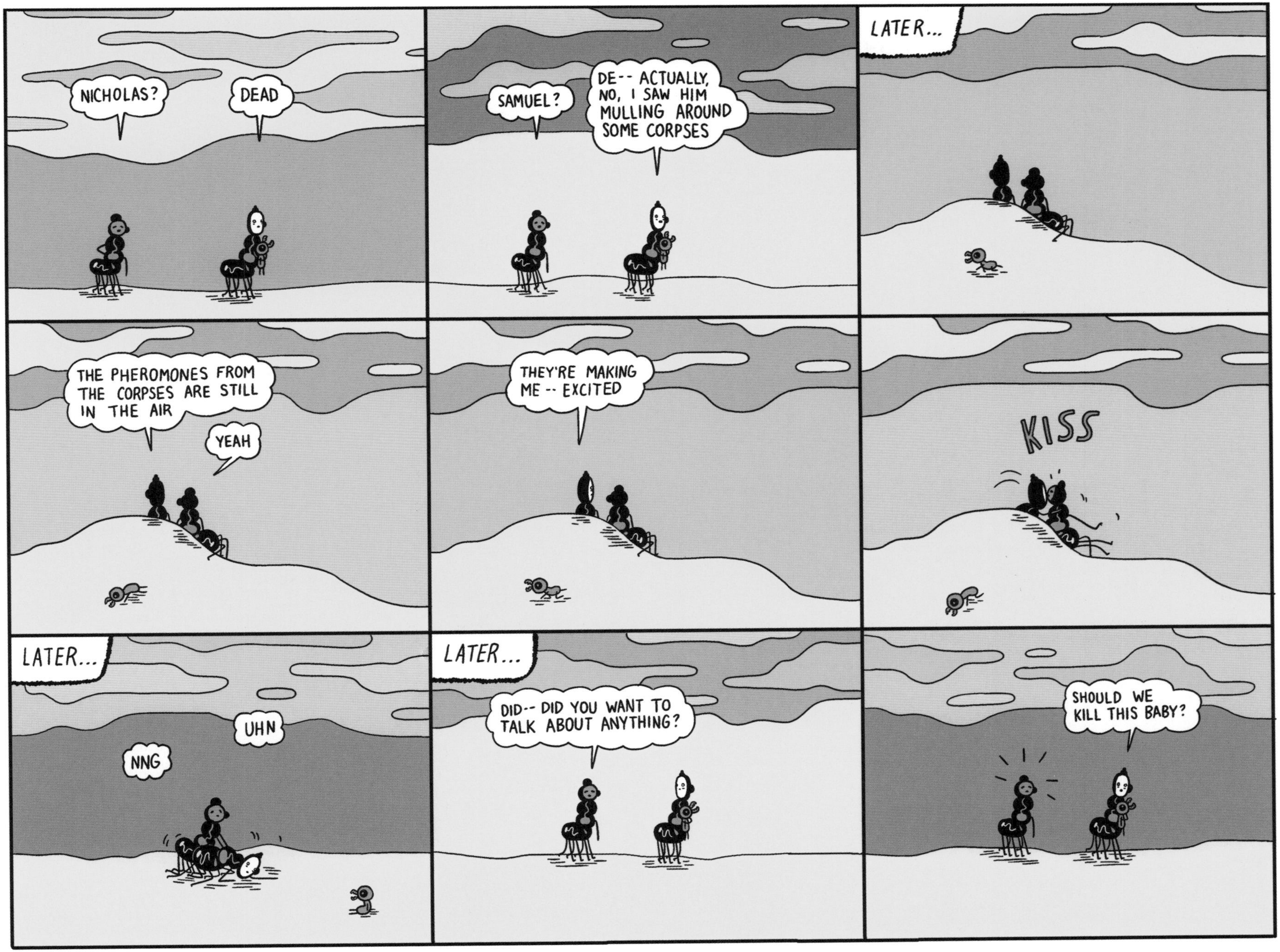
NICHOLAS?
DEAD
SAMUEL?
DE-- ACTUALLY, NO, I SAW HIM MULLING AROUND SOME CORPSES
LATER...
THE PHEROMONES FROM THE CORPSES ARE STILL IN THE AIR
YEAH
THEY'RE MAKING ME -- EXCITED
KISS
LATER...
UHN
NNG
LATER...
DID-- DID YOU WANT TO TALK ABOUT ANYTHING?
SHOULD WE KILL THIS BABY?

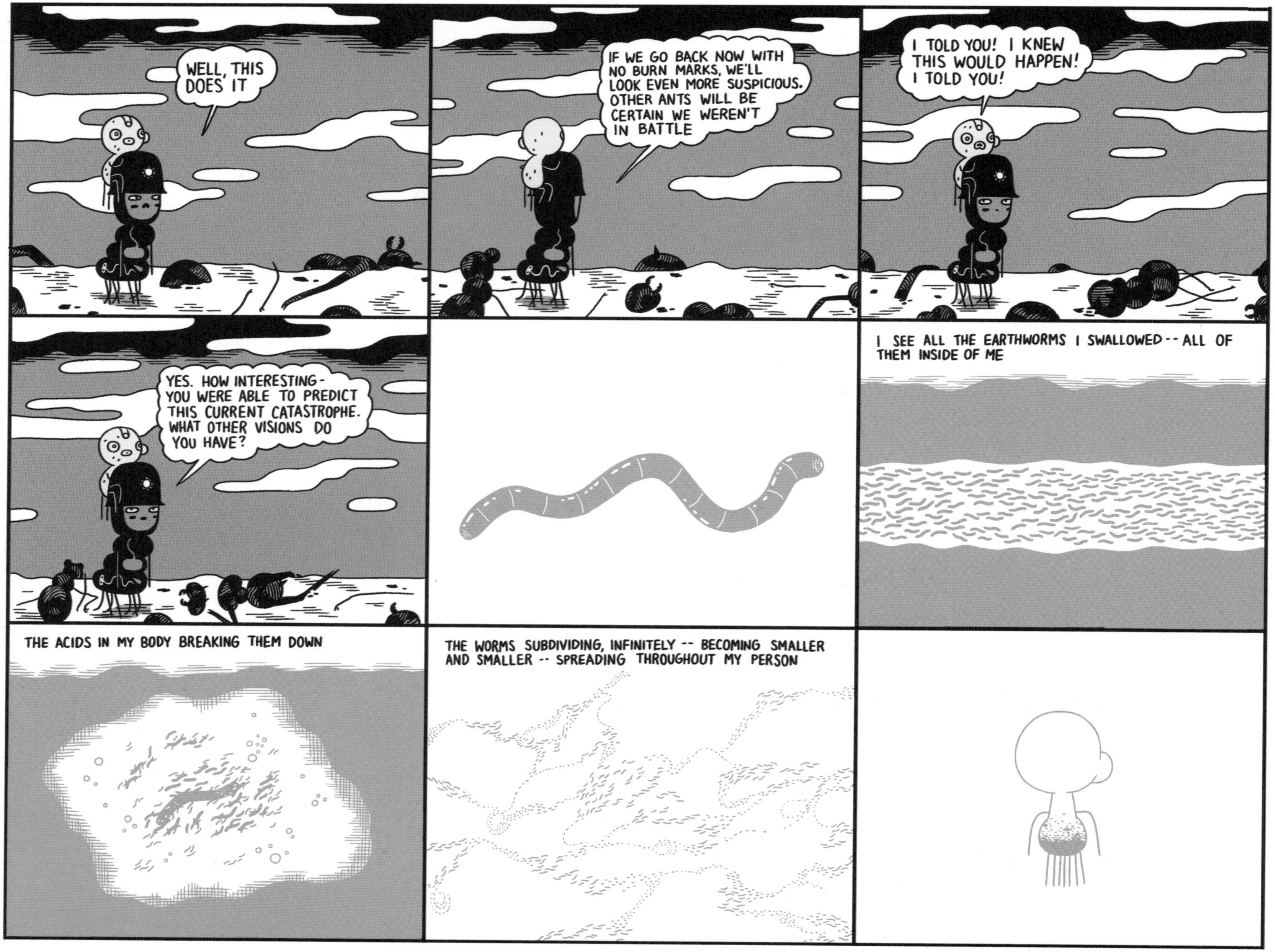
WELL, THIS DOES IT
IF WE GO BACK NOW WITH NO BURN MARKS, WE'LL LOOK EVEN MORE SUSPICIOUS. OTHER ANTS WILL BE CERTAIN WE WEREN'T IN BATTLE
I TOLD YOU! I KNEW THIS WOULD HAPPEN! I TOLD YOU!
YES. HOW INTERESTING - YOU WERE ABLE TO PREDICT THIS CURRENT CATASTROPHE. WHAT OTHER VISIONS DO YOU HAVE?
I SEE ALL THE EARTHWORMS I SWALLOWED -- ALL OF THEM INSIDE OF ME
THE ACIDS IN MY BODY BREAKING THEM DOWN
THE WORMS SUBDIVIDING, INFINITELY -- BECOMING SMALLER AND SMALLER -- SPREADING THROUGHOUT MY PERSON

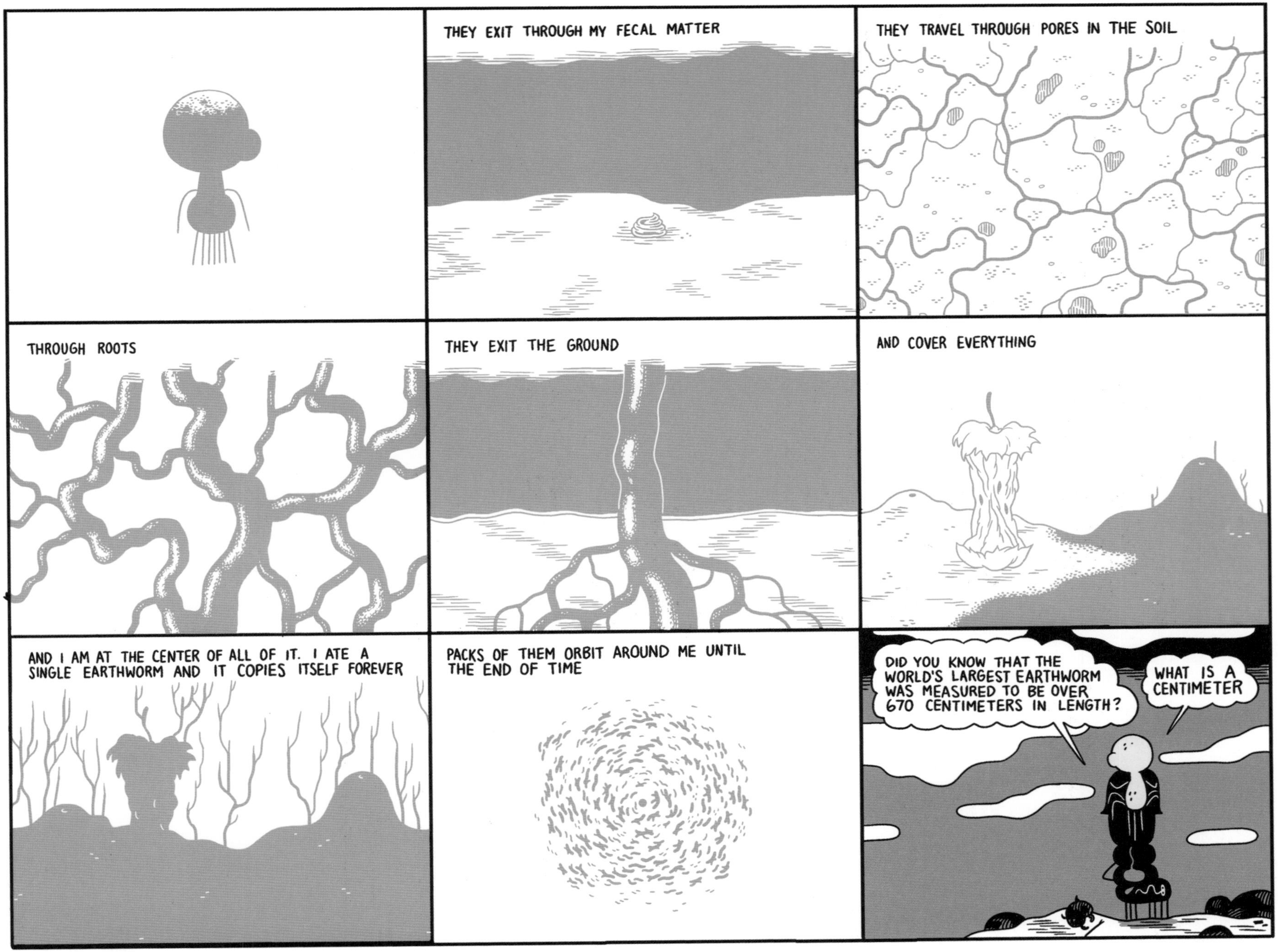
THEY EXIT THROUGH MY FECAL MATTER
THEY TRAVEL THROUGH PORES IN THE SOIL
THROUGH ROOTS
THEY EXIT THE GROUND
AND COVER EVERYTHING
AND I AM AT THE CENTER OF ALL OF IT. I ATE A SINGLE EARTHWORM AND IT COPIES ITSELF FOREVER
PACKS OF THEM ORBIT AROUND ME UNTIL THE END OF TIME
DID YOU KNOW THAT THE WORLD'S LARGEST EARTHWORM WAS MEASURED TO BE OVER 670 CENTIMETERS IN LENGTH?
WHAT IS A CENTIMETER

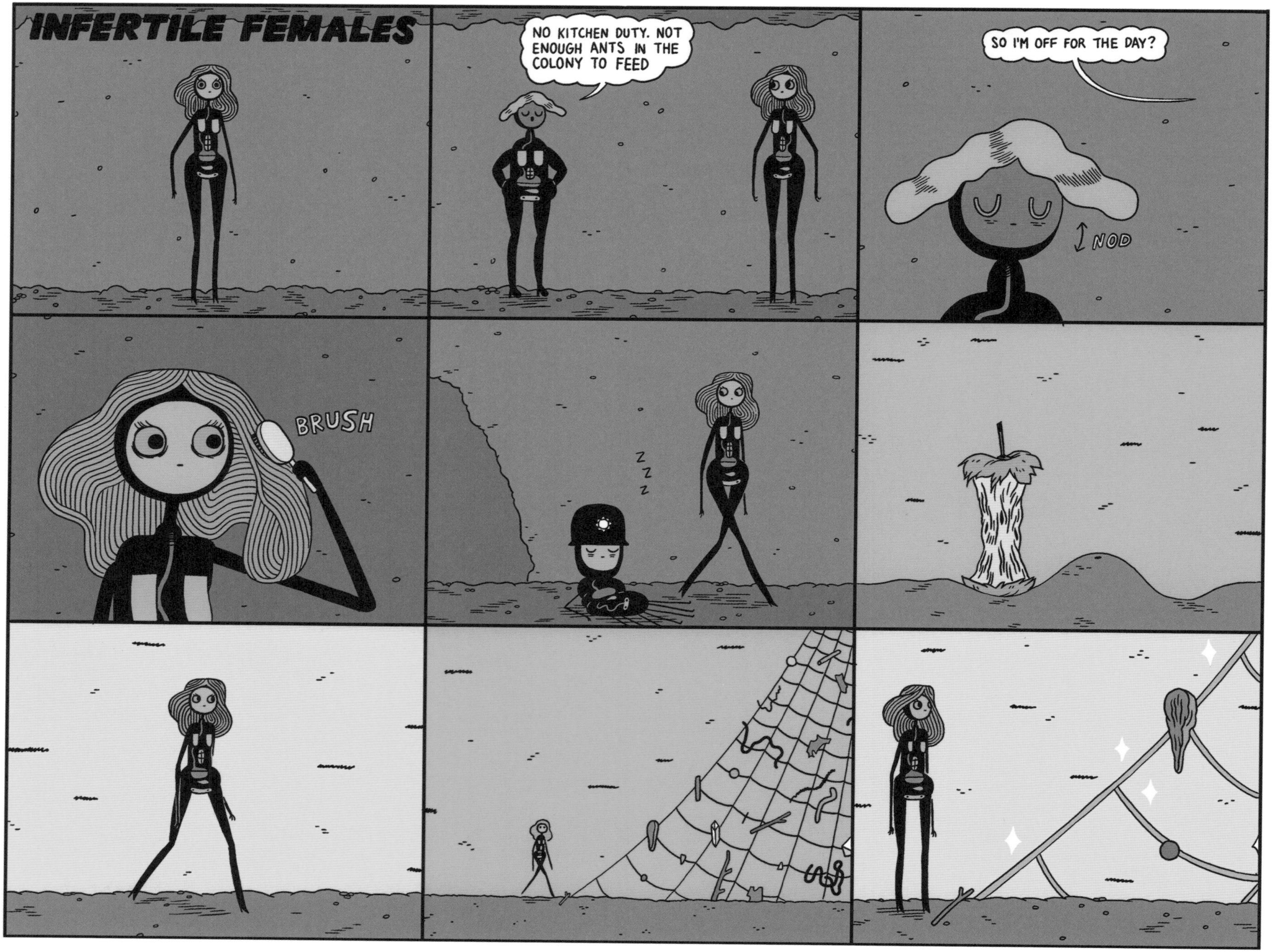
INFERTILE FEMALES
NO KITCHEN DUTY. NOT ENOUGH ANTS IN THE COLONY TO FEED
SO I'M OFF FOR THE DAY?
NOD
BRUSH
Z Z Z

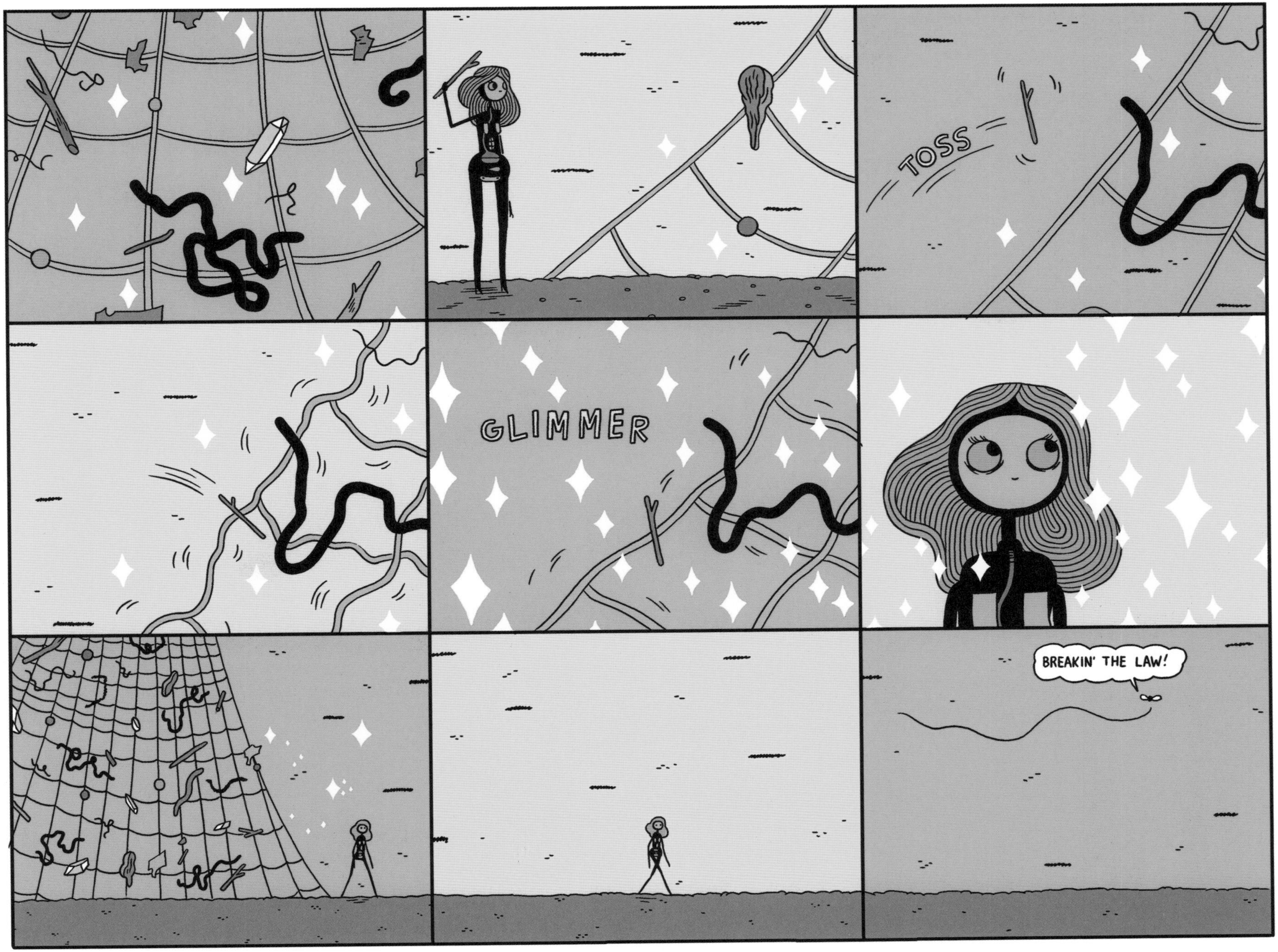
TOSS
GLIMMER
BREAKIN' THE LAW!

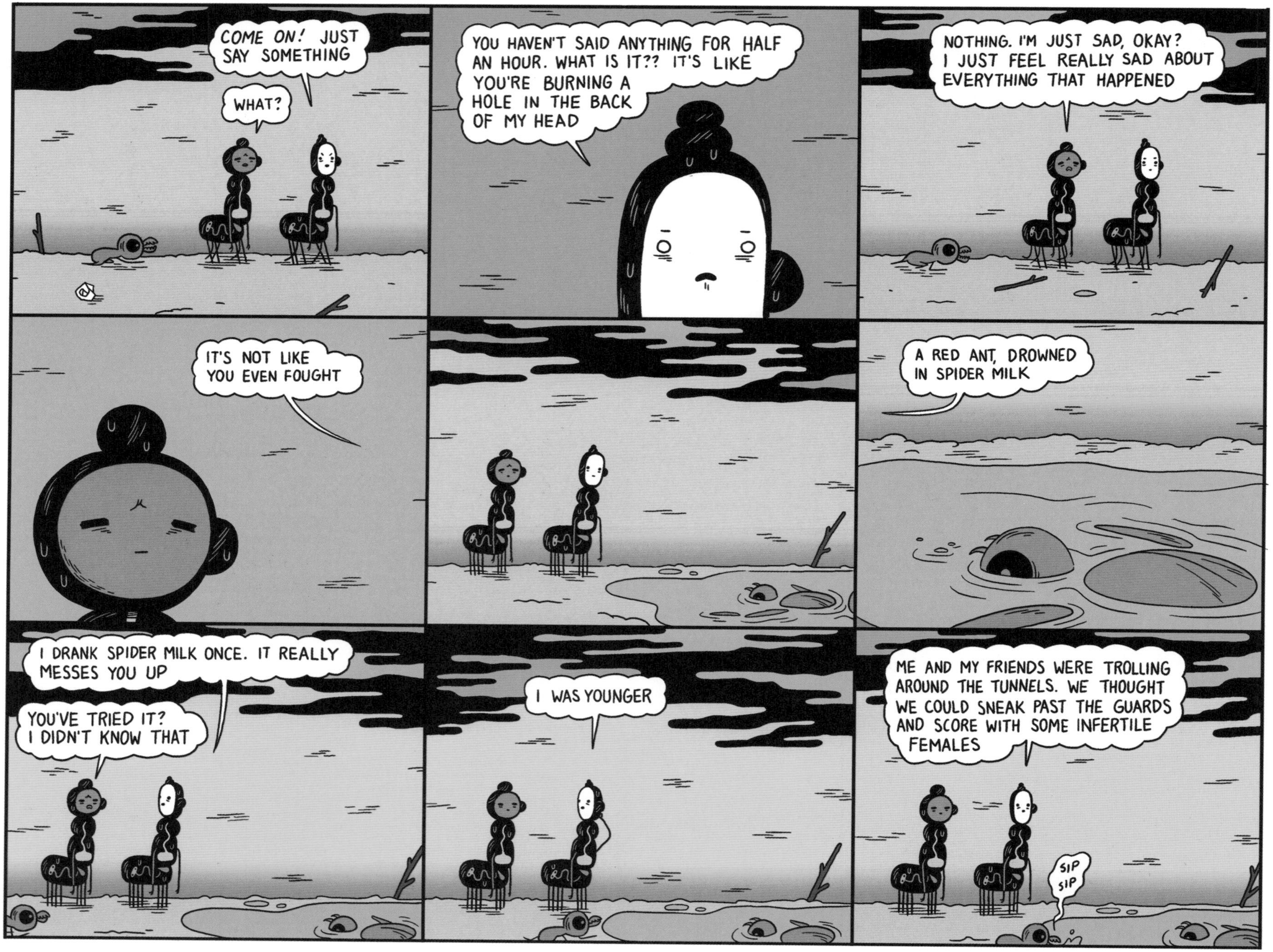
COME ON! JUST SAY SOMETHING
WHAT?
YOU HAVEN'T SAID ANYTHING FOR HALF AN HOUR. WHAT IS IT?? IT'S LIKE YOU'RE BURNING A HOLE IN THE BACK OF MY HEAD
NOTHING. I'M JUST SAD, OKAY? I JUST FEEL REALLY SAD ABOUT EVERYTHING THAT HAPPENED
IT'S NOT LIKE YOU EVEN FOUGHT
A RED ANT, DROWNED IN SPIDER MILK
I DRANK SPIDER MILK ONCE. IT REALLY MESSES YOU UP
YOU'VE TRIED IT? I DIDN'T KNOW THAT
I WAS YOUNGER
ME AND MY FRIENDS WERE TROLLING AROUND THE TUNNELS. WE THOUGHT WE COULD SNEAK PAST THE GUARDS AND SCORE WITH SOME INFERTILE FEMALES
SIP SIP

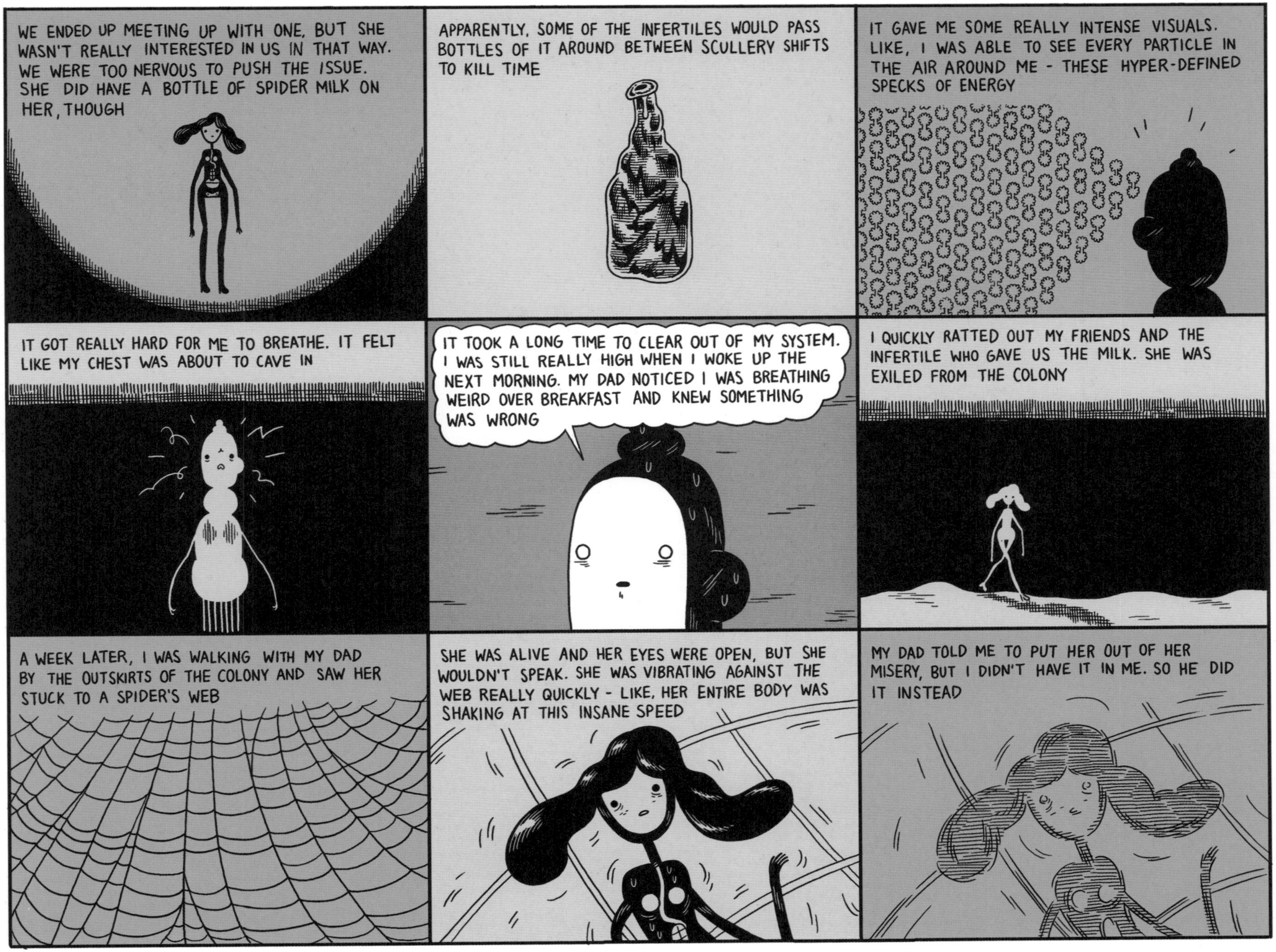
WE ENDED UP MEETING UP WITH ONE, BUT SHE WASN'T REALLY INTERESTED IN US IN THAT WAY. WE WERE TOO NERVOUS TO PUSH THE ISSUE. SHE DID HAVE A BOTTLE OF SPIDER MILK ON HER, THOUGH
APPARENTLY, SOME OF THE INFERTILES WOULD PASS BOTTLES OF IT AROUND BETWEEN SCULLERY SHIFTS TO KILL TIME
IT GAVE ME SOME REALLY INTENSE VISUALS. LIKE, I WAS ABLE TO SEE EVERY PARTICLE IN THE AIR AROUND ME - THESE HYPER-DEFINED SPECKS OF ENERGY
IT GOT REALLY HARD FOR ME TO BREATHE. IT FELT LIKE MY CHEST WAS ABOUT TO CAVE IN
IT TOOK A LONG TIME TO CLEAR OUT OF MY SYSTEM. I WAS STILL REALLY HIGH WHEN I WOKE UP THE NEXT MORNING. MY DAD NOTICED I WAS BREATHING WEIRD OVER BREAKFAST AND KNEW SOMETHING WAS WRONG
I QUICKLY RATTED OUT MY FRIENDS AND THE INFERTILE WHO GAVE US THE MILK. SHE WAS EXILED FROM THE COLONY
A WEEK LATER, I WAS WALKING WITH MY DAD BY THE OUTSKIRTS OF THE COLONY AND SAW HER STUCK TO A SPIDER'S WEB
SHE WAS ALIVE AND HER EYES WERE OPEN, BUT SHE WOULDN'T SPEAK. SHE WAS VIBRATING AGAINST THE WEB REALLY QUICKLY - LIKE, HER ENTIRE BODY WAS SHAKING AT THIS INSANE SPEED
MY DAD TOLD ME TO PUT HER OUT OF HER MISERY, BUT I DIDN'T HAVE IT IN ME. SO HE DID IT INSTEAD

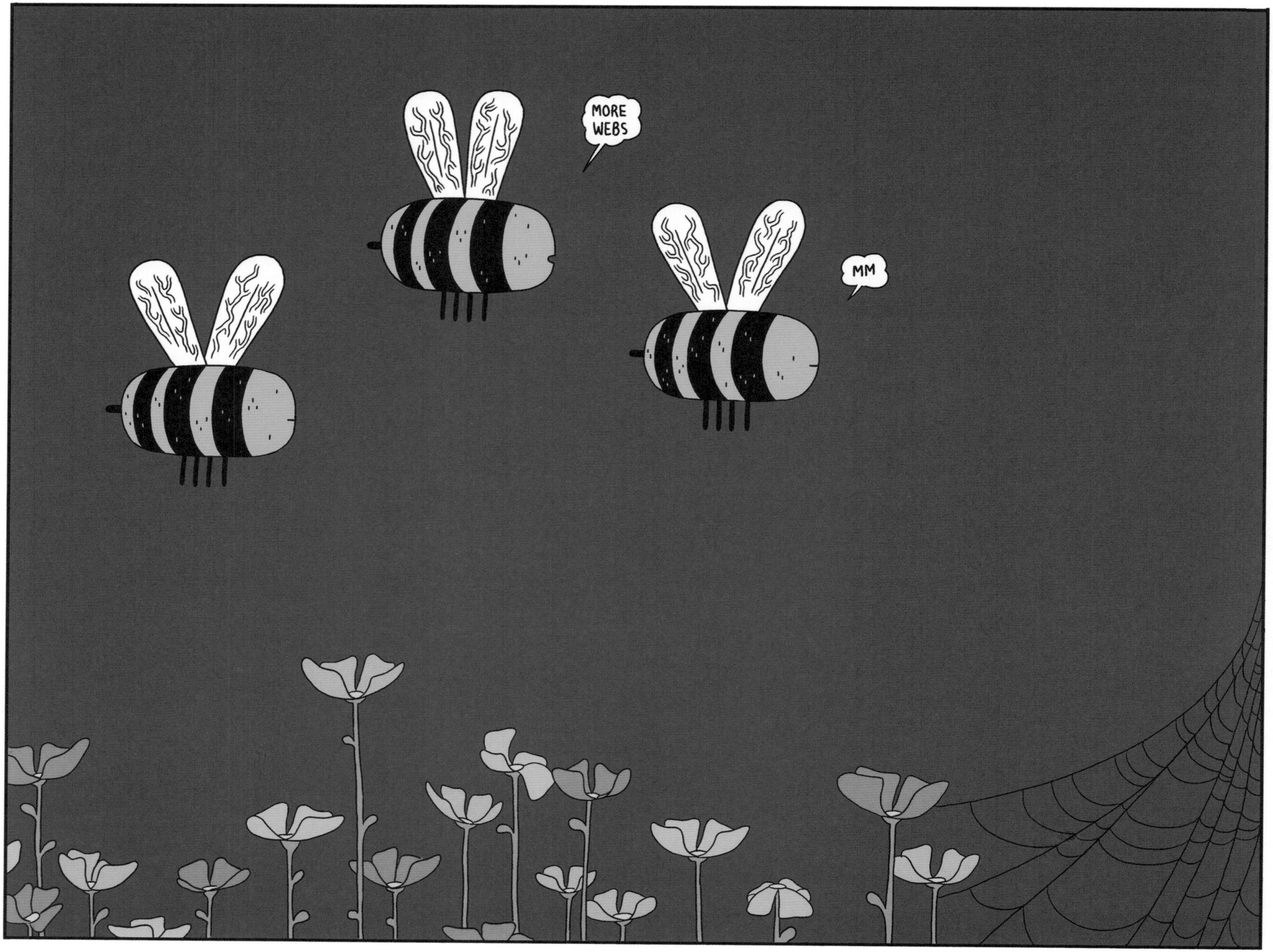
MORE WEBS
MM

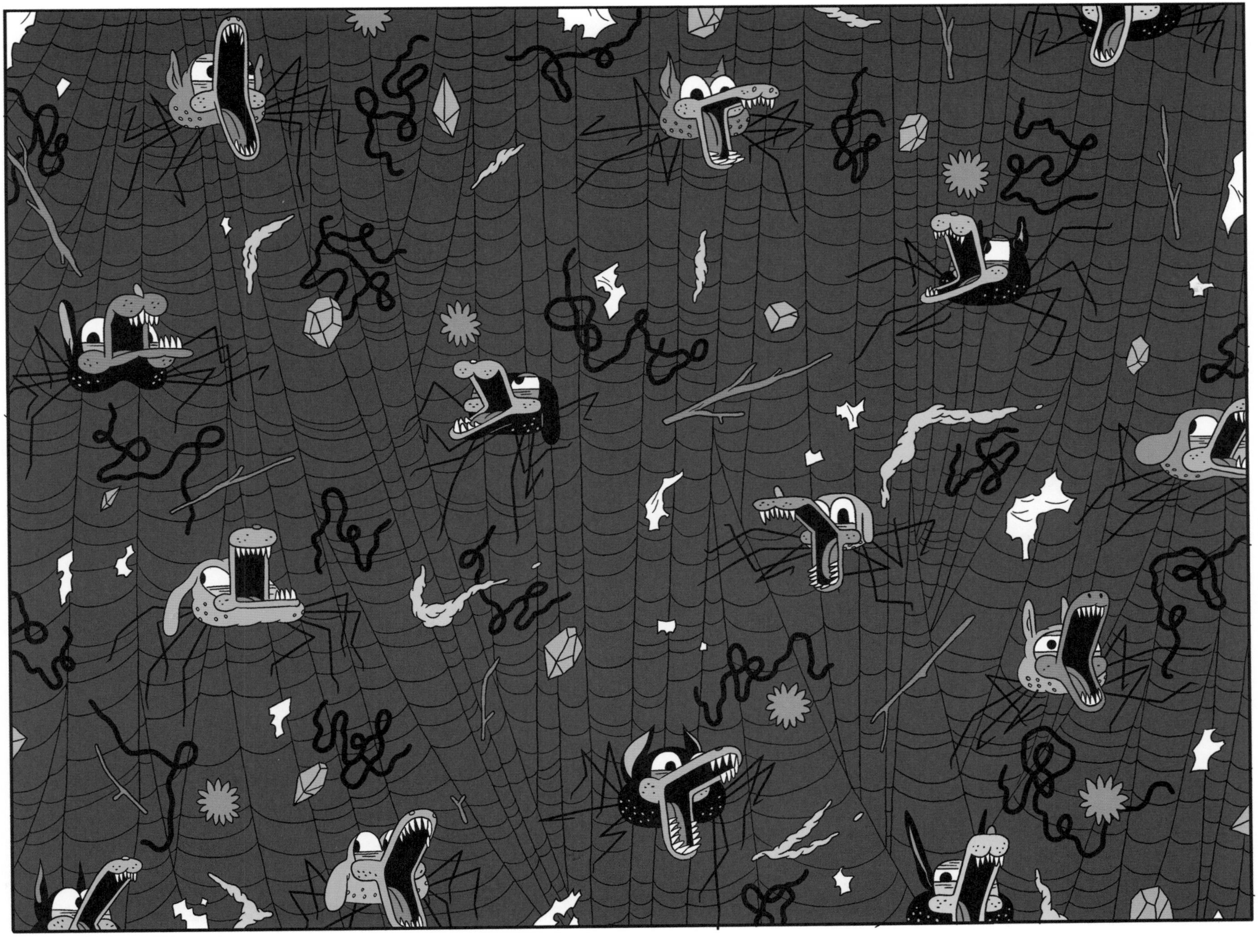

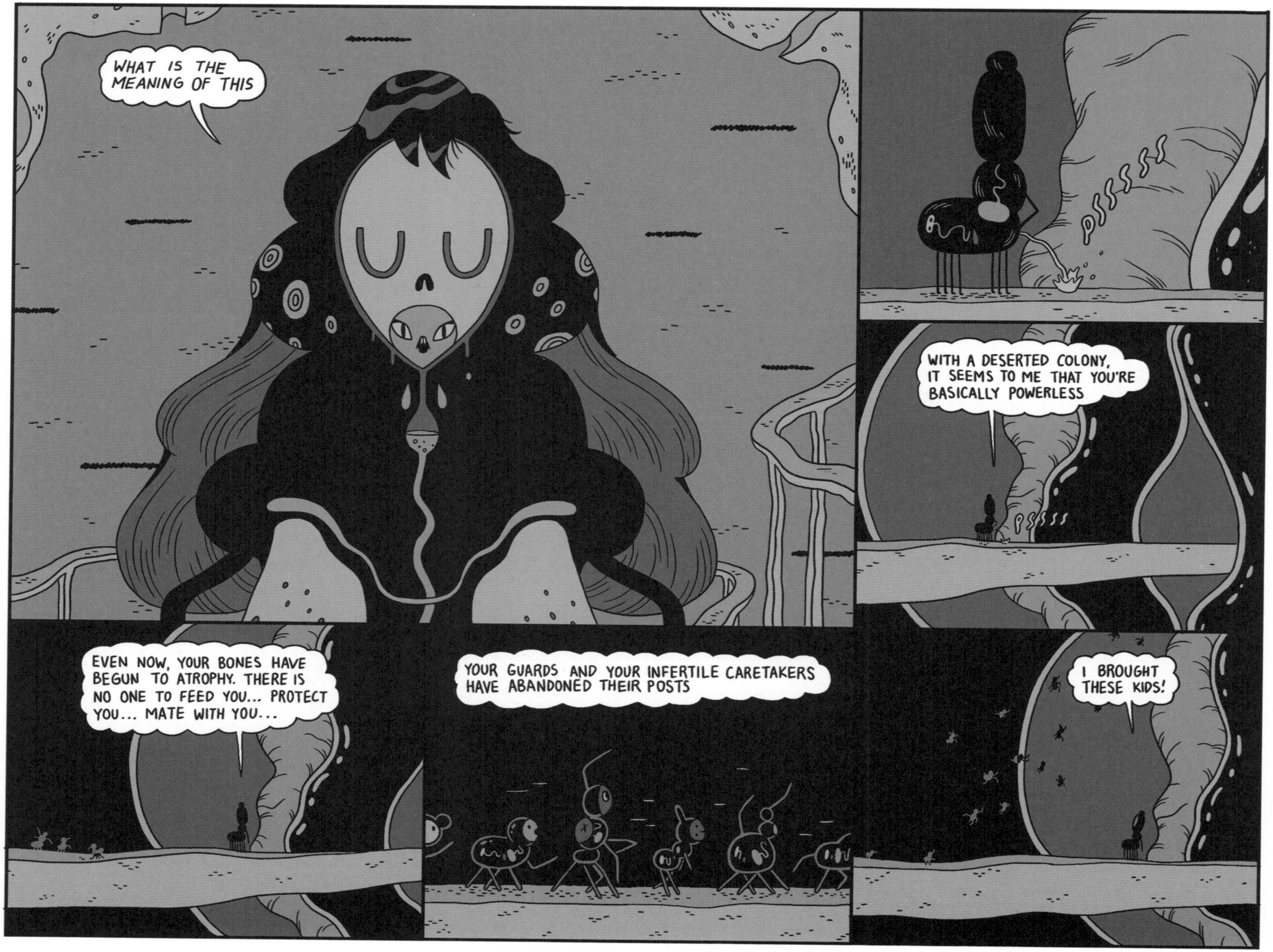
WHAT IS THE MEANING OF THIS
PSSSSS
WITH A DESERTED COLONY, IT SEEMS TO ME THAT YOU'RE BASICALLY POWERLESS
PSSSS
EVEN NOW, YOUR BONES HAVE BEGUN TO ATROPHY. THERE IS NO ONE TO FEED YOU... PROTECT YOU... MATE WITH YOU...
YOUR GUARDS AND YOUR INFERTILE CARETAKERS HAVE ABANDONED THEIR POSTS
I BROUGHT THESE KIDS!

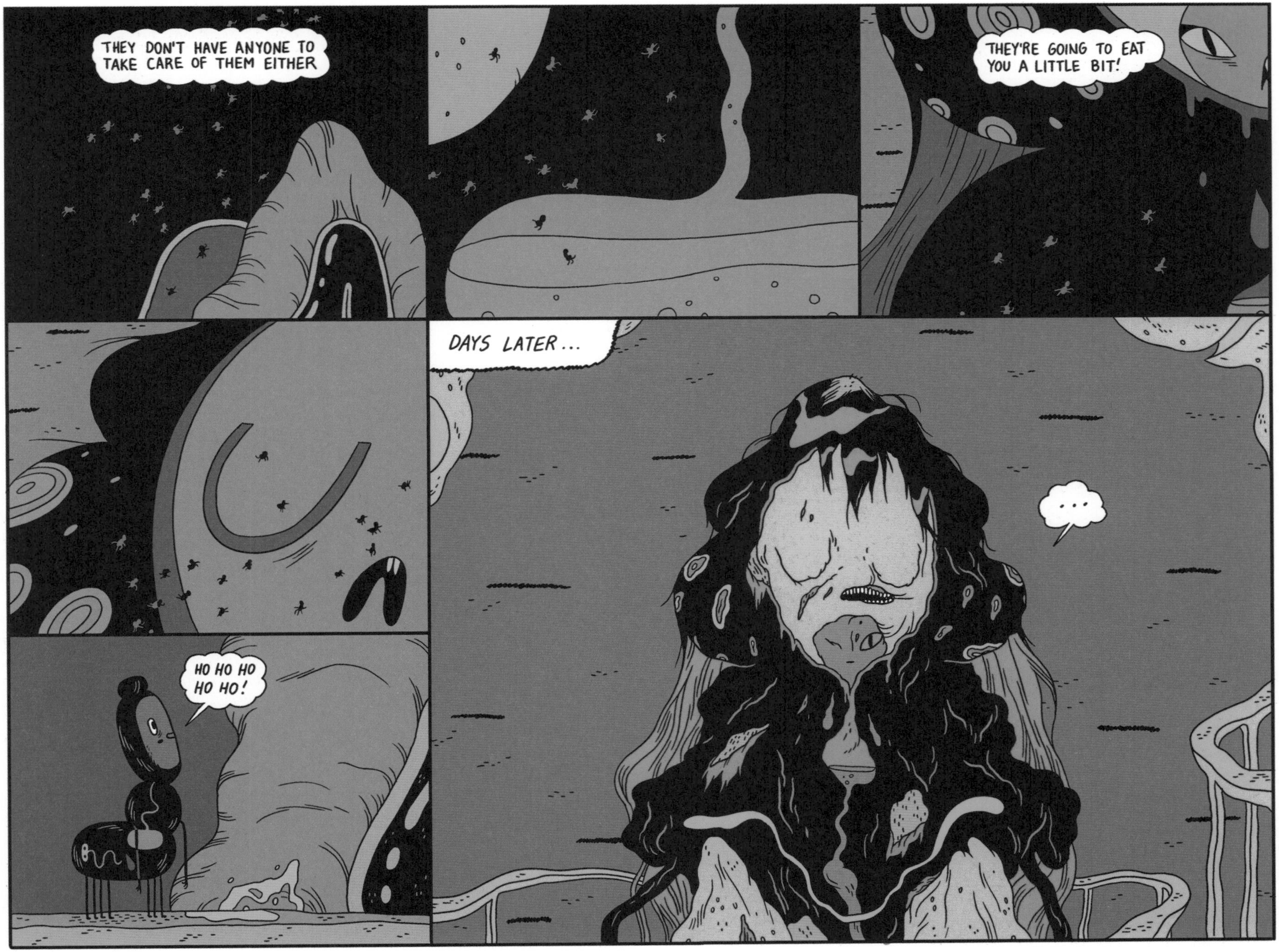
THEY DON'T HAVE ANYONE TO TAKE CARE OF THEM EITHER
THEY'RE GOING TO EAT YOU A LITTLE BIT!
DAYS LATER...
HO HO HO HO HO!
...

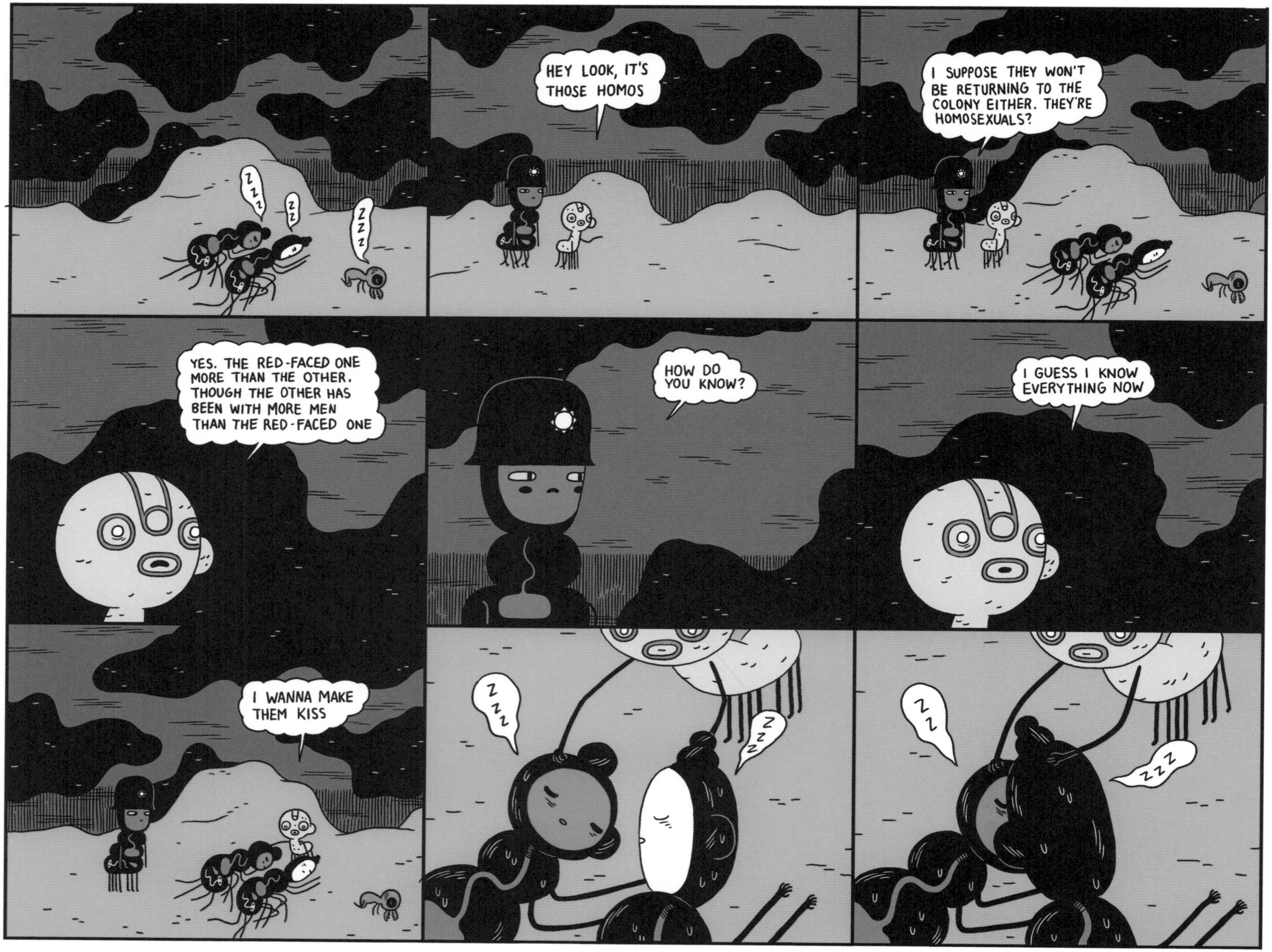
Z Z Z
Z Z
Z Z Z
HEY LOOK, IT'S THOSE HOMOS
I SUPPOSE THEY WON'T BE RETURNING TO THE COLONY EITHER. THEY'RE HOMOSEXUALS?
YES. THE RED-FACED ONE MORE THAN THE OTHER. THOUGH THE OTHER HAS BEEN WITH MORE MEN THAN THE RED-FACED ONE
HOW DO YOU KNOW?
I GUESS I KNOW EVERYTHING NOW
I WANNA MAKE THEM KISS
Z Z Z
Z Z Z
Z Z
Z Z Z

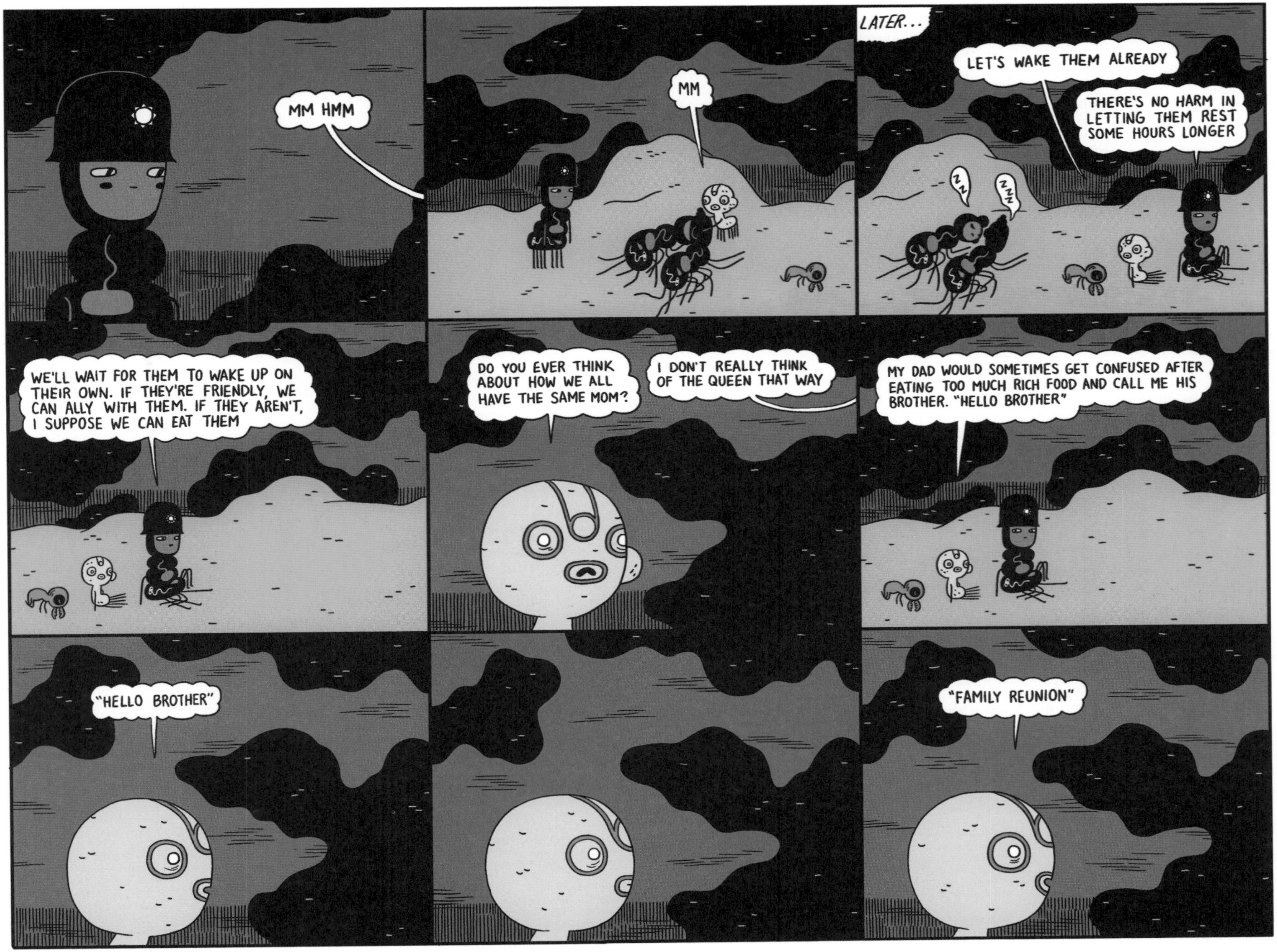
MM HMM
MM
LATER...
LET'S WAKE THEM ALREADY
THERE'S NO HARM IN LETTING THEM REST SOME HOURS LONGER
Z Z
Z Z Z
WE'LL WAIT FOR THEM TO WAKE UP ON THEIR OWN. IF THEY'RE FRIENDLY, WE CAN ALLY WITH THEM. IF THEY AREN'T, I SUPPOSE WE CAN EAT THEM
DO YOU EVER THINK ABOUT HOW WE ALL HAVE THE SAME MOM?
I DON'T REALLY THINK OF THE QUEEN THAT WAY
MY DAD WOULD SOMETIMES GET CONFUSED AFTER EATING TOO MUCH RICH FOOD AND CALL ME HIS BROTHER. "HELLO BROTHER"
"HELLO BROTHER"
"FAMILY REUNION"

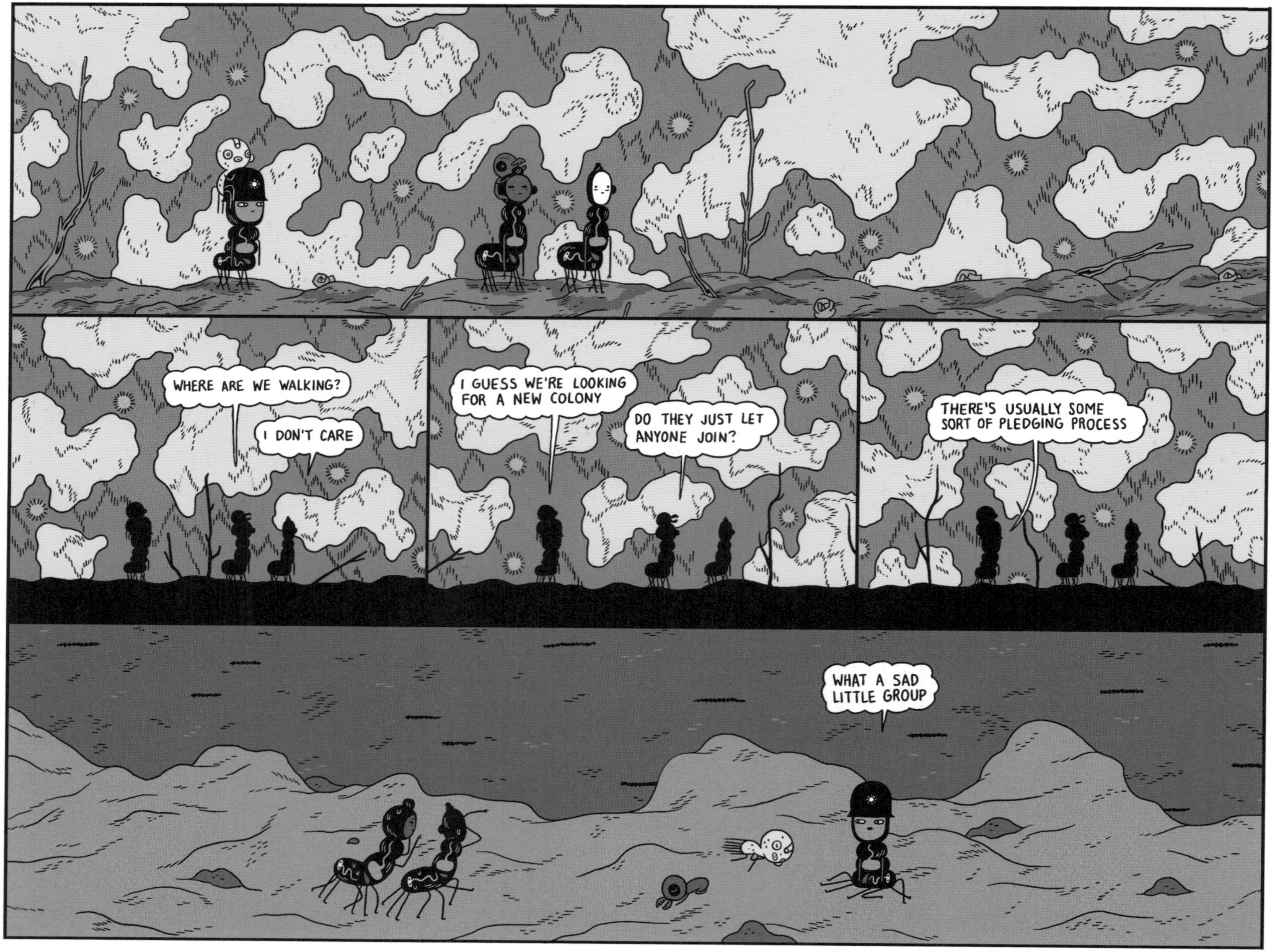
WHERE ARE WE WALKING?
I DON'T CARE
I GUESS WE'RE LOOKING FOR A NEW COLONY
DO THEY JUST LET ANYONE JOIN?
THERE'S USUALLY SOME SORT OF PLEDGING PROCESS
WHAT A SAD LITTLE GROUP

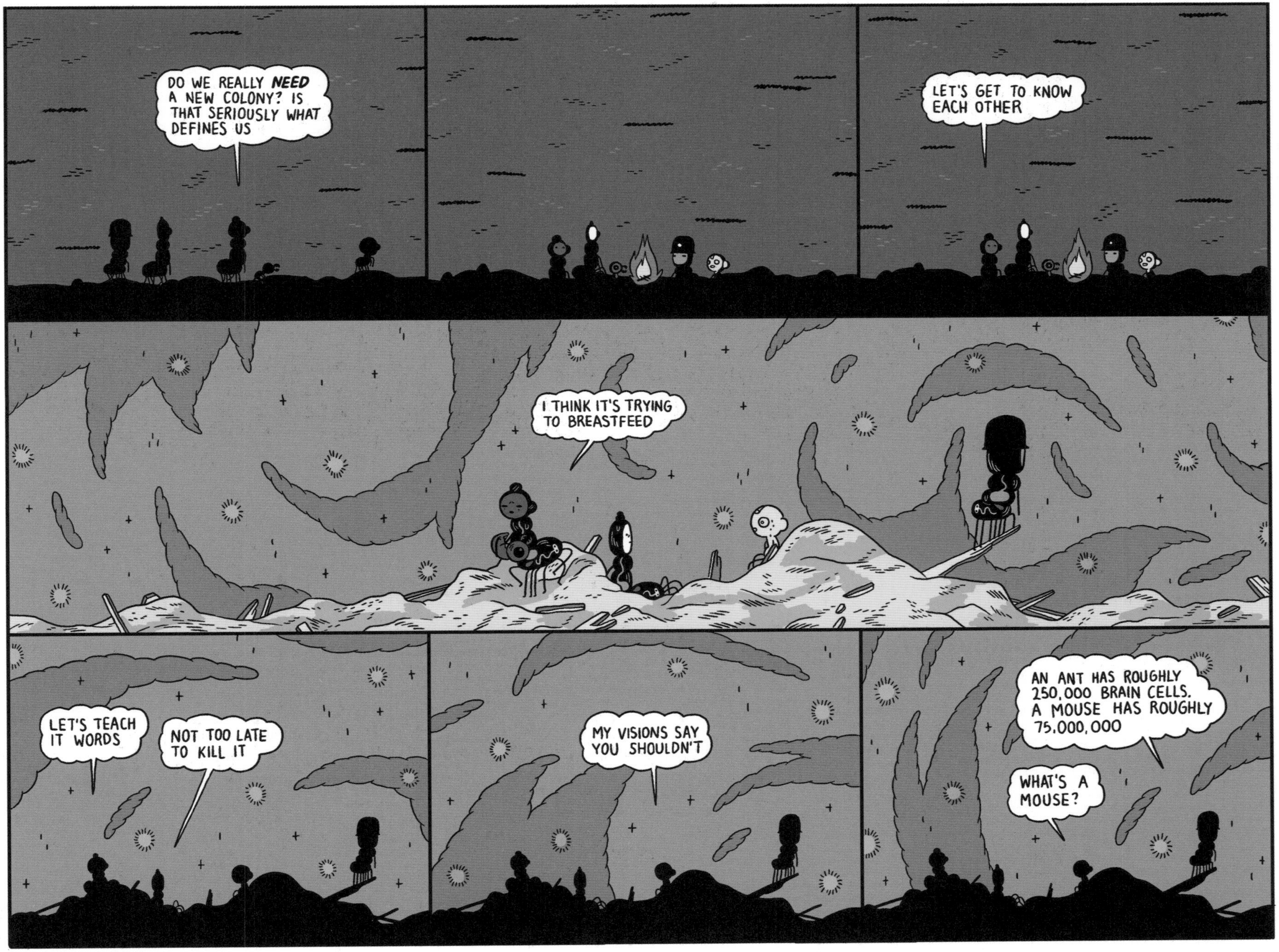
DO WE REALLY **NEED** A NEW COLONY? IS THAT SERIOUSLY WHAT DEFINES US
LET'S GET TO KNOW EACH OTHER
I THINK IT'S TRYING TO BREASTFEED
LET'S TEACH IT WORDS
NOT TOO LATE TO KILL IT
MY VISIONS SAY YOU SHOULDN'T
AN ANT HAS ROUGHLY 250,000 BRAIN CELLS. A MOUSE HAS ROUGHLY 75,000,000
WHAT'S A MOUSE?

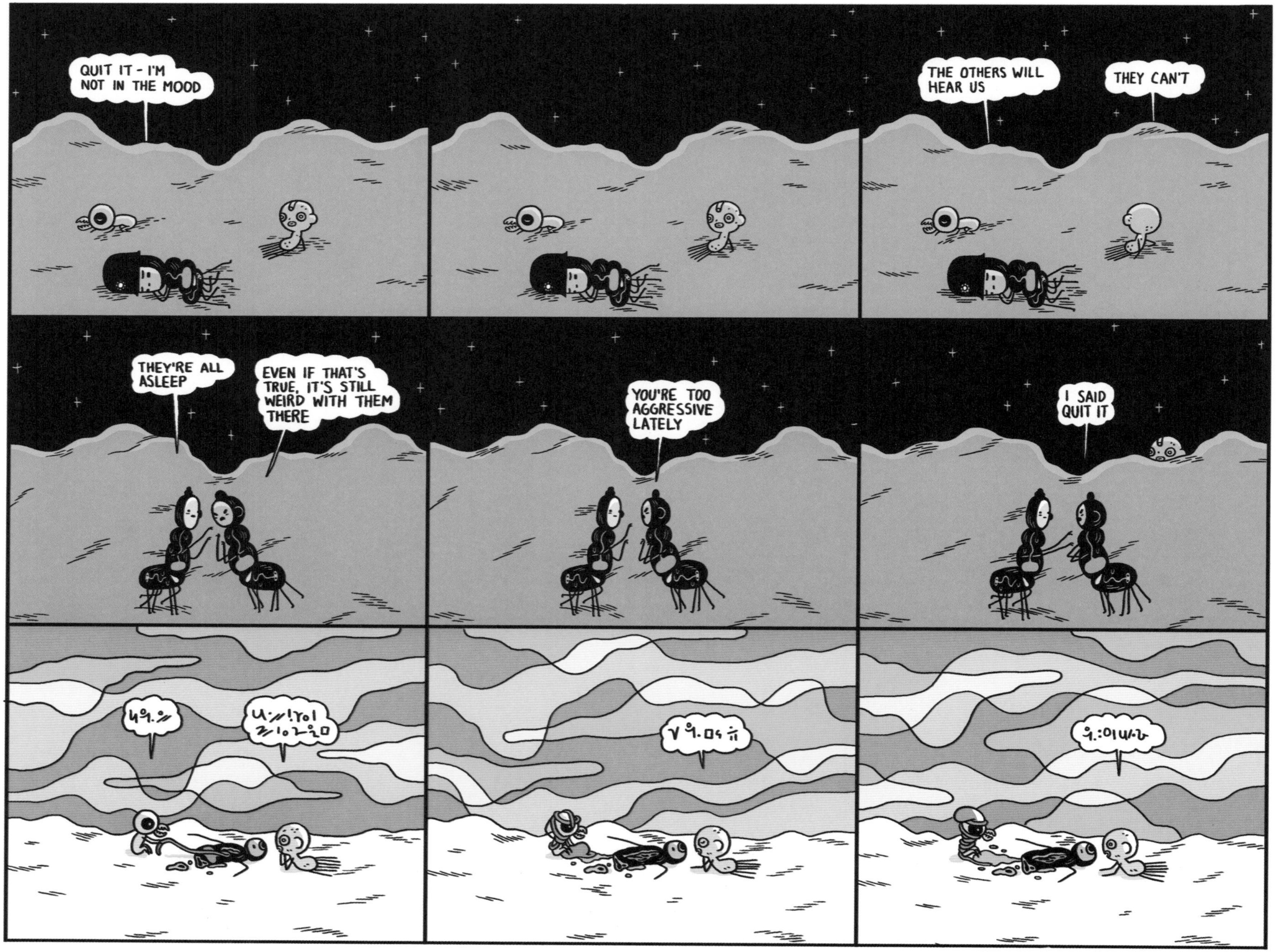
QUIT IT - I'M NOT IN THE MOOD
THE OTHERS WILL HEAR US
THEY CAN'T
THEY'RE ALL ASLEEP
EVEN IF THAT'S TRUE, IT'S STILL WEIRD WITH THEM THERE
YOU'RE TOO AGGRESSIVE LATELY
I SAID QUIT IT

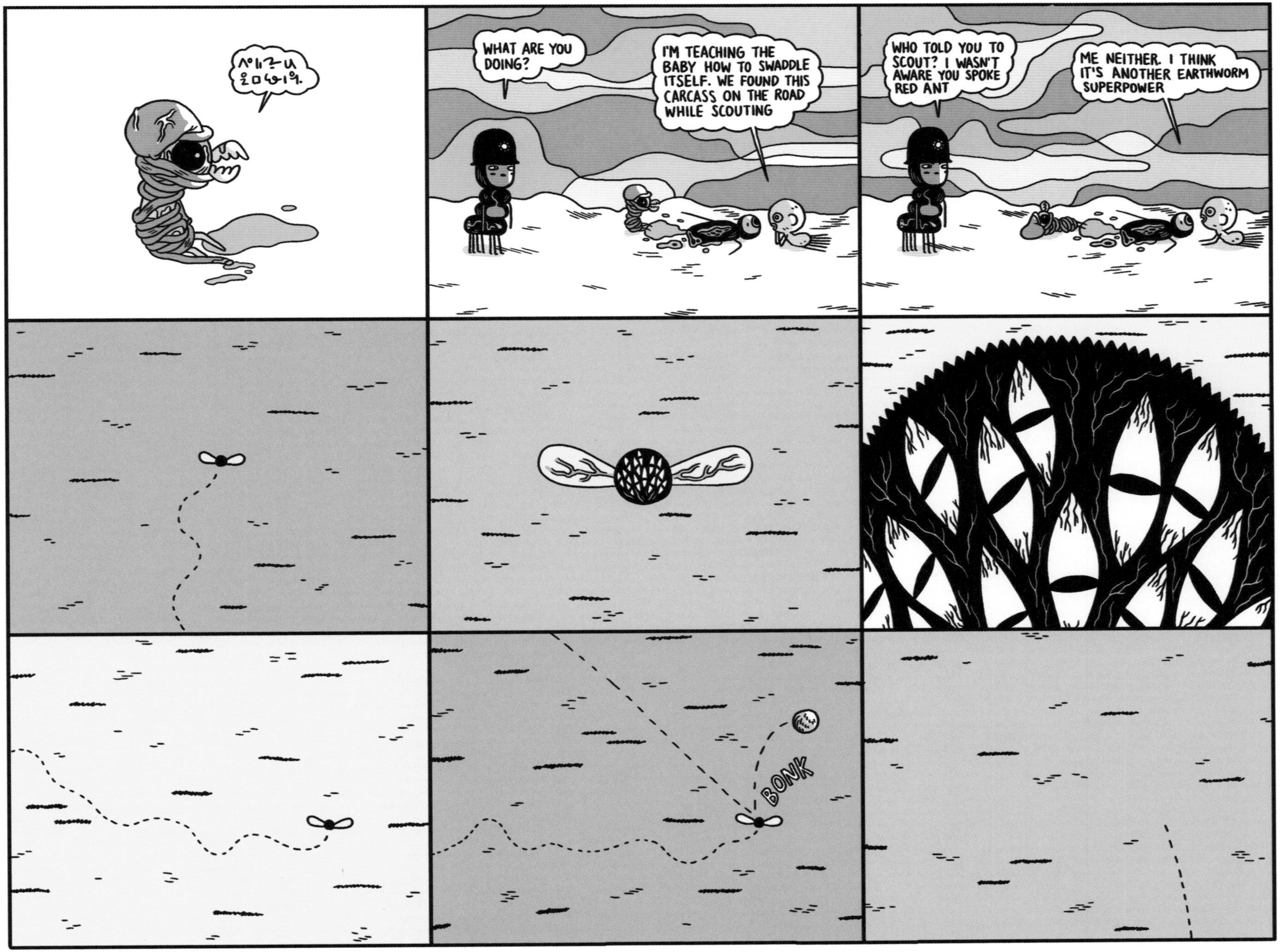
WHAT ARE YOU DOING?
I'M TEACHING THE BABY HOW TO SWADDLE ITSELF. WE FOUND THIS CARCASS ON THE ROAD WHILE SCOUTING
WHO TOLD YOU TO SCOUT? I WASN'T AWARE YOU SPOKE RED ANT
ME NEITHER. I THINK IT'S ANOTHER EARTHWORM SUPERPOWER
BONK

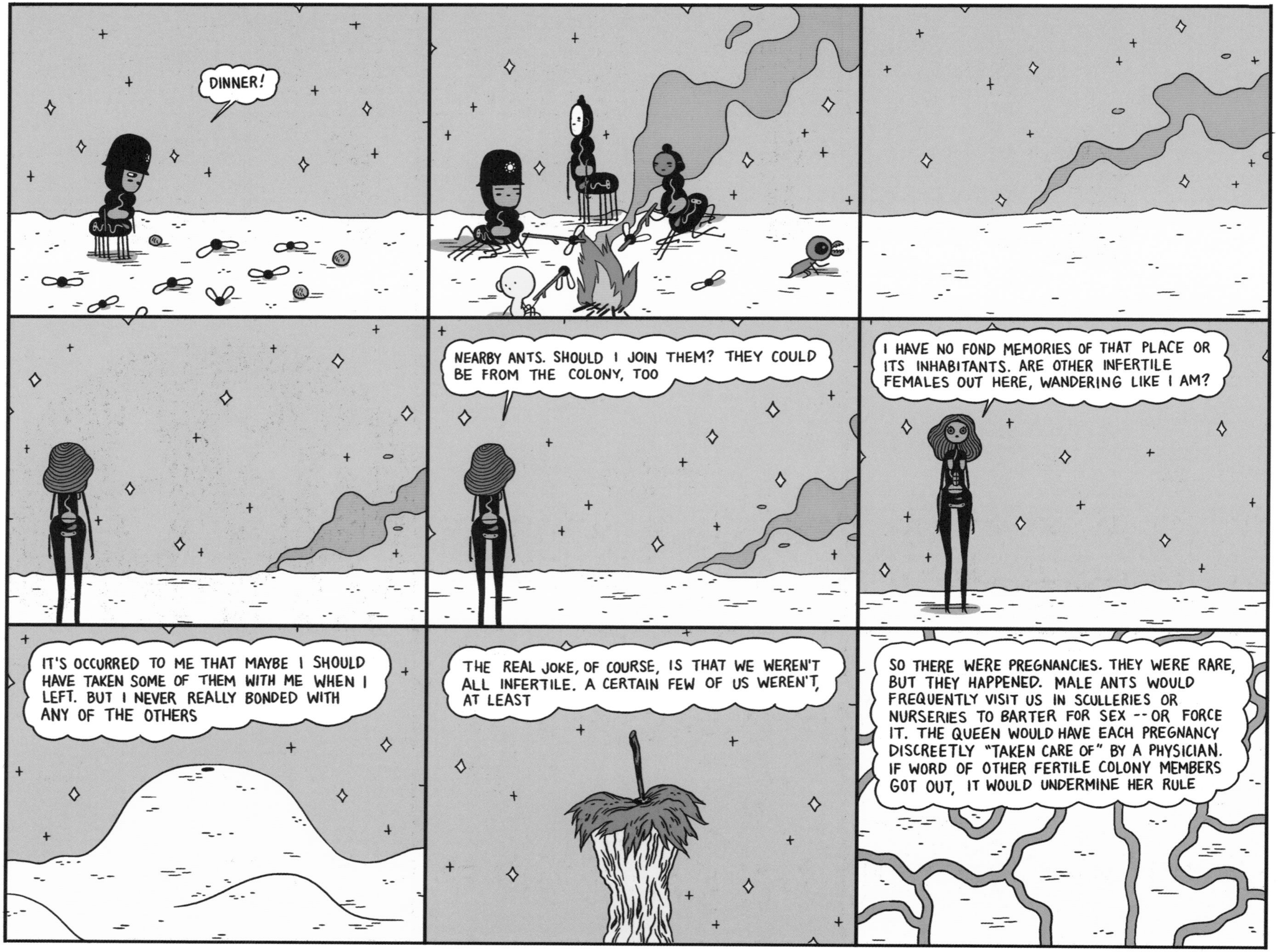
DINNER!
NEARBY ANTS. SHOULD I JOIN THEM? THEY COULD BE FROM THE COLONY, TOO
I HAVE NO FOND MEMORIES OF THAT PLACE OR ITS INHABITANTS. ARE OTHER INFERTILE FEMALES OUT HERE, WANDERING LIKE I AM?
IT'S OCCURRED TO ME THAT MAYBE I SHOULD HAVE TAKEN SOME OF THEM WITH ME WHEN I LEFT. BUT I NEVER REALLY BONDED WITH ANY OF THE OTHERS
THE REAL JOKE, OF COURSE, IS THAT WE WEREN'T ALL INFERTILE. A CERTAIN FEW OF US WEREN'T, AT LEAST
SO THERE WERE PREGNANCIES. THEY WERE RARE, BUT THEY HAPPENED. MALE ANTS WOULD FREQUENTLY VISIT US IN SCULLERIES OR NURSERIES TO BARTER FOR SEX -- OR FORCE IT. THE QUEEN WOULD HAVE EACH PREGNANCY DISCREETLY "TAKEN CARE OF" BY A PHYSICIAN. IF WORD OF OTHER FERTILE COLONY MEMBERS GOT OUT, IT WOULD UNDERMINE HER RULE

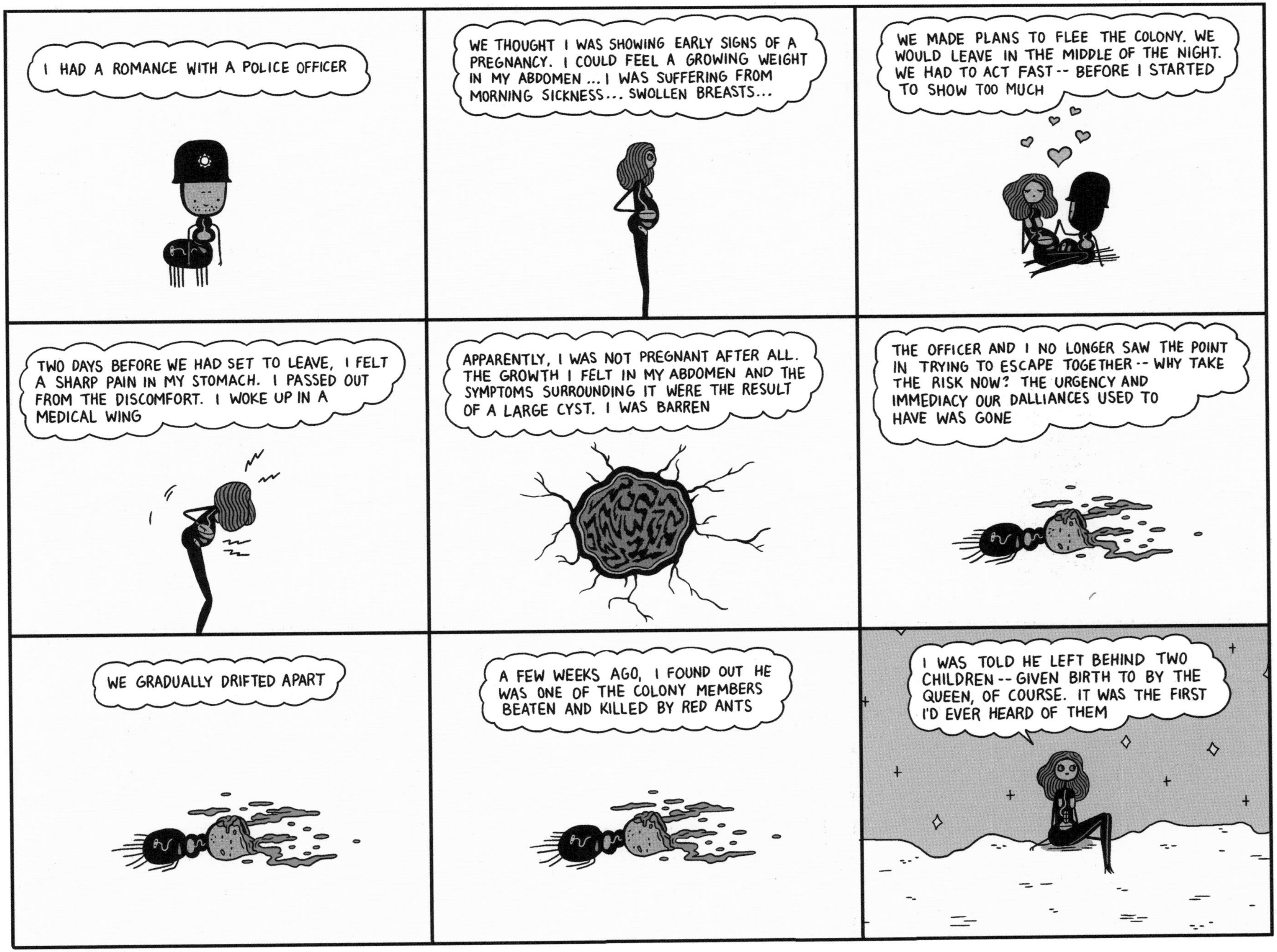
I HAD A ROMANCE WITH A POLICE OFFICER
WE THOUGHT I WAS SHOWING EARLY SIGNS OF A PREGNANCY. I COULD FEEL A GROWING WEIGHT IN MY ABDOMEN ... I WAS SUFFERING FROM MORNING SICKNESS... SWOLLEN BREASTS...
WE MADE PLANS TO FLEE THE COLONY. WE WOULD LEAVE IN THE MIDDLE OF THE NIGHT. WE HAD TO ACT FAST -- BEFORE I STARTED TO SHOW TOO MUCH
TWO DAYS BEFORE WE HAD SET TO LEAVE, I FELT A SHARP PAIN IN MY STOMACH. I PASSED OUT FROM THE DISCOMFORT. I WOKE UP IN A MEDICAL WING
APPARENTLY, I WAS NOT PREGNANT AFTER ALL. THE GROWTH I FELT IN MY ABDOMEN AND THE SYMPTOMS SURROUNDING IT WERE THE RESULT OF A LARGE CYST. I WAS BARREN
THE OFFICER AND I NO LONGER SAW THE POINT IN TRYING TO ESCAPE TOGETHER -- WHY TAKE THE RISK NOW? THE URGENCY AND IMMEDIACY OUR DALLIANCES USED TO HAVE WAS GONE
WE GRADUALLY DRIFTED APART
A FEW WEEKS AGO, I FOUND OUT HE WAS ONE OF THE COLONY MEMBERS BEATEN AND KILLED BY RED ANTS
I WAS TOLD HE LEFT BEHIND TWO CHILDREN -- GIVEN BIRTH TO BY THE QUEEN, OF COURSE. IT WAS THE FIRST I'D EVER HEARD OF THEM

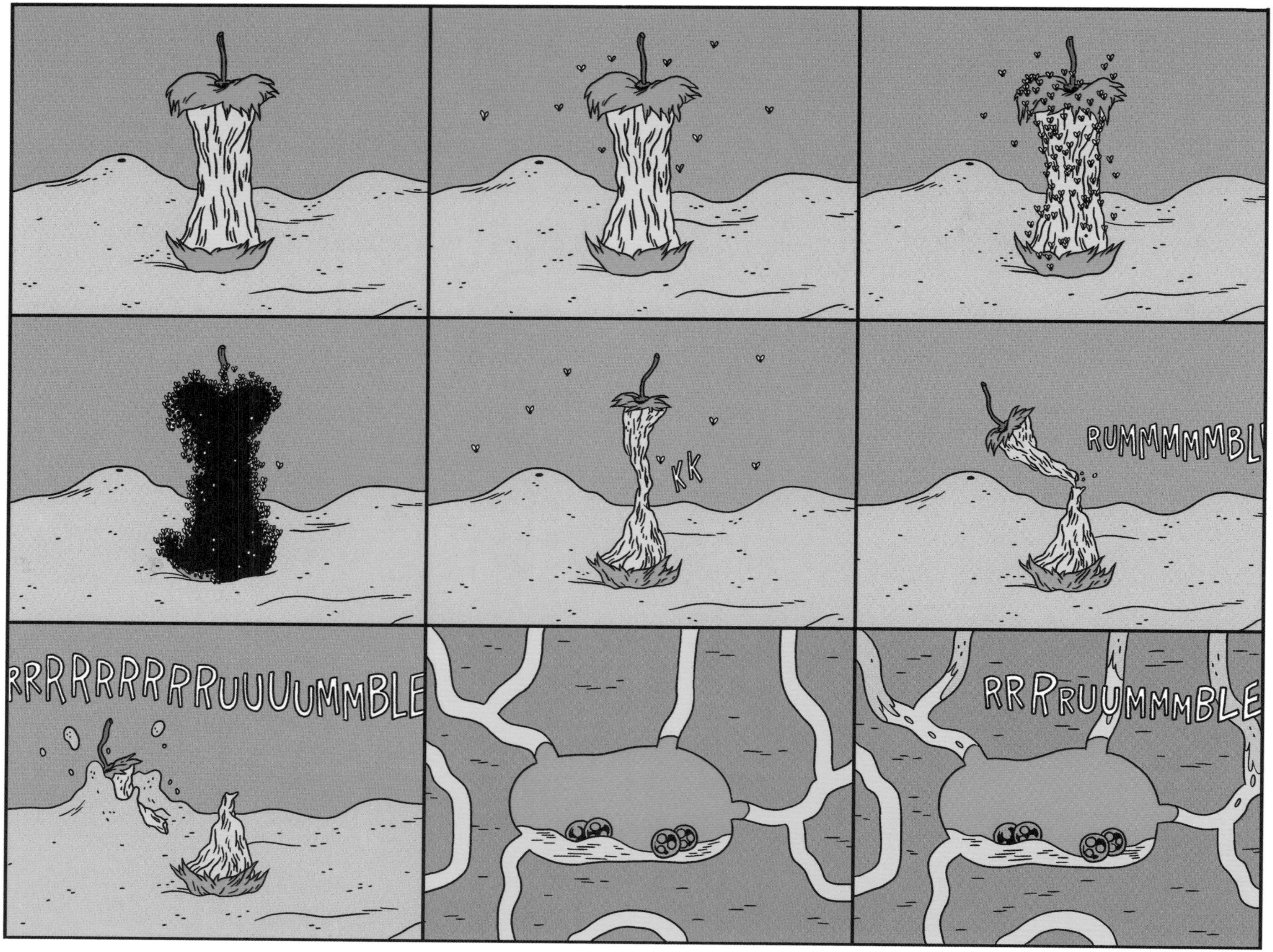
KK
RUMMMMMMBL
RRRRRRRRRRUUUUMMBLE
RRRRUUMMMMBLE

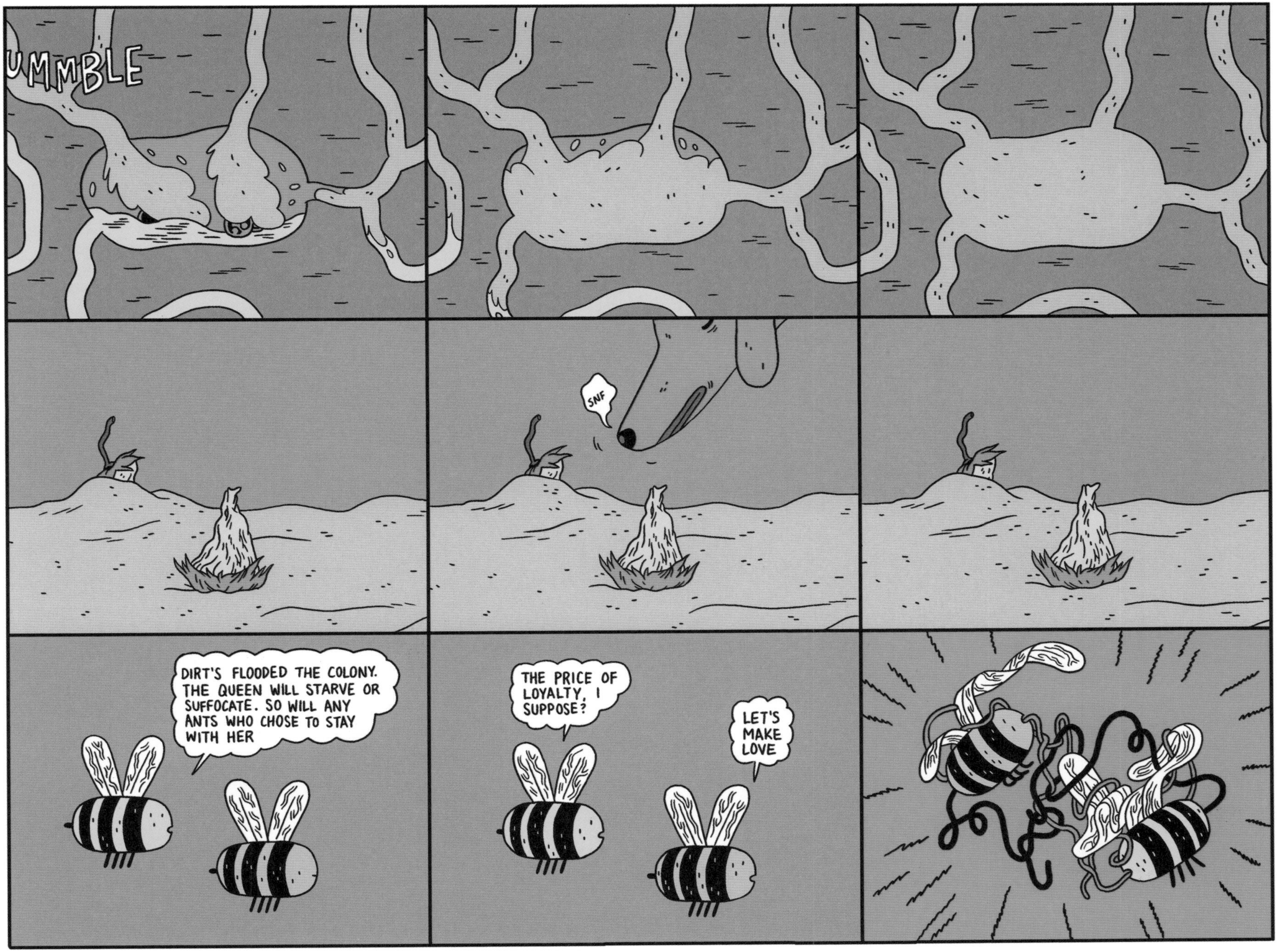
UMMBLE
SNF
DIRT'S FLOODED THE COLONY. THE QUEEN WILL STARVE OR SUFFOCATE. SO WILL ANY ANTS WHO CHOSE TO STAY WITH HER
THE PRICE OF LOYALTY, I SUPPOSE?
LET'S MAKE LOVE

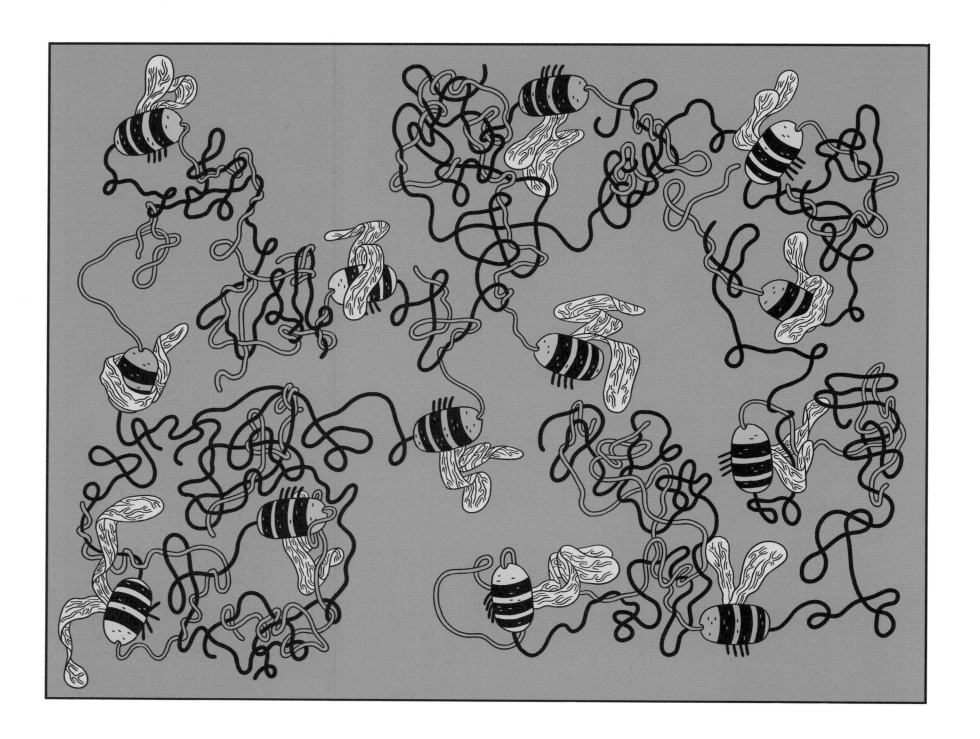

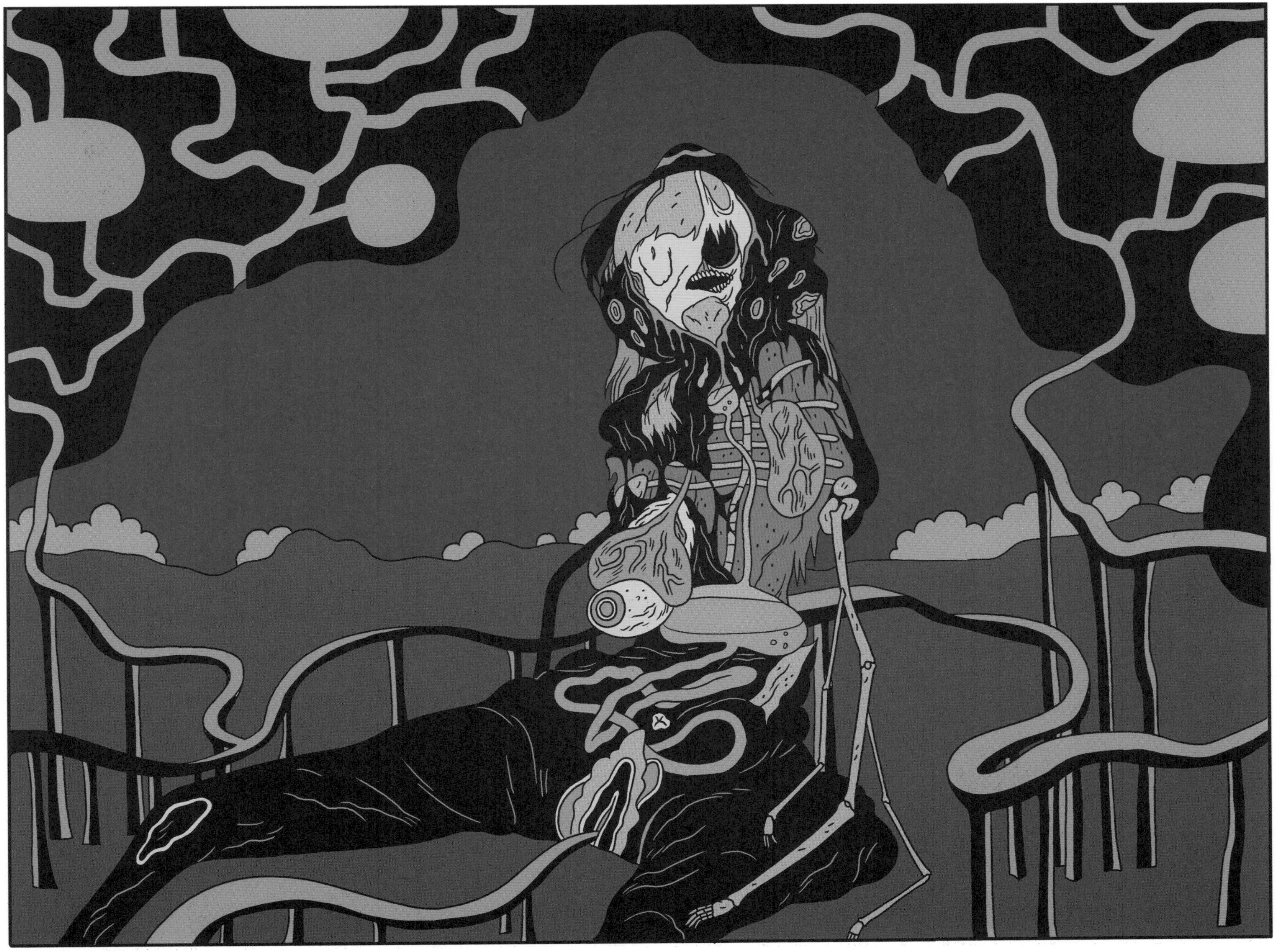

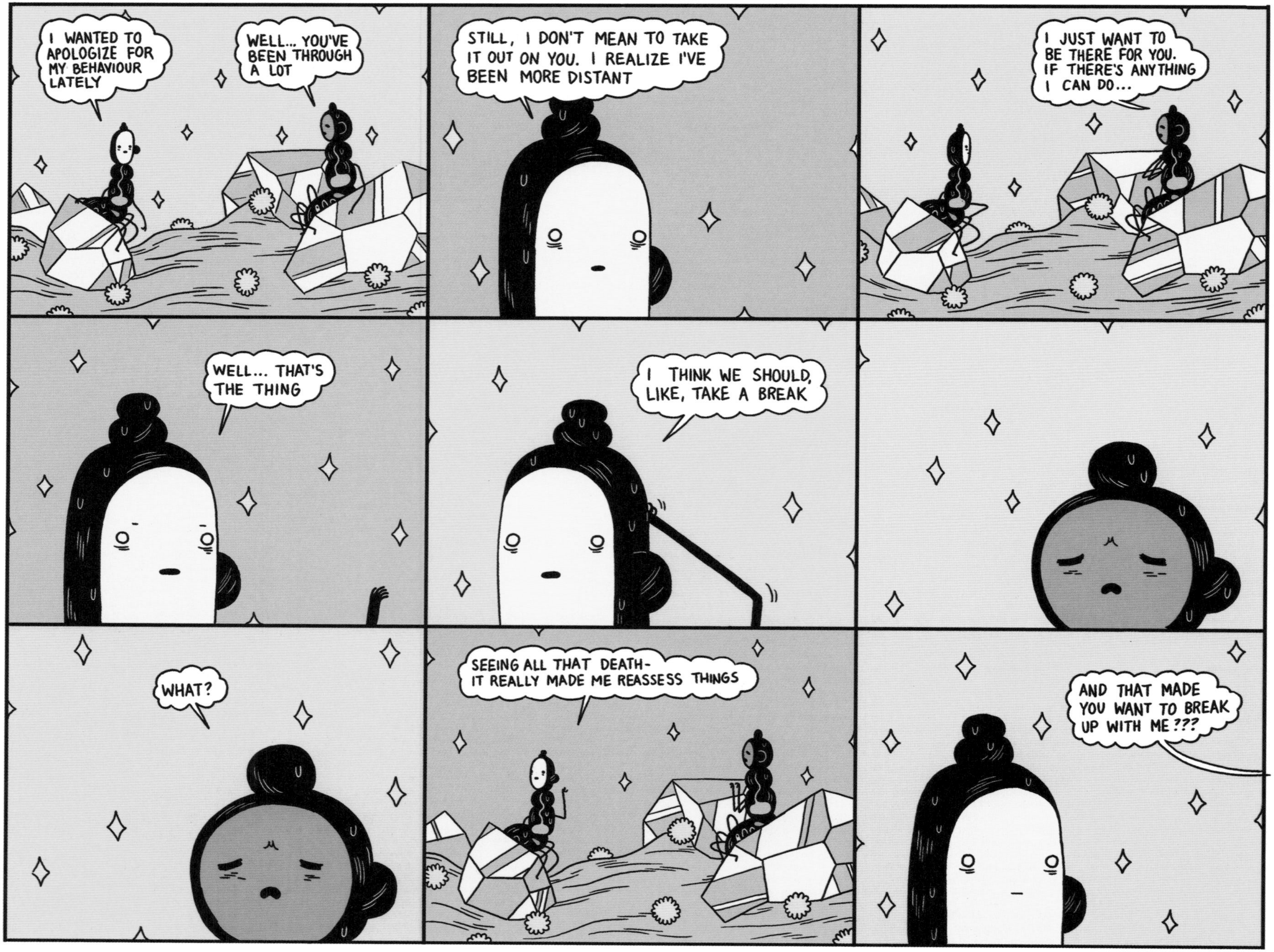
I WANTED TO APOLOGIZE FOR MY BEHAVIOUR LATELY
WELL... YOU'VE BEEN THROUGH A LOT
STILL, I DON'T MEAN TO TAKE IT OUT ON YOU. I REALIZE I'VE BEEN MORE DISTANT
I JUST WANT TO BE THERE FOR YOU. IF THERE'S ANYTHING I CAN DO...
WELL... THAT'S THE THING
I THINK WE SHOULD, LIKE, TAKE A BREAK
WHAT?
SEEING ALL THAT DEATH- IT REALLY MADE ME REASSESS THINGS
AND THAT MADE YOU WANT TO BREAK UP WITH ME???

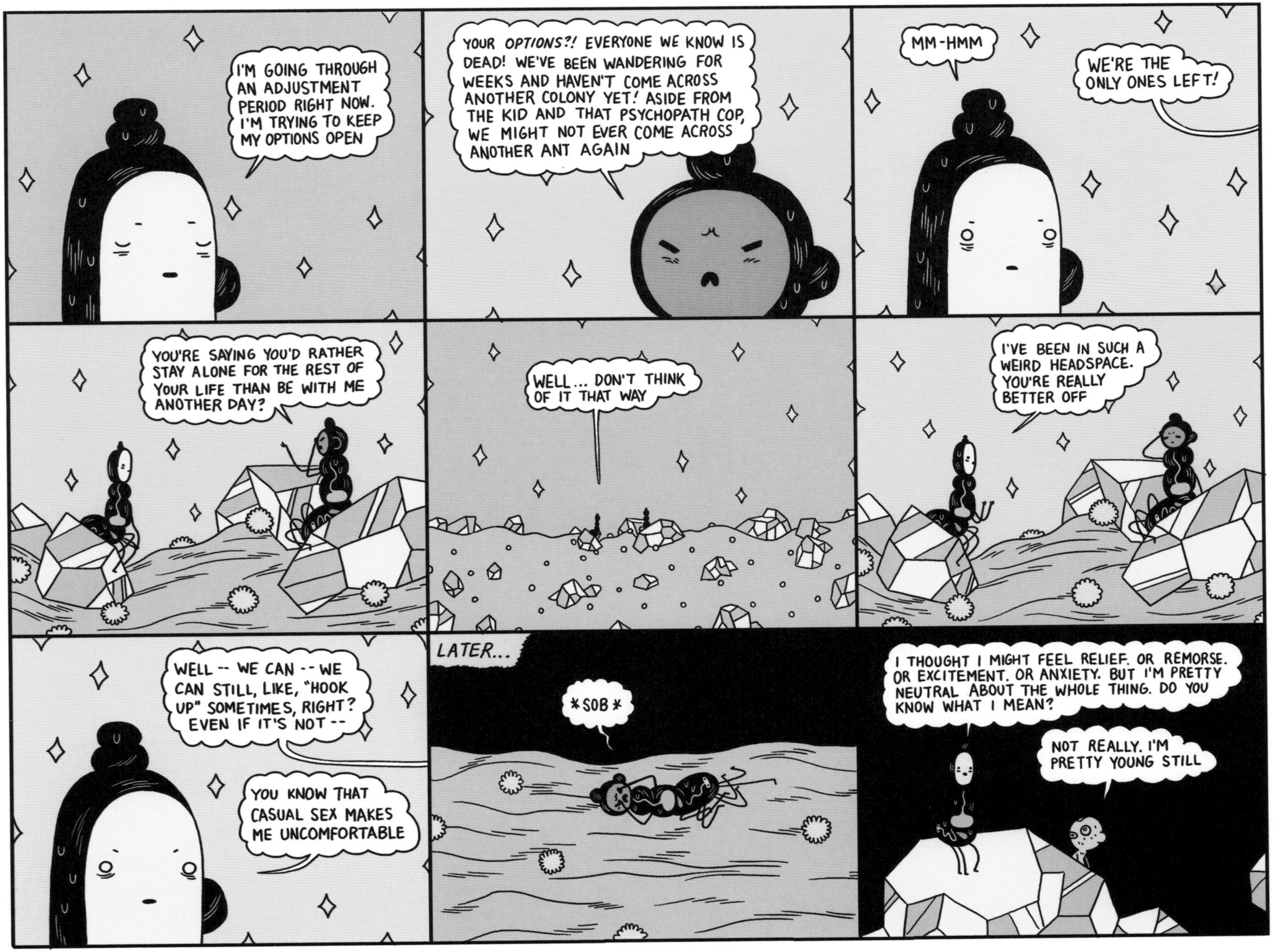
I'M GOING THROUGH AN ADJUSTMENT PERIOD RIGHT NOW. I'M TRYING TO KEEP MY OPTIONS OPEN
YOUR *OPTIONS?!* EVERYONE WE KNOW IS DEAD! WE'VE BEEN WANDERING FOR WEEKS AND HAVEN'T COME ACROSS ANOTHER COLONY YET! ASIDE FROM THE KID AND THAT PSYCHOPATH COP, WE MIGHT NOT EVER COME ACROSS ANOTHER ANT AGAIN
MM-HMM
WE'RE THE ONLY ONES LEFT!
YOU'RE SAYING YOU'D RATHER STAY ALONE FOR THE REST OF YOUR LIFE THAN BE WITH ME ANOTHER DAY?
WELL... DON'T THINK OF IT THAT WAY
I'VE BEEN IN SUCH A WEIRD HEADSPACE. YOU'RE REALLY BETTER OFF
WELL -- WE CAN -- WE CAN STILL, LIKE, "HOOK UP" SOMETIMES, RIGHT? EVEN IF IT'S NOT --
YOU KNOW THAT CASUAL SEX MAKES ME UNCOMFORTABLE
LATER...
SOB
I THOUGHT I MIGHT FEEL RELIEF. OR REMORSE. OR EXCITEMENT. OR ANXIETY. BUT I'M PRETTY NEUTRAL ABOUT THE WHOLE THING. DO YOU KNOW WHAT I MEAN?
NOT REALLY. I'M PRETTY YOUNG STILL

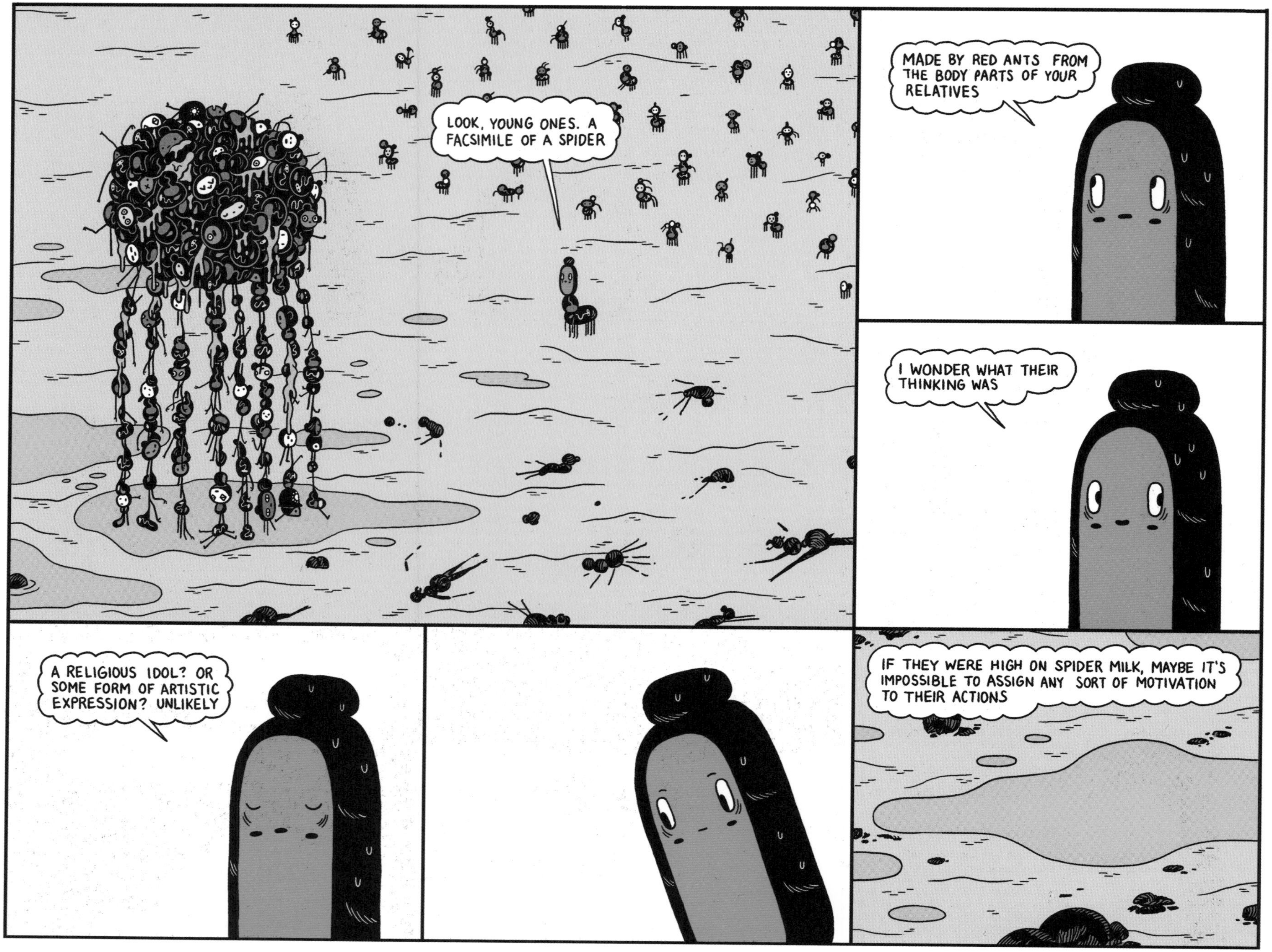
LOOK, YOUNG ONES. A FACSIMILE OF A SPIDER
MADE BY RED ANTS FROM THE BODY PARTS OF YOUR RELATIVES
I WONDER WHAT THEIR THINKING WAS
A RELIGIOUS IDOL? OR SOME FORM OF ARTISTIC EXPRESSION? UNLIKELY
IF THEY WERE HIGH ON SPIDER MILK, MAYBE IT'S IMPOSSIBLE TO ASSIGN ANY SORT OF MOTIVATION TO THEIR ACTIONS

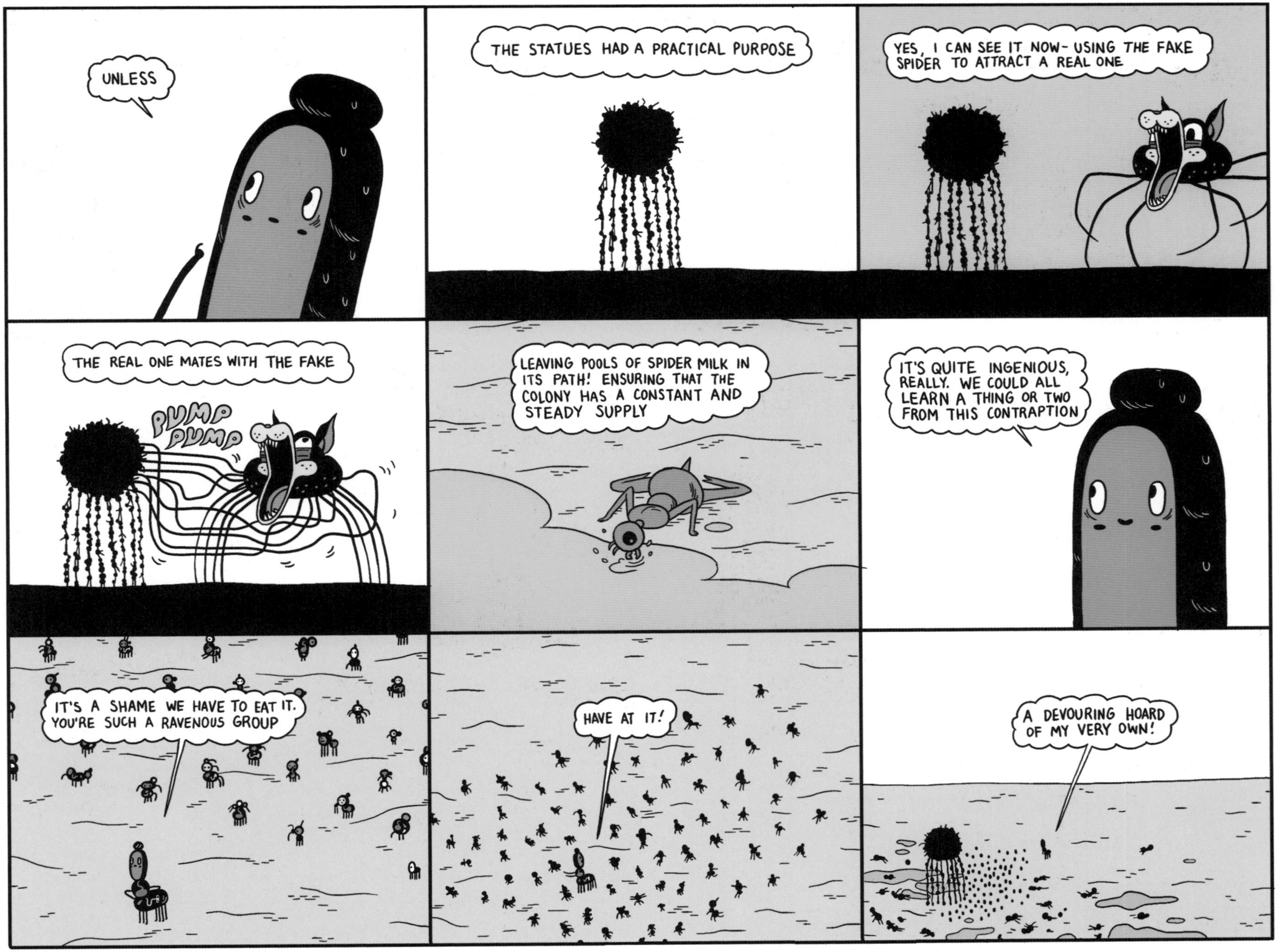
UNLESS
THE STATUES HAD A PRACTICAL PURPOSE
YES, I CAN SEE IT NOW- USING THE FAKE SPIDER TO ATTRACT A REAL ONE
THE REAL ONE MATES WITH THE FAKE
PUMP PUMP
LEAVING POOLS OF SPIDER MILK IN ITS PATH! ENSURING THAT THE COLONY HAS A CONSTANT AND STEADY SUPPLY
IT'S QUITE INGENIOUS, REALLY. WE COULD ALL LEARN A THING OR TWO FROM THIS CONTRAPTION
IT'S A SHAME WE HAVE TO EAT IT. YOU'RE SUCH A RAVENOUS GROUP
HAVE AT IT!
A DEVOURING HOARD OF MY VERY OWN!

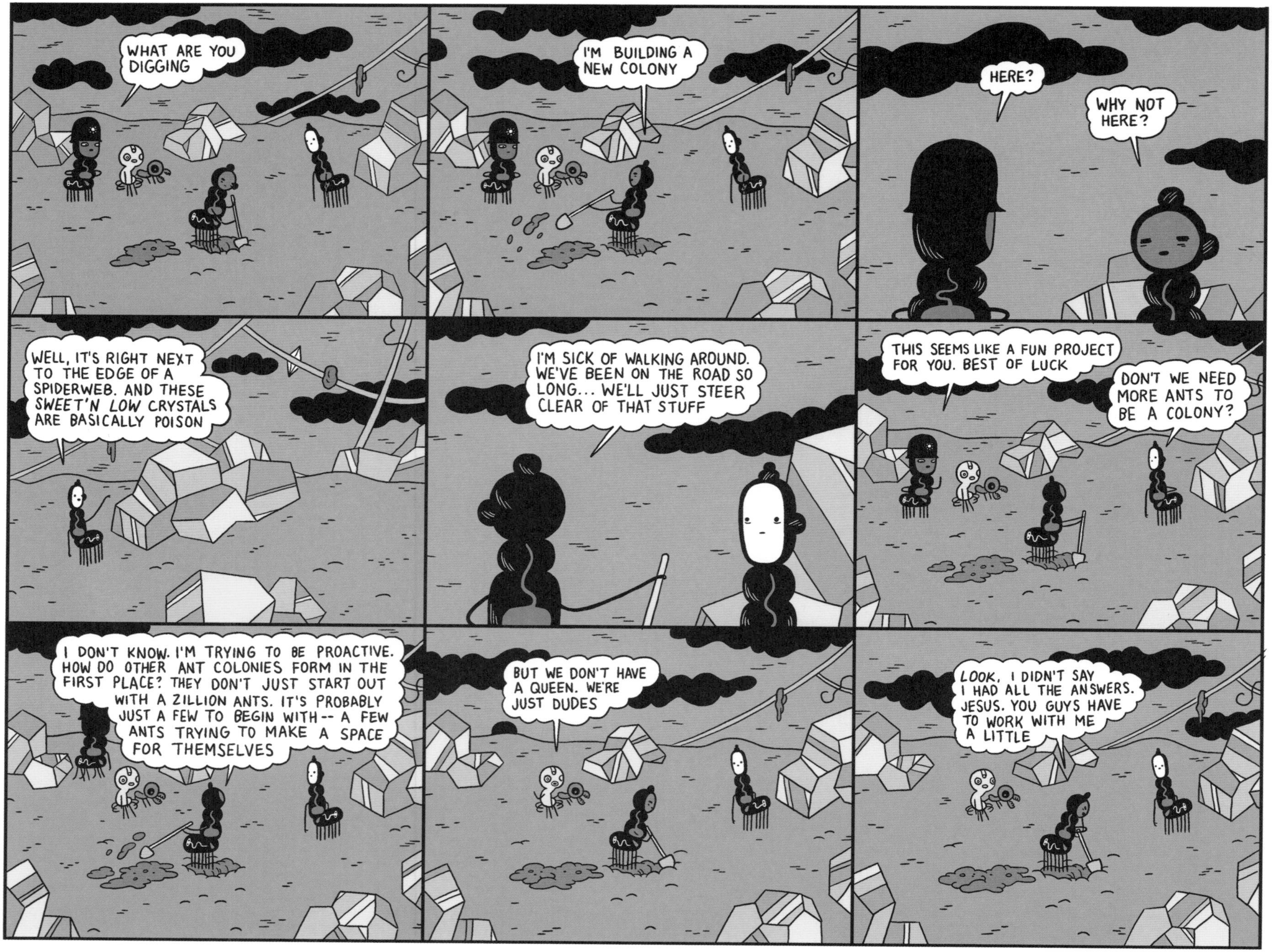
WHAT ARE YOU DIGGING
I'M BUILDING A NEW COLONY
HERE?
WHY NOT HERE?
WELL, IT'S RIGHT NEXT TO THE EDGE OF A SPIDERWEB. AND THESE *SWEET'N LOW* CRYSTALS ARE BASICALLY POISON
I'M SICK OF WALKING AROUND. WE'VE BEEN ON THE ROAD SO LONG... WE'LL JUST STEER CLEAR OF THAT STUFF
THIS SEEMS LIKE A FUN PROJECT FOR YOU. BEST OF LUCK
DON'T WE NEED MORE ANTS TO BE A COLONY?
I DON'T KNOW. I'M TRYING TO BE PROACTIVE. HOW DO OTHER ANT COLONIES FORM IN THE FIRST PLACE? THEY DON'T JUST START OUT WITH A ZILLION ANTS. IT'S PROBABLY JUST A FEW TO BEGIN WITH -- A FEW ANTS TRYING TO MAKE A SPACE FOR THEMSELVES
BUT WE DON'T HAVE A QUEEN. WE'RE JUST DUDES
LOOK, I DIDN'T SAY I HAD ALL THE ANSWERS. JESUS. YOU GUYS HAVE TO WORK WITH ME A LITTLE

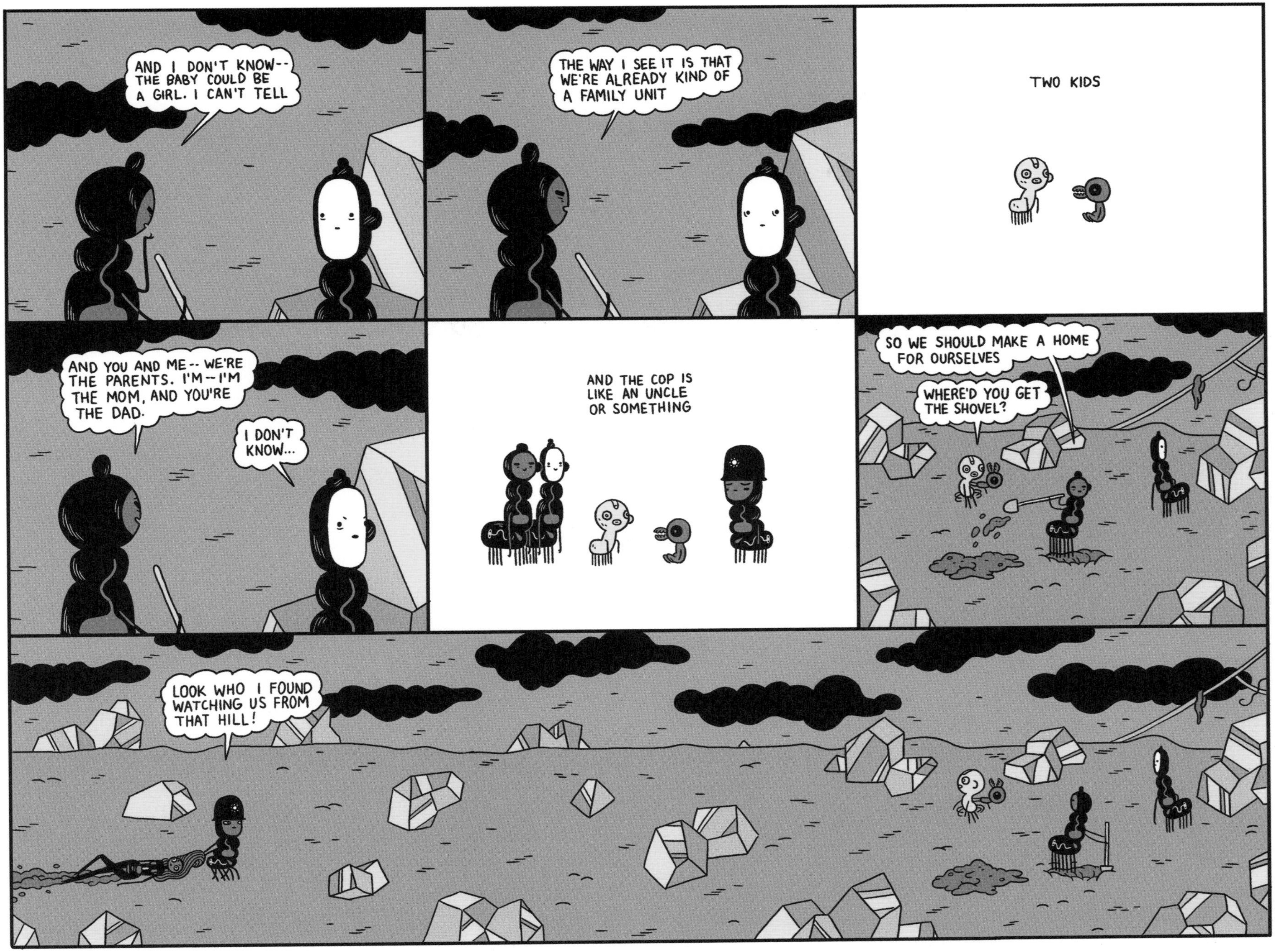
AND I DON'T KNOW-- THE BABY COULD BE A GIRL. I CAN'T TELL
THE WAY I SEE IT IS THAT WE'RE ALREADY KIND OF A FAMILY UNIT
TWO KIDS
AND YOU AND ME-- WE'RE THE PARENTS. I'M--I'M THE MOM, AND YOU'RE THE DAD.
I DON'T KNOW...
AND THE COP IS LIKE AN UNCLE OR SOMETHING
SO WE SHOULD MAKE A HOME FOR OURSELVES
WHERE'D YOU GET THE SHOVEL?
LOOK WHO I FOUND WATCHING US FROM THAT HILL!

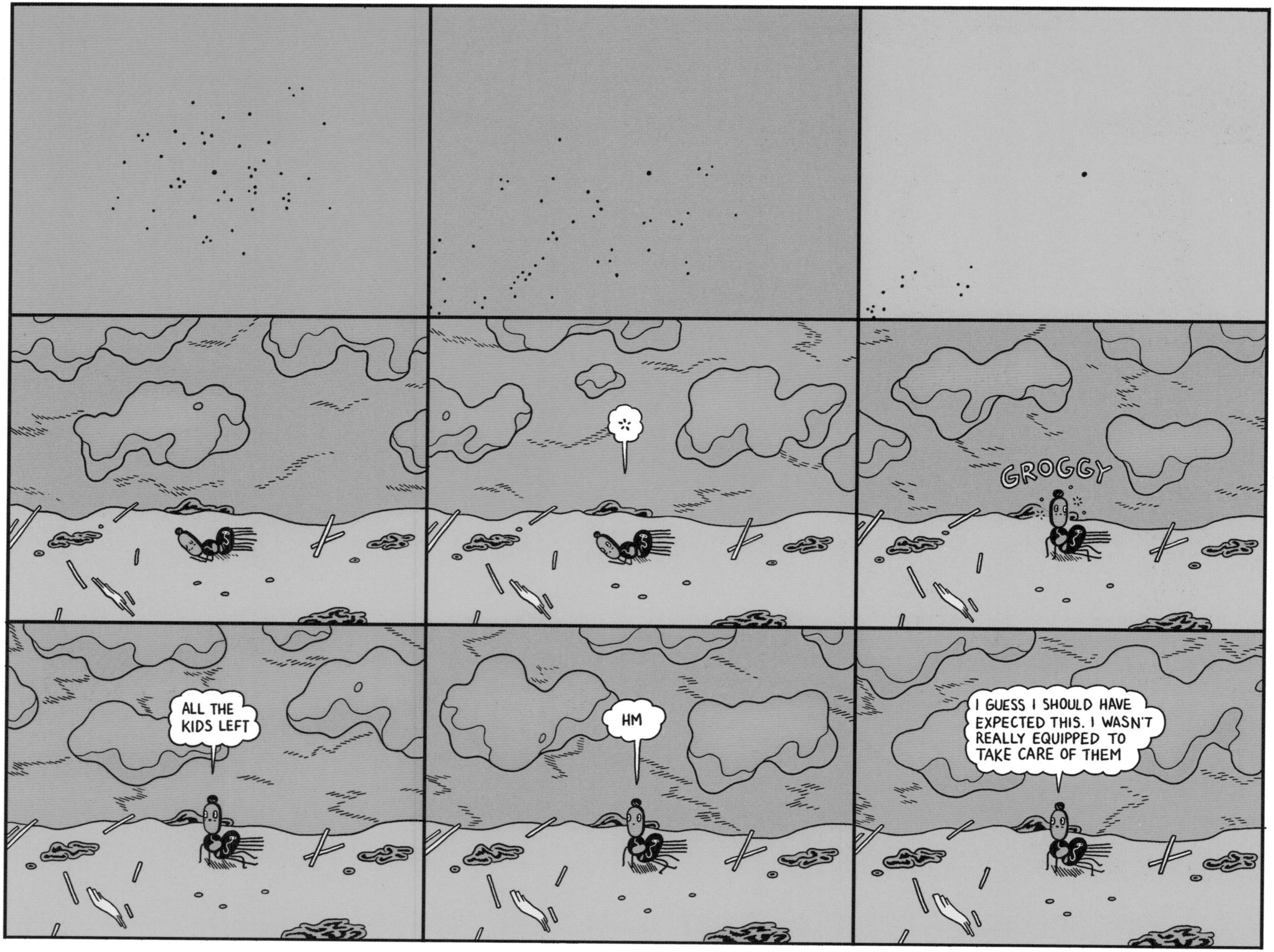
GROGGY
ALL THE KIDS LEFT
HM
I GUESS I SHOULD HAVE EXPECTED THIS. I WASN'T REALLY EQUIPPED TO TAKE CARE OF THEM

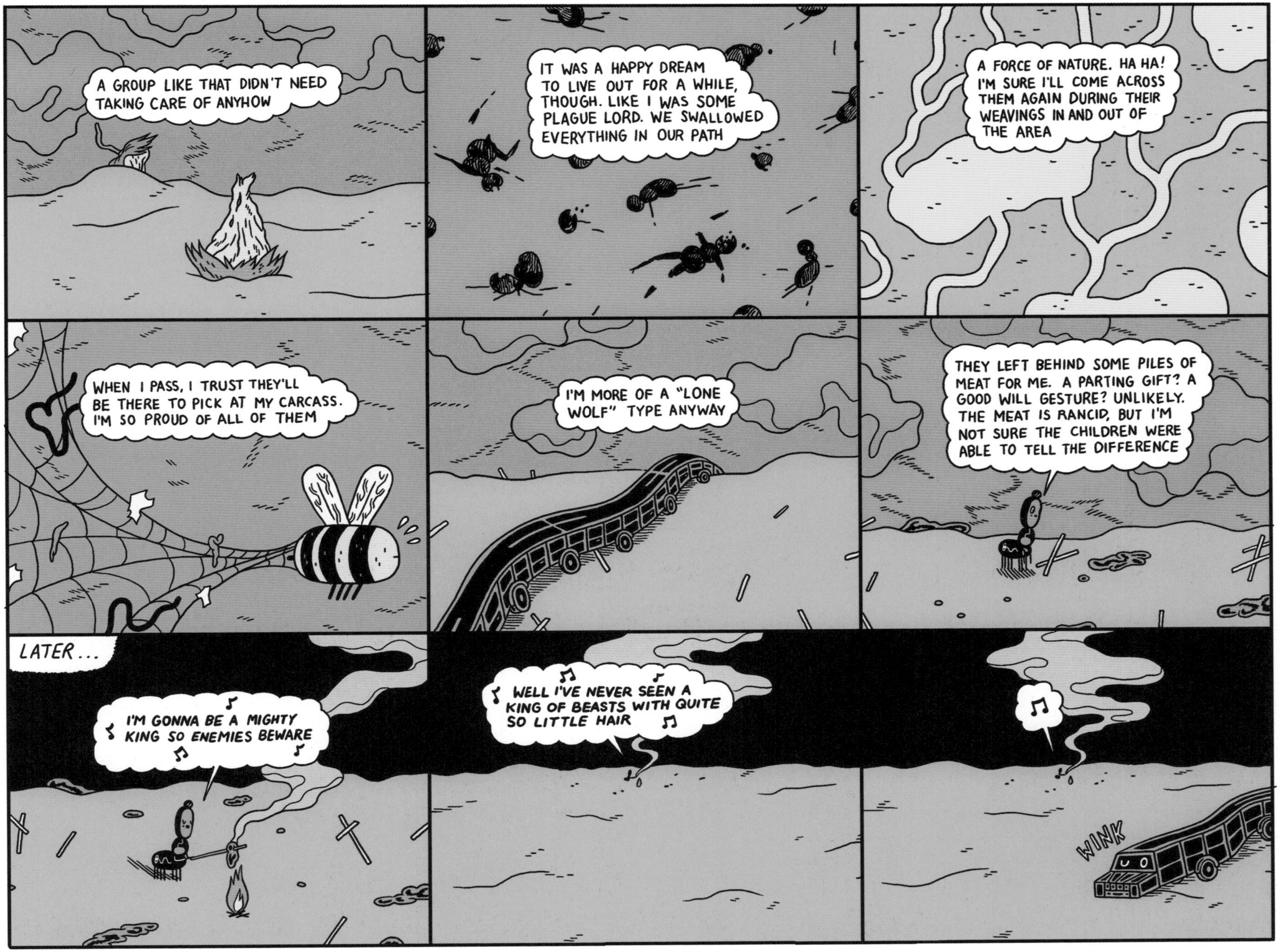
A GROUP LIKE THAT DIDN'T NEED TAKING CARE OF ANYHOW
IT WAS A HAPPY DREAM TO LIVE OUT FOR A WHILE, THOUGH. LIKE I WAS SOME PLAGUE LORD. WE SWALLOWED EVERYTHING IN OUR PATH
A FORCE OF NATURE. HA HA! I'M SURE I'LL COME ACROSS THEM AGAIN DURING THEIR WEAVINGS IN AND OUT OF THE AREA
WHEN I PASS, I TRUST THEY'LL BE THERE TO PICK AT MY CARCASS. I'M SO PROUD OF ALL OF THEM
I'M MORE OF A "LONE WOLF" TYPE ANYWAY
THEY LEFT BEHIND SOME PILES OF MEAT FOR ME. A PARTING GIFT? A GOOD WILL GESTURE? UNLIKELY. THE MEAT IS RANCID, BUT I'M NOT SURE THE CHILDREN WERE ABLE TO TELL THE DIFFERENCE
LATER...
I'M GONNA BE A MIGHTY KING SO ENEMIES BEWARE
WELL I'VE NEVER SEEN A KING OF BEASTS WITH QUITE SO LITTLE HAIR
WINK

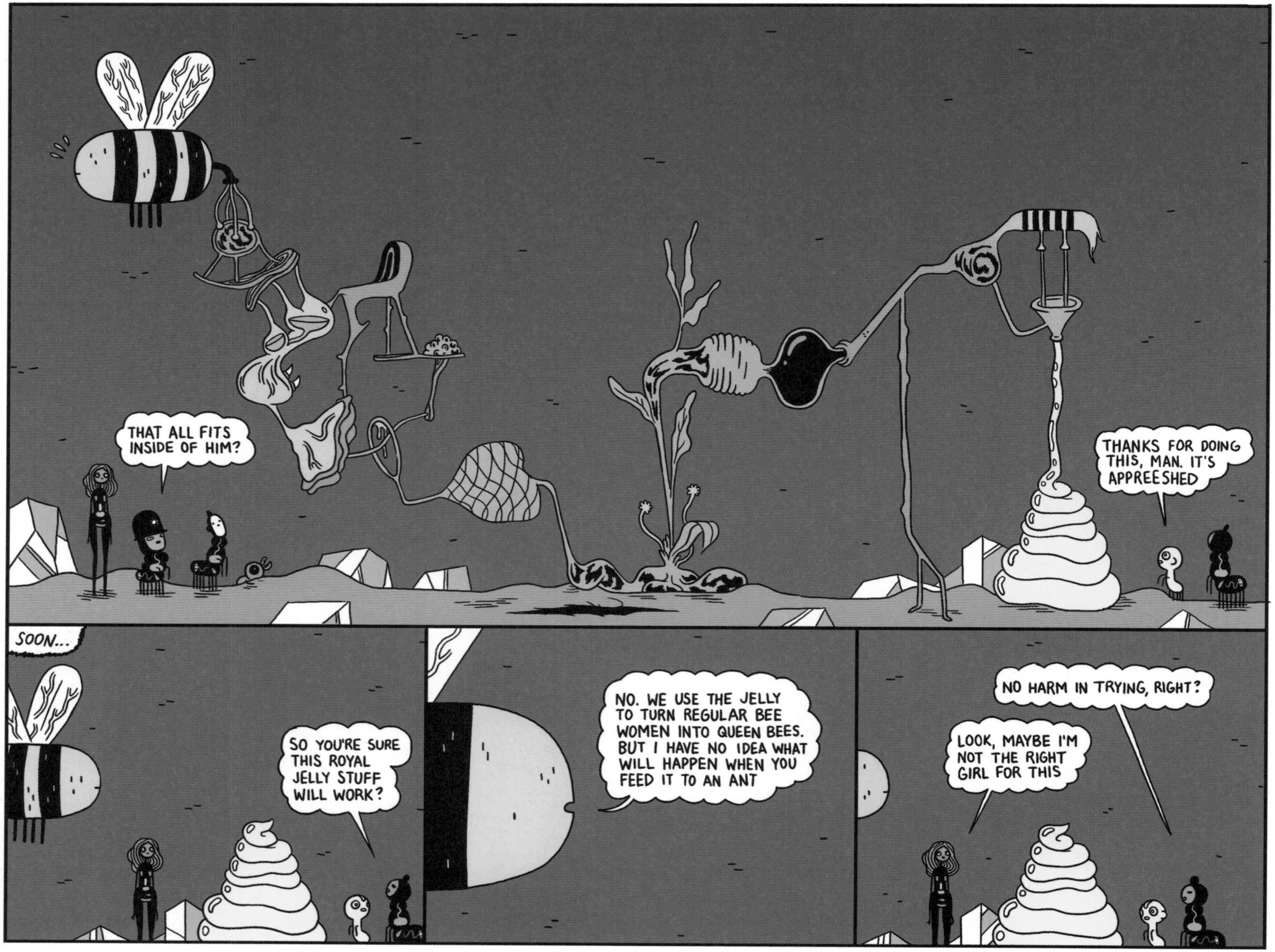
THAT ALL FITS INSIDE OF HIM?
THANKS FOR DOING THIS, MAN. IT'S APPREESHED
SOON...
SO YOU'RE SURE THIS ROYAL JELLY STUFF WILL WORK?
NO. WE USE THE JELLY TO TURN REGULAR BEE WOMEN INTO QUEEN BEES. BUT I HAVE NO IDEA WHAT WILL HAPPEN WHEN YOU FEED IT TO AN ANT
LOOK, MAYBE I'M NOT THE RIGHT GIRL FOR THIS
NO HARM IN TRYING, RIGHT?

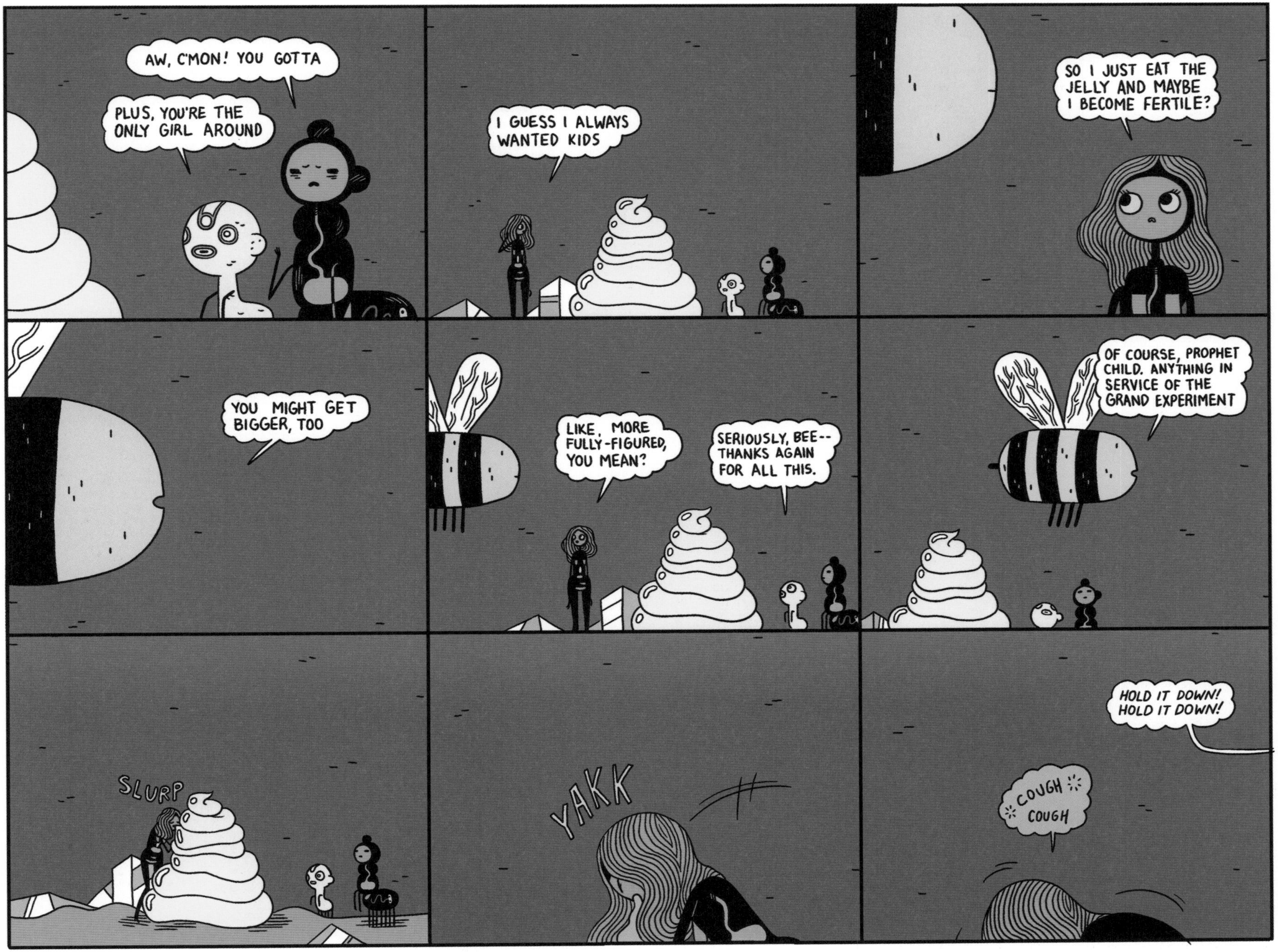
AW, C'MON! YOU GOTTA
PLUS, YOU'RE THE ONLY GIRL AROUND
I GUESS I ALWAYS WANTED KIDS
SO I JUST EAT THE JELLY AND MAYBE I BECOME FERTILE?
YOU MIGHT GET BIGGER, TOO
LIKE, MORE FULLY-FIGURED, YOU MEAN?
SERIOUSLY, BEE-- THANKS AGAIN FOR ALL THIS.
OF COURSE, PROPHET CHILD. ANYTHING IN SERVICE OF THE GRAND EXPERIMENT
SLURP
YAKK
HOLD IT DOWN! HOLD IT DOWN!
COUGH COUGH

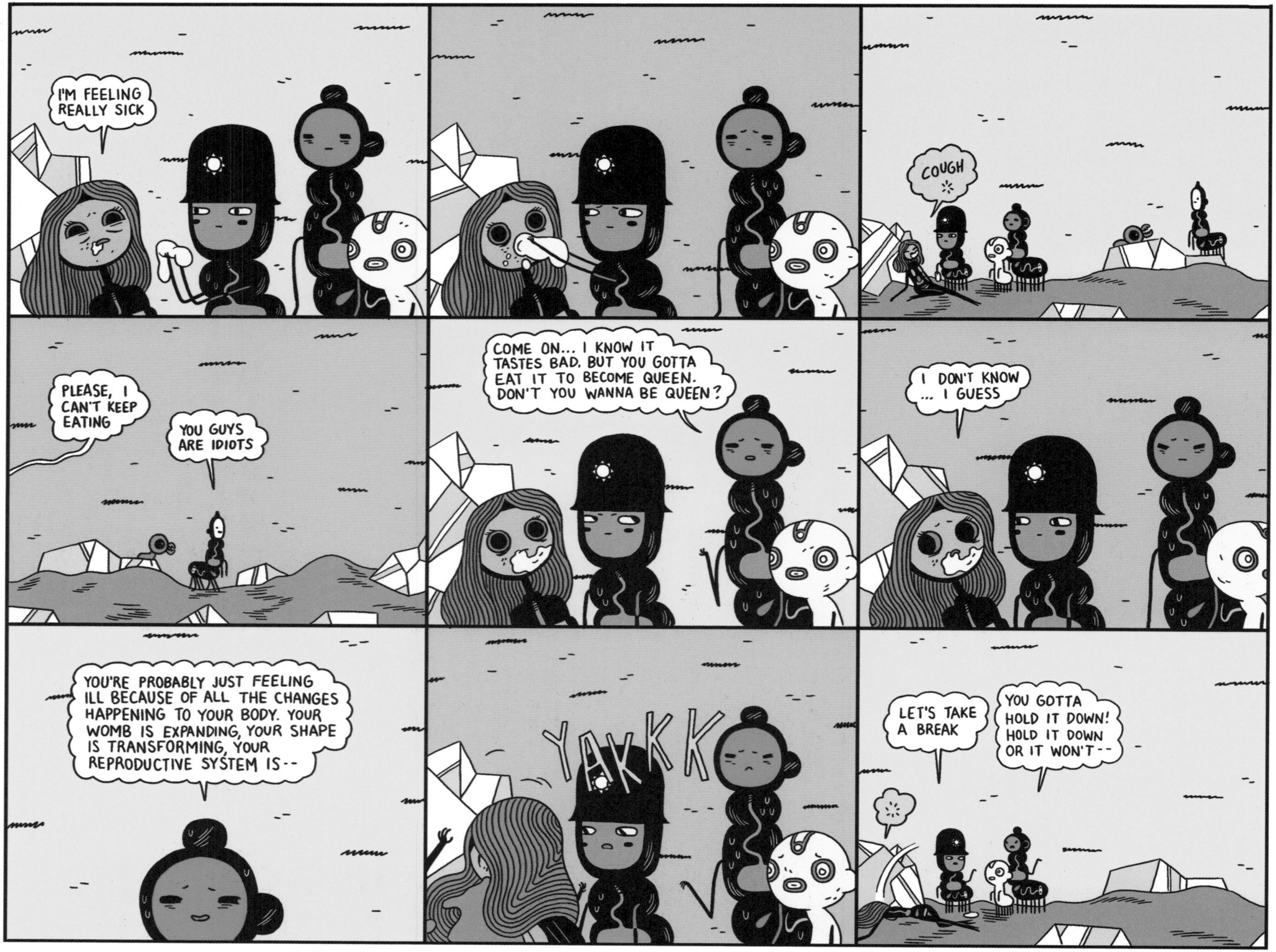
I'M FEELING REALLY SICK
COUGH
PLEASE, I CAN'T KEEP EATING
YOU GUYS ARE IDIOTS
COME ON... I KNOW IT TASTES BAD. BUT YOU GOTTA EAT IT TO BECOME QUEEN. DON'T YOU WANNA BE QUEEN?
I DON'T KNOW ... I GUESS
YOU'RE PROBABLY JUST FEELING ILL BECAUSE OF ALL THE CHANGES HAPPENING TO YOUR BODY. YOUR WOMB IS EXPANDING, YOUR SHAPE IS TRANSFORMING, YOUR REPRODUCTIVE SYSTEM IS--
YAKKK
LET'S TAKE A BREAK
YOU GOTTA HOLD IT DOWN! HOLD IT DOWN OR IT WON'T--

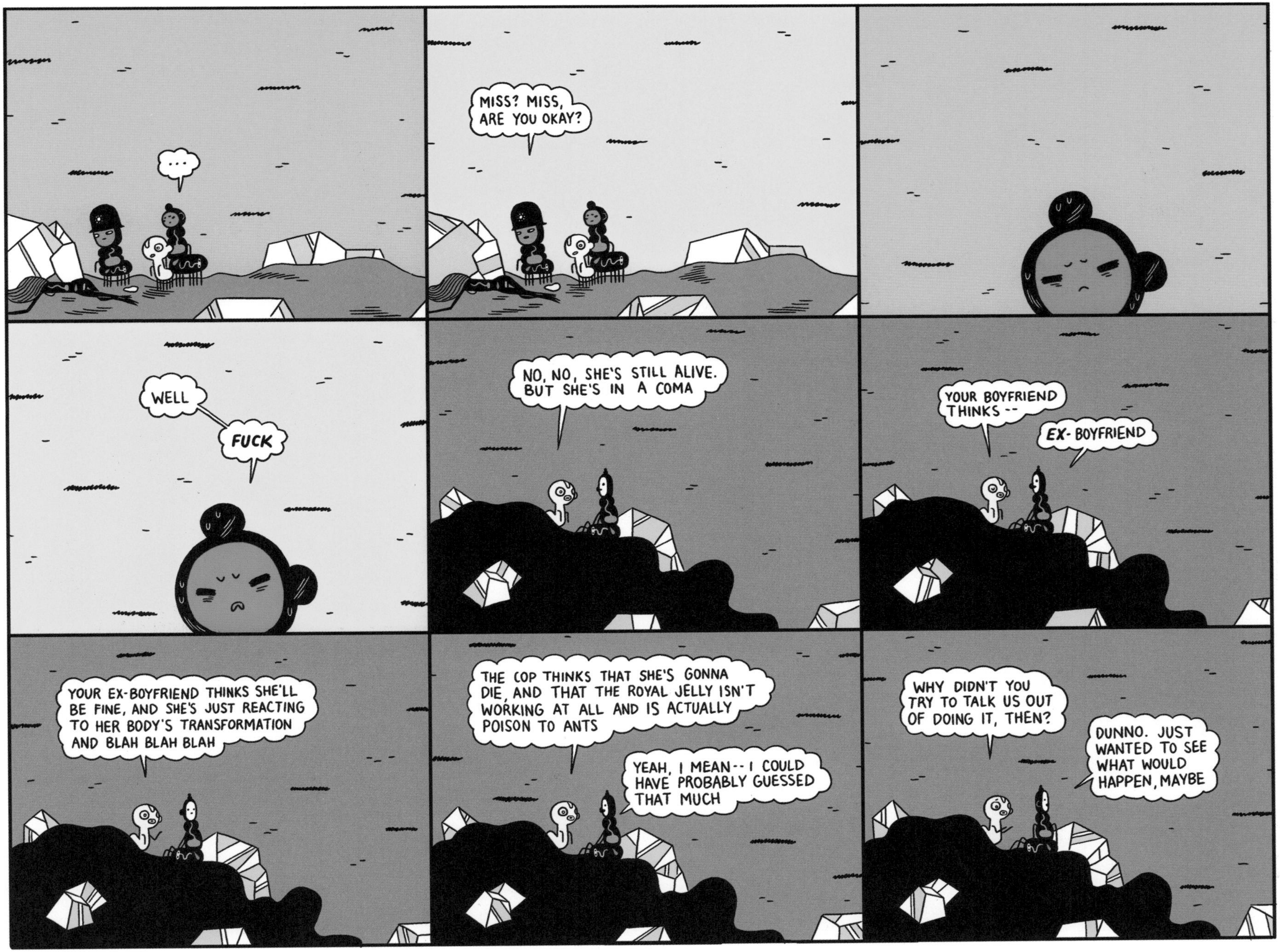
...
MISS? MISS, ARE YOU OKAY?
WELL
FUCK
NO, NO, SHE'S STILL ALIVE. BUT SHE'S IN A COMA
YOUR BOYFRIEND THINKS --
EX-BOYFRIEND
YOUR EX-BOYFRIEND THINKS SHE'LL BE FINE, AND SHE'S JUST REACTING TO HER BODY'S TRANSFORMATION AND BLAH BLAH BLAH
THE COP THINKS THAT SHE'S GONNA DIE, AND THAT THE ROYAL JELLY ISN'T WORKING AT ALL AND IS ACTUALLY POISON TO ANTS
YEAH, I MEAN-- I COULD HAVE PROBABLY GUESSED THAT MUCH
WHY DIDN'T YOU TRY TO TALK US OUT OF DOING IT, THEN?
DUNNO. JUST WANTED TO SEE WHAT WOULD HAPPEN, MAYBE

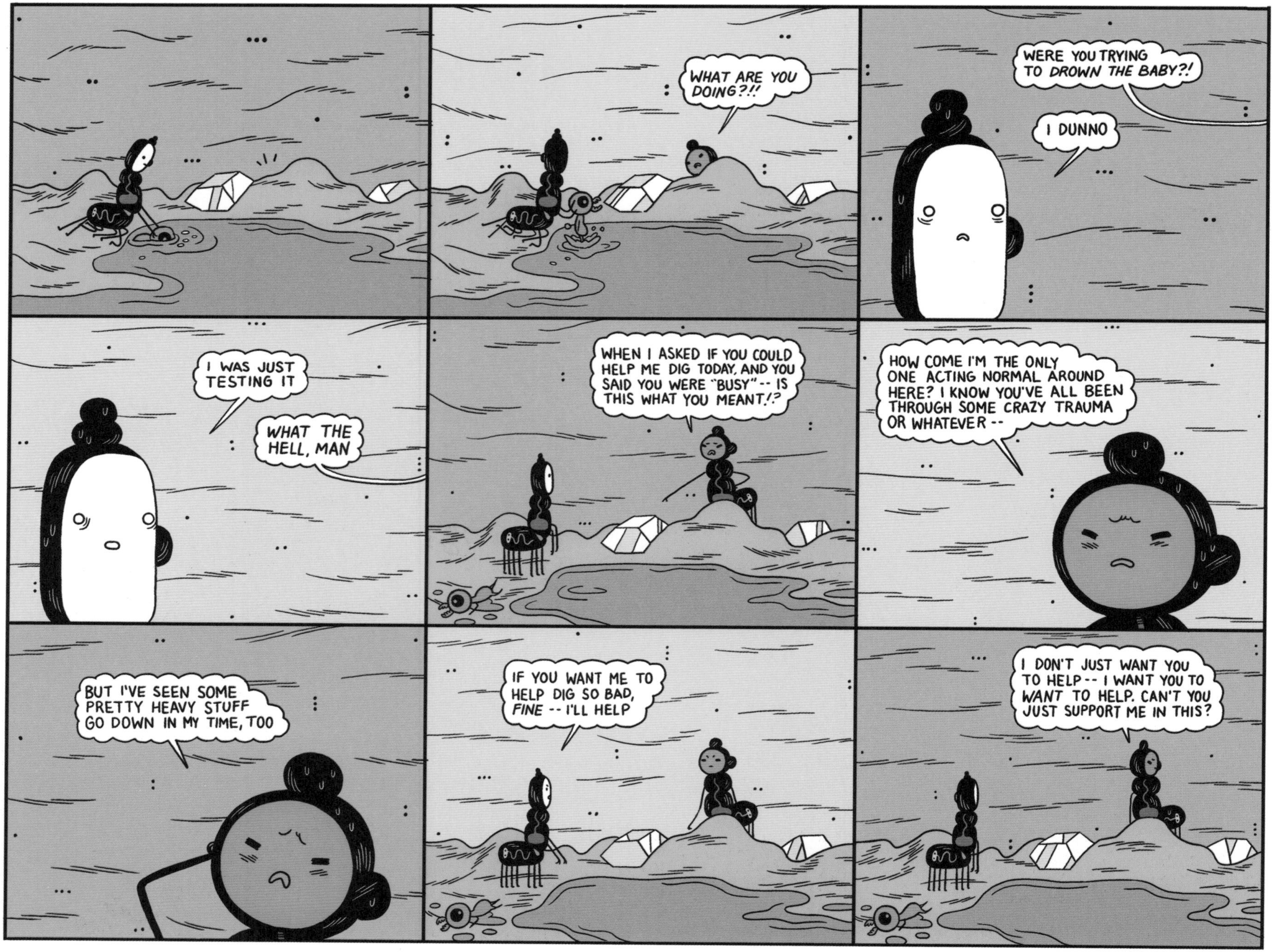
WHAT ARE YOU DOING?!!
WERE YOU TRYING TO *DROWN THE BABY?!*
I DUNNO
I WAS JUST TESTING IT
WHAT THE HELL, MAN
WHEN I ASKED IF YOU COULD HELP ME DIG TODAY, AND YOU SAID YOU WERE "BUSY" -- IS THIS WHAT YOU MEANT!?
HOW COME I'M THE ONLY ONE ACTING NORMAL AROUND HERE? I KNOW YOU'VE ALL BEEN THROUGH SOME CRAZY TRAUMA OR WHATEVER --
BUT I'VE SEEN SOME PRETTY HEAVY STUFF GO DOWN IN MY TIME, TOO
IF YOU WANT ME TO HELP DIG SO BAD, *FINE* -- I'LL HELP
I DON'T JUST WANT YOU TO HELP -- I WANT YOU TO *WANT* TO HELP. CAN'T YOU JUST SUPPORT ME IN THIS?

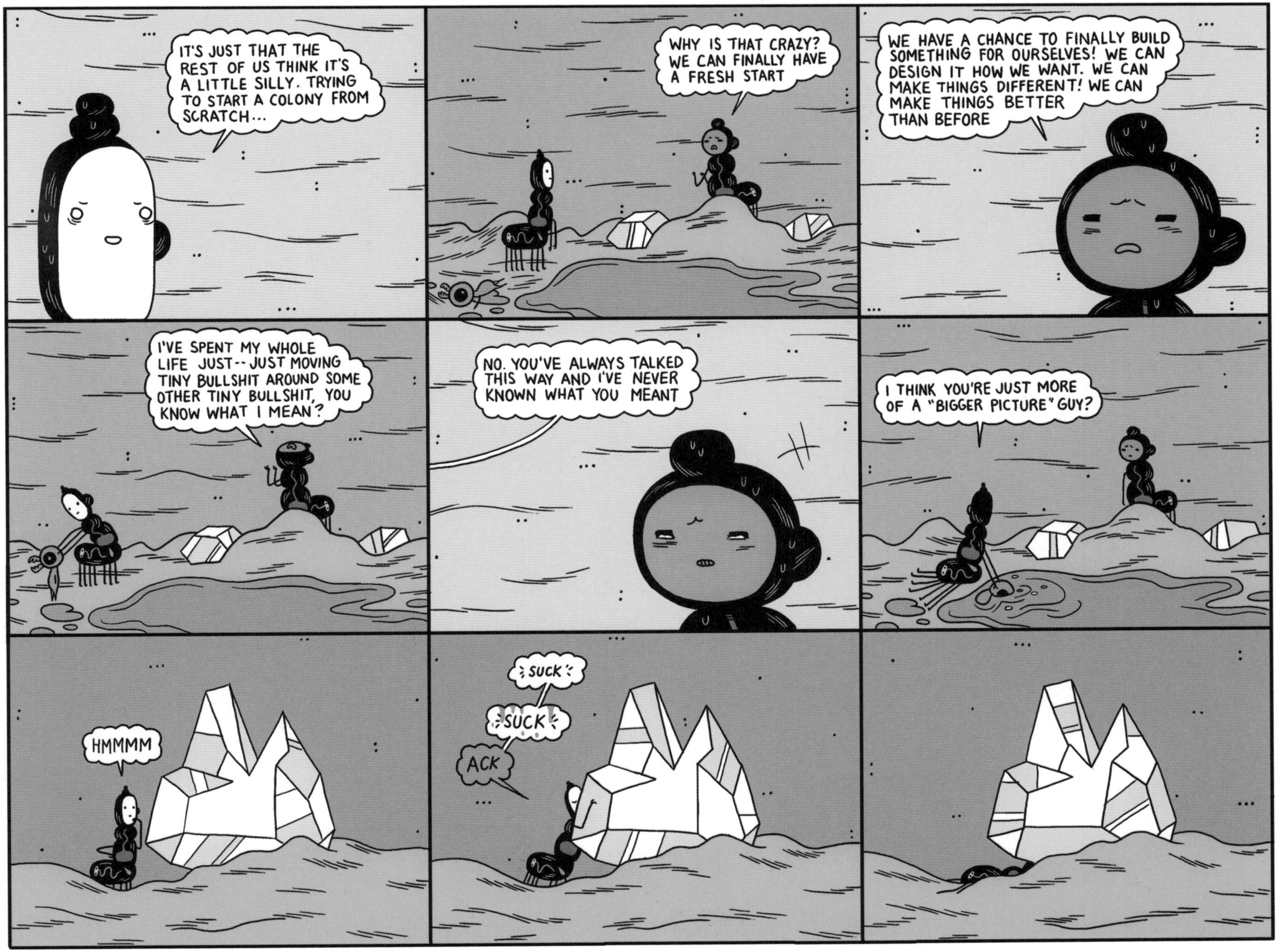
IT'S JUST THAT THE REST OF US THINK IT'S A LITTLE SILLY. TRYING TO START A COLONY FROM SCRATCH...
WHY IS THAT CRAZY? WE CAN FINALLY HAVE A FRESH START
WE HAVE A CHANCE TO FINALLY BUILD SOMETHING FOR OURSELVES! WE CAN DESIGN IT HOW WE WANT. WE CAN MAKE THINGS DIFFERENT! WE CAN MAKE THINGS BETTER THAN BEFORE
I'VE SPENT MY WHOLE LIFE JUST--JUST MOVING TINY BULLSHIT AROUND SOME OTHER TINY BULLSHIT, YOU KNOW WHAT I MEAN?
NO. YOU'VE ALWAYS TALKED THIS WAY AND I'VE NEVER KNOWN WHAT YOU MEANT
I THINK YOU'RE JUST MORE OF A "BIGGER PICTURE" GUY?
HMMMM
SUCK
SUCK
ACK

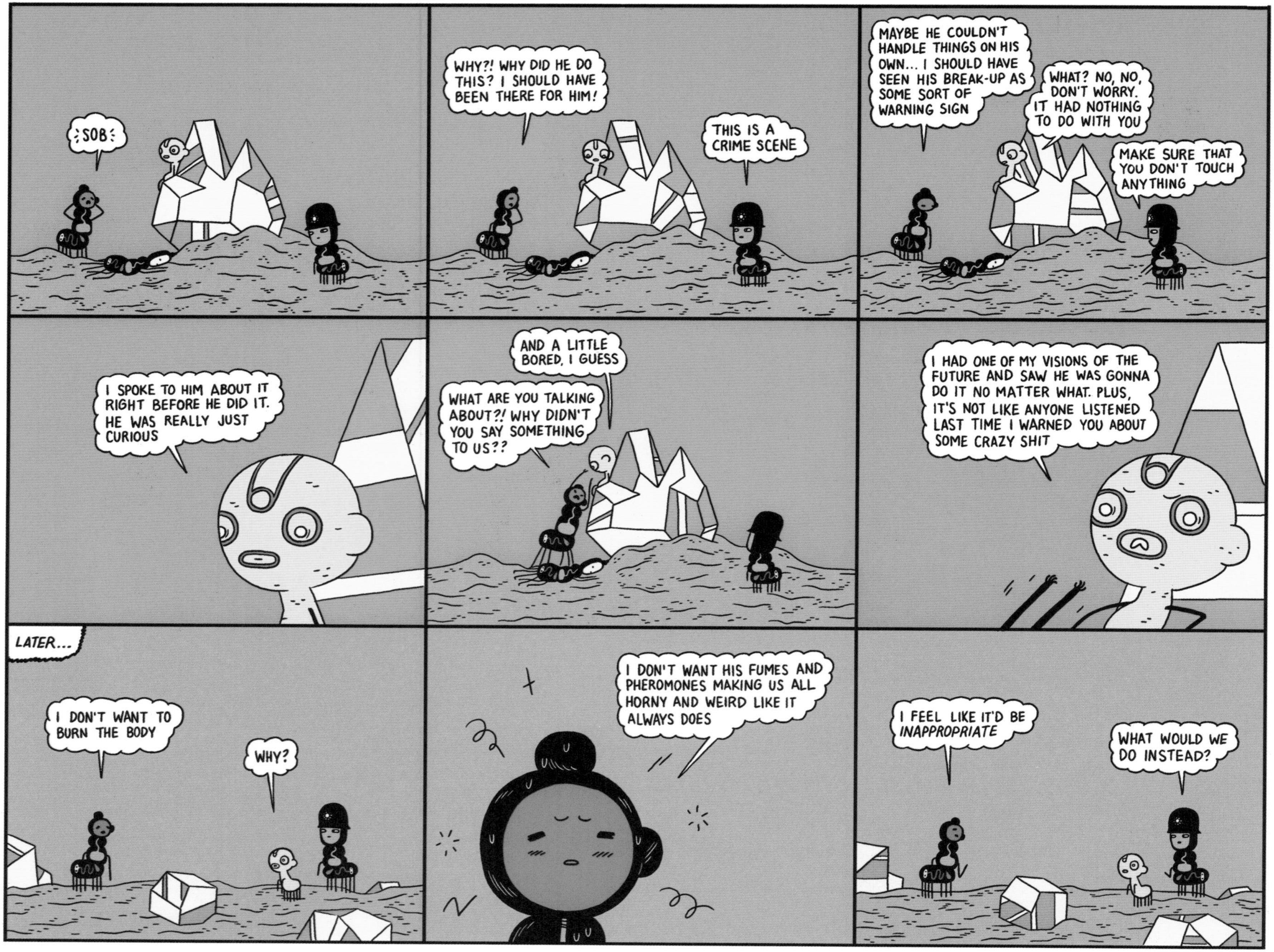
SOB
WHY?! WHY DID HE DO THIS? I SHOULD HAVE BEEN THERE FOR HIM!
THIS IS A CRIME SCENE
MAYBE HE COULDN'T HANDLE THINGS ON HIS OWN... I SHOULD HAVE SEEN HIS BREAK-UP AS SOME SORT OF WARNING SIGN
WHAT? NO, NO, DON'T WORRY. IT HAD NOTHING TO DO WITH YOU
MAKE SURE THAT YOU DON'T TOUCH ANYTHING
I SPOKE TO HIM ABOUT IT RIGHT BEFORE HE DID IT. HE WAS REALLY JUST CURIOUS
AND A LITTLE BORED, I GUESS
WHAT ARE YOU TALKING ABOUT?! WHY DIDN'T YOU SAY SOMETHING TO US??
I HAD ONE OF MY VISIONS OF THE FUTURE AND SAW HE WAS GONNA DO IT NO MATTER WHAT. PLUS, IT'S NOT LIKE ANYONE LISTENED LAST TIME I WARNED YOU ABOUT SOME CRAZY SHIT
LATER...
I DON'T WANT TO BURN THE BODY
WHY?
I DON'T WANT HIS FUMES AND PHEROMONES MAKING US ALL HORNY AND WEIRD LIKE IT ALWAYS DOES
I FEEL LIKE IT'D BE INAPPROPRIATE
WHAT WOULD WE DO INSTEAD?

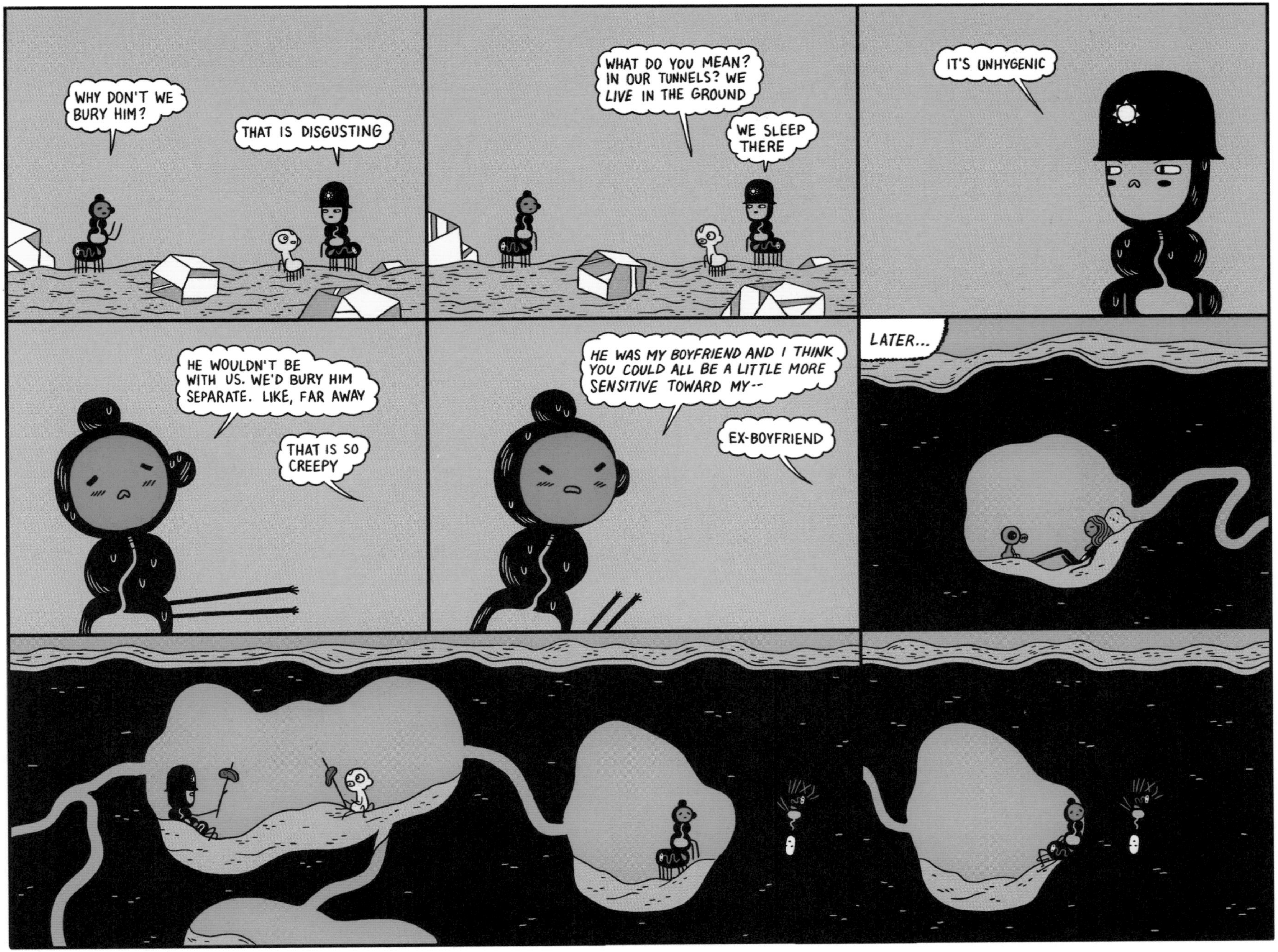
WHY DON'T WE BURY HIM?
THAT IS DISGUSTING
WHAT DO YOU MEAN? IN OUR TUNNELS? WE LIVE IN THE GROUND
WE SLEEP THERE
IT'S UNHYGENIC
HE WOULDN'T BE WITH US. WE'D BURY HIM SEPARATE. LIKE, FAR AWAY
THAT IS SO CREEPY
HE WAS MY BOYFRIEND AND I THINK YOU COULD ALL BE A LITTLE MORE SENSITIVE TOWARD MY--
EX-BOYFRIEND
LATER...

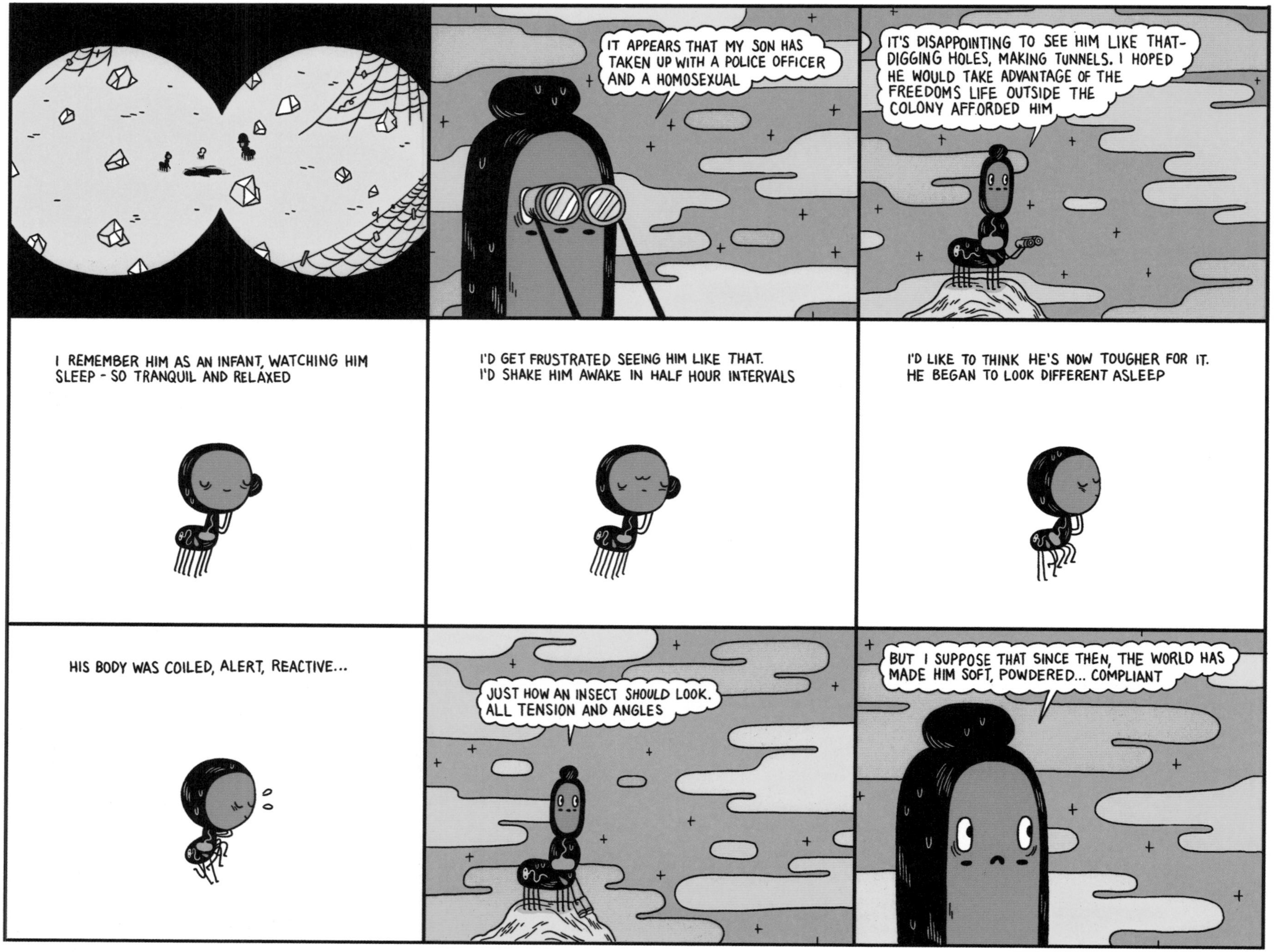
IT APPEARS THAT MY SON HAS TAKEN UP WITH A POLICE OFFICER AND A HOMOSEXUAL
IT'S DISAPPOINTING TO SEE HIM LIKE THAT- DIGGING HOLES, MAKING TUNNELS. I HOPED HE WOULD TAKE ADVANTAGE OF THE FREEDOMS LIFE OUTSIDE THE COLONY AFFORDED HIM
I REMEMBER HIM AS AN INFANT, WATCHING HIM SLEEP - SO TRANQUIL AND RELAXED
I'D GET FRUSTRATED SEEING HIM LIKE THAT. I'D SHAKE HIM AWAKE IN HALF HOUR INTERVALS
I'D LIKE TO THINK HE'S NOW TOUGHER FOR IT. HE BEGAN TO LOOK DIFFERENT ASLEEP
HIS BODY WAS COILED, ALERT, REACTIVE...
JUST HOW AN INSECT SHOULD LOOK. ALL TENSION AND ANGLES
BUT I SUPPOSE THAT SINCE THEN, THE WORLD HAS MADE HIM SOFT, POWDERED... COMPLIANT

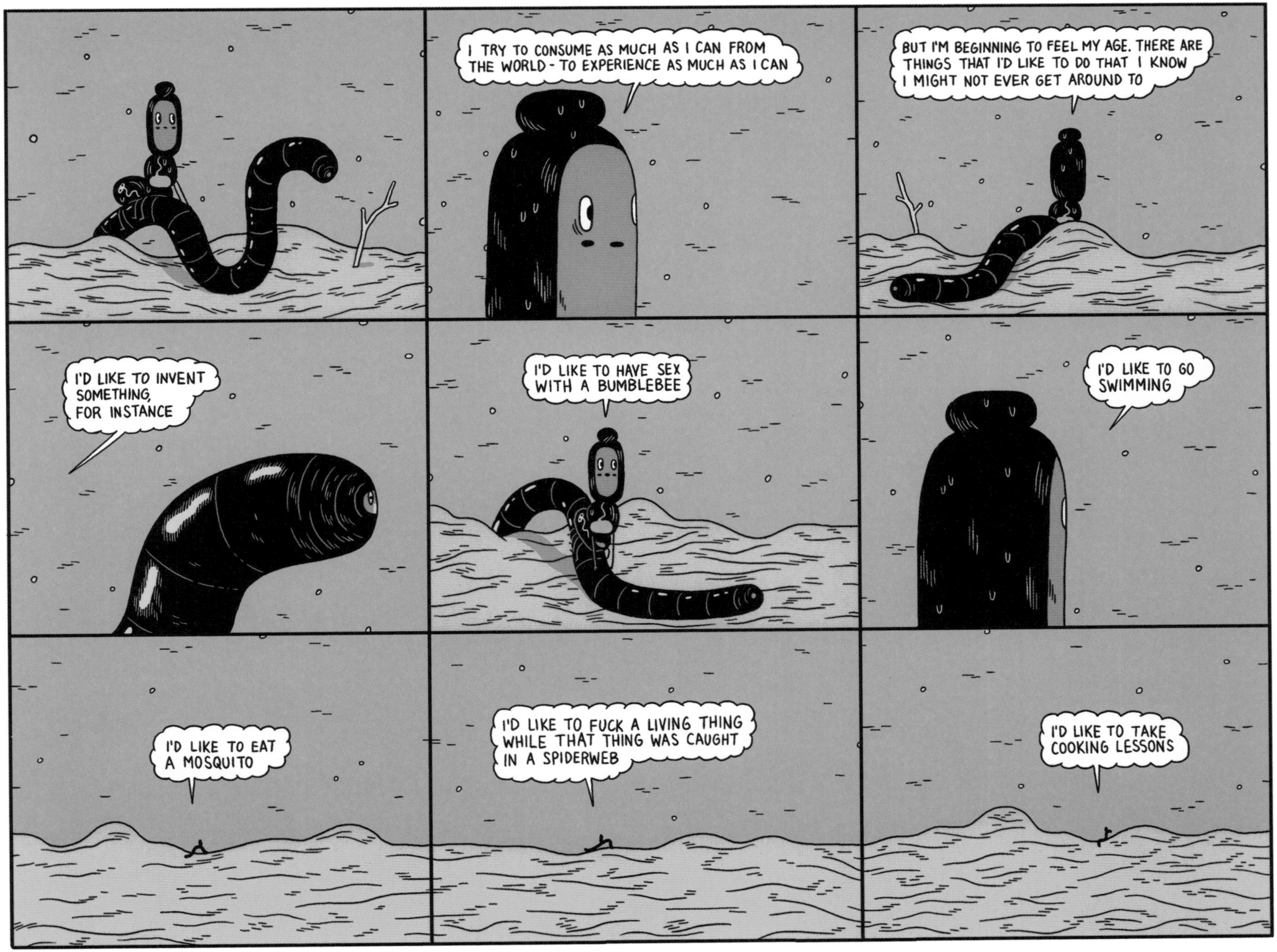
I TRY TO CONSUME AS MUCH AS I CAN FROM THE WORLD - TO EXPERIENCE AS MUCH AS I CAN
BUT I'M BEGINNING TO FEEL MY AGE. THERE ARE THINGS THAT I'D LIKE TO DO THAT I KNOW I MIGHT NOT EVER GET AROUND TO
I'D LIKE TO INVENT SOMETHING, FOR INSTANCE
I'D LIKE TO HAVE SEX WITH A BUMBLEBEE
I'D LIKE TO GO SWIMMING
I'D LIKE TO EAT A MOSQUITO
I'D LIKE TO FUCK A LIVING THING WHILE THAT THING WAS CAUGHT IN A SPIDERWEB
I'D LIKE TO TAKE COOKING LESSONS

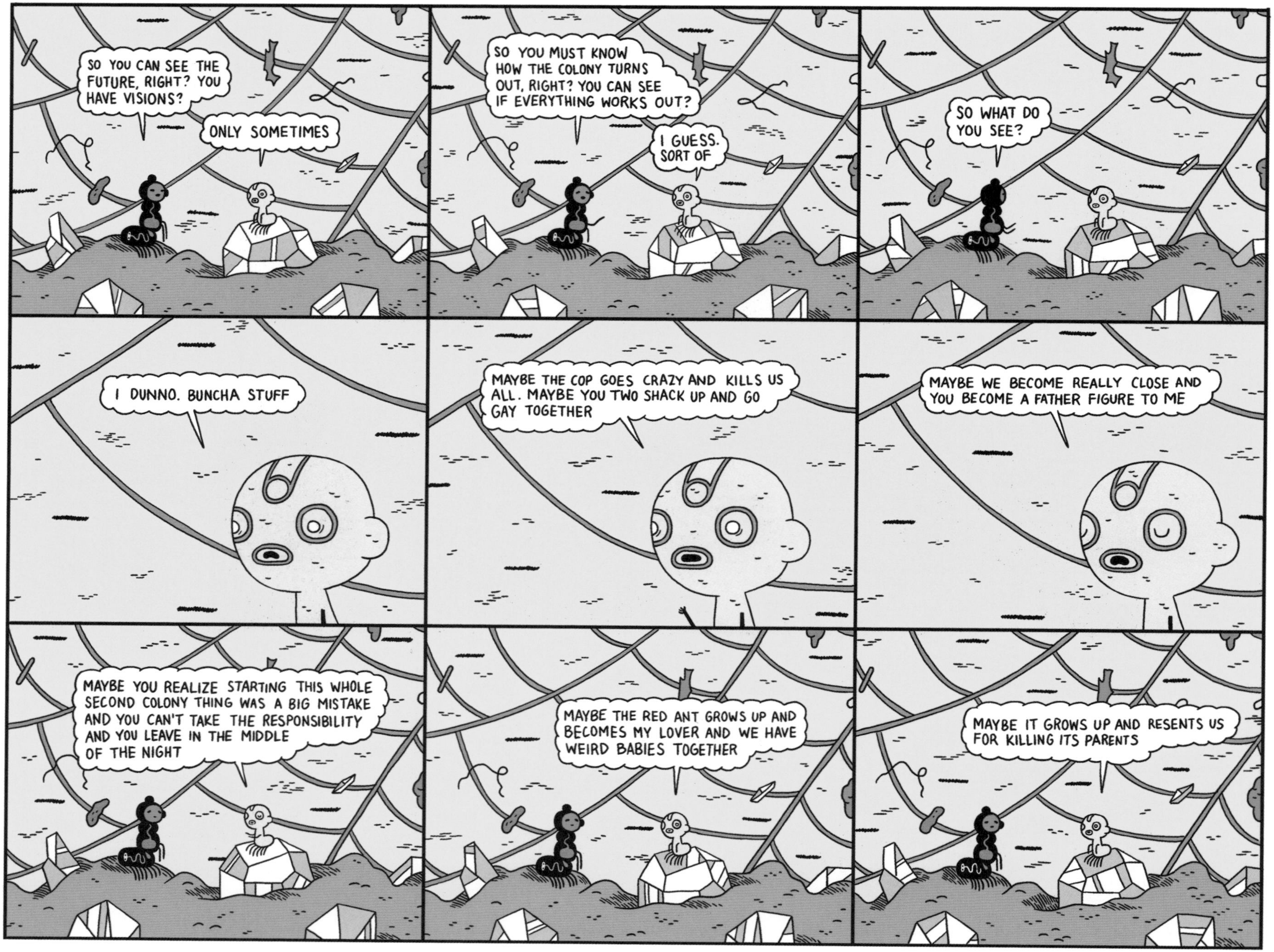
SO YOU CAN SEE THE FUTURE, RIGHT? YOU HAVE VISIONS?
ONLY SOMETIMES
SO YOU MUST KNOW HOW THE COLONY TURNS OUT, RIGHT? YOU CAN SEE IF EVERYTHING WORKS OUT?
I GUESS. SORT OF
SO WHAT DO YOU SEE?
I DUNNO. BUNCHA STUFF
MAYBE THE COP GOES CRAZY AND KILLS US ALL. MAYBE YOU TWO SHACK UP AND GO GAY TOGETHER
MAYBE WE BECOME REALLY CLOSE AND YOU BECOME A FATHER FIGURE TO ME
MAYBE YOU REALIZE STARTING THIS WHOLE SECOND COLONY THING WAS A BIG MISTAKE AND YOU CAN'T TAKE THE RESPONSIBILITY AND YOU LEAVE IN THE MIDDLE OF THE NIGHT
MAYBE THE RED ANT GROWS UP AND BECOMES MY LOVER AND WE HAVE WEIRD BABIES TOGETHER
MAYBE IT GROWS UP AND RESENTS US FOR KILLING ITS PARENTS

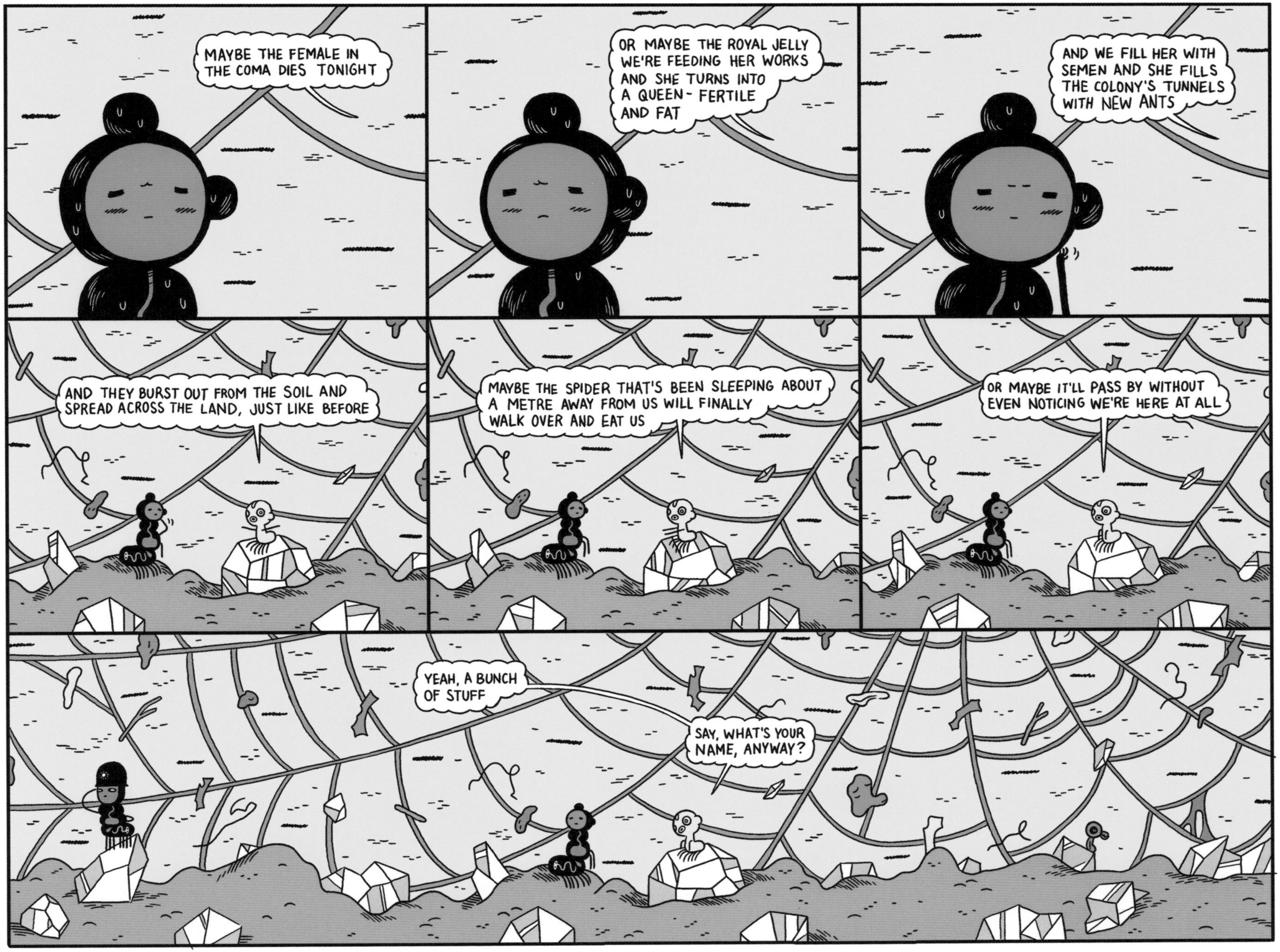
MAYBE THE FEMALE IN THE COMA DIES TONIGHT
OR MAYBE THE ROYAL JELLY WE'RE FEEDING HER WORKS AND SHE TURNS INTO A QUEEN- FERTILE AND FAT
AND WE FILL HER WITH SEMEN AND SHE FILLS THE COLONY'S TUNNELS WITH NEW ANTS
AND THEY BURST OUT FROM THE SOIL AND SPREAD ACROSS THE LAND, JUST LIKE BEFORE
MAYBE THE SPIDER THAT'S BEEN SLEEPING ABOUT A METRE AWAY FROM US WILL FINALLY WALK OVER AND EAT US
OR MAYBE IT'LL PASS BY WITHOUT EVEN NOTICING WE'RE HERE AT ALL
YEAH, A BUNCH OF STUFF
SAY, WHAT'S YOUR NAME, ANYWAY?

MICHAEL DEFORGE WAS BORN IN 1987.
HE DRAWS COMICS IN TORONTO, ONTARIO.

THANKS TO DRAWN AND QUARTERLY, LESLIE,
PATRICK, RYAN, KEITH, ROBIN, GINETTE, ANNE,
THE BEGUILING AND MY FAMILY.